KT-199-925

NEW IDEAS FOR FAMILY MEALS

LOUISE STEELE

New Ideas For Family Meals

TREASURE PRESS

First published in Great Britain in 1984 by
Octopus Books Limited under the title
Cooking for the Family

This edition published in 1988 by
Treasure Press
Michelin House
81 Fulham Road
London SW3 6RB

© 1984 Octopus Books Limited

ISBN 1 85051 341 4

Printed by Mandarin Offset in Hong Kong

CONTENTS

INTRODUCTION

*L*ove it; hate it; a pleasure, or a chore – cooking brings out mixed reactions in most people, and family cooking is no exception. No wonder busy housewives and mothers, who may have a job as well as a home and family to cope with, welcome all the inspiration they can get to help them with budgeting, shopping and catering for the ever-changing fads of modern-day tastes.

Most women have a good fundamental knowledge of what their family likes to eat, but all the same they will be all too familiar with the cry – 'Oh no, not that again'! Producing wholesome, yet tasty and popular meals on a day-to-day basis is no easy task, especially when time is at a premium, ideas are running thin – and so is the housekeeping money! And men may face the same problem too, for with the recent changes in our economic structure, many more men are taking on the responsibility of catering for the family as well as making ends meet in the household budget.

All the basic foods we require for a well-balanced diet are now readily available, so all that's needed is plenty of ideas to ring the changes and make them more exciting and nutritious. The recipes given here do just that, from breakfast to supper, from winter to autumn, week in and week out. They are designed to make the job of cooking for the family a pleasure, and not a chore.

Food is one of the major items of housekeeping expenditure and should therefore be budgeted for accordingly. Be sure to include on your shopping list foods that are nutritionally adequate (see the chart on page 11), and you'll find that, with careful planning, wise shopping and interesting, varied cooking, you and your family can eat extremely well, even on a limited budget! It certainly makes sense to plan menus ahead, say a week at a time, for this way you not only save yourself time and money, but can link one day's meals to the next by making the most of any leftovers. For example, leftover meat from a roast chicken can be made into a tasty chicken and ham, or chicken and mushroom pie, pasties for a packed lunch or a chicken and vegetable curry. Even the carcass need not be wasted, but used to make a good tasty stock for the basis of a nourishing homemade soup.

Planning in advance also enables you to make the most of your oven, whenever it's in use, with a big saving on the cost of fuel. Every so often plan a breadmaking session, or a batch bake of cakes, pies, puddings and biscuits; double up on casserole and soup quantities to freeze away ready for large family gatherings – or to bring out when time is short.

A little imagination and clever choice of cuts means you can come up with many good, meaty dishes that are still easy on the purse. The lower-priced, less tender cuts of meat, like braising and stewing steak – although requiring a little more preparation and a longer, slower cooking time – produce an enormous variety of delicious dishes, ranging from hearty casseroles to tempting pie fillings. The clever housewife will prepare and cook these dishes when she has a few minutes to spare – perhaps at the weekend for the freezer, or maybe the previous evening, ready to reheat and serve in minutes when required. Don't forget too, all those super 'boosters' like batter, pie crusts, dumplings, pulses, pasta and rice that help stretch a meal and are very popular too.

Recipes which involve fiddly preparation and complicated cooking techniques are just not suitable for the busy cook with a hungry family to feed – it's the easy-to-follow, simple to cook, convenient ideas she needs to add to her repertoire. And remember, the cost of convenience foods like ready prepared bought meals, or quick-to-cook steak and chops is high, so these foods should be kept to a minimum or for special occasions only.

WELL-BALANCED MEALS

When planning weekly menus include recipes to complement each other in flavour, texture and colour: a crunchy dish with a softer texture; a highly seasoned one with a more bland one. Remember, too, not to serve up the same meals too often (unless, of course, it happens to be a family favourite). A well-balanced diet means supplying the family with a mixture of foods to give them the right amount of calories for energy (too many and they are stored as fat, remember) plus the necessary nutrients for health (see chart, page 11). Daily meals should contain fibrous carbohydrate foods, such as wholegrain cereals and potatoes, plenty of fruit and vegetables to provide some of the necessary vitamins and minerals, some protein-rich foods and energy-rich foods, which should be eaten in correct amounts to satisfy the appetite and to maintain correct body weights. It's worth bearing in mind that the cost of an ingredient is no indication of its nutritional content: a 100 g (4 oz) piece of stewing beef contains the same amount of protein as a 100 g (4 oz) piece of rump steak, and a pound of coley the same as a pound of plaice.

Start off with a good breakfast and whenever possible, aim to have two smaller meals during the day, rather than a light snack at lunchtime and a large evening meal.

Try to cut out fried foods in favour of grilling or baking.

Include green vegetables or a fresh salad every day and/or raw vegetables as often as possible and eat plenty of fresh

fruit, especially oranges and grapefruit. Encourage the whole family to eat fresh fruit as a snack instead of biscuits, buns or crisps.

Serve wholemeal breads and bran products and cereals to provide plenty of fibre and reduce calorie intakes.

Encourage the family to cut down on fizzy drinks, tea and coffee – it's far better for them to drink tap or mineral water or fruit juices instead. Although sweet, sugary foods are popular, especially with youngsters, do ration these and avoid giving sugary snacks between meals. If children are trained from an early age to eat a healthy diet, it will become a way of life for them, and they will soon begin to accept and appreciate that they are what they eat!

Balance dishes at mealtimes to make them as appetizing and interesting as possible – for example, you wouldn't want to serve a thick, hearty soup followed by a casserole; or a curry and rice followed by a rice pudding; or a chicken pie followed by apple pie for dessert. And on the subject of balance, if you serve a really substantial main course, like a steak and kidney pudding, plus vegetables, then a light refreshing dessert, or just a piece of fresh fruit is all you need, whereas a jam roly-poly would be far too heavy.

Many meat, fish and poultry dishes can be 'stretched' and made more filling and substantial. A savoury mince mixture goes further if topped with a pastry lid or mashed potato, or served with pasta shapes or rice. A little braising steak goes a long way if minced and made into small patties, turnovers or pasties. A boned shoulder or breast of lamb is extra delicious if stuffed before roasting; a chicken goes further if taken off the bone, cut into thin strips, added to a selection of crisp vegetables and mixed with mayonnaise. A few fish fillets 'stretch' well if cut into cubes or strips then dipped in egg and breadcrumbs before frying, but as mentioned earlier, do not eat fried foods too often.

FADS AND FANCIES

It's sensible to start off as you wish to continue when feeding the family. It's important to remember to tempt children to eat as wide a range of foods as possible to ensure that they get the right balance of all the nutrients their bodies require and adjust to adult meals more readily, too. So start when the children are very young – as early as the weaning stage, when they are being introduced to new textures and flavours. It's certainly more economical to prepare these foods yourself, using the freshly cooked foods you've prepared for the rest of the family (puréeing, mincing or chopping it finely, depending on the age of the child), but avoiding anything highly seasoned or salty. As they get older, discourage them from becoming fussy faddy eaters – so often their dislikes are triggered off at an early age by something as simple as the appearance of a particular dish. It's important to make their meals as appealing and attractive as possible, perhaps with the addition of a pretty garnish, such as a tomato lily or carrot curl.

Many youngsters don't like vegetables – even if they've never tried them! – but children are very often lazy eaters and can't be bothered with a large helping. Put just one Brussels sprout, a carrot or a few peas on their plate and make sure they eat them up – by a process of elimination you will soon discover those which are acceptable and those which genuinely aren't liked.

A common problem facing most mums is coping with youngsters' ever-changing needs, including how to make

foods interesting for grownups, yet still palatable for children of varying ages. This means choosing dishes which lend themselves to flexibility. For example, a beef casserole cooked in wine would meet with an adult's approval, but would probably not be popular with youngsters. The problem can be overcome, however, by dividing the mixture in half, or into the number of portions needed, and cooking half in wine and the other in stock. Obviously this involves a few extra minutes' preparation time, but is well worth the effort and is a necessary part of family catering.

Some of the more 'unpopular' flavourings with children, best avoided altogether or kept to a minimum, are as follows: too much garlic; hot mustards (although they usually enjoy the mild burger-type); spices and highly-seasoned dishes, such as curries and chillies (so keep these mild); too many oily salad dressings (better to serve the dressing separately); anchovies (though their saltiness can be reduced quite considerably by soaking them in milk for 30 minutes before use); olives.

Teenagers can be especially demanding by arriving home at odd times to fit in with their after school activities – and what's more, often with a hungry friend or two in tow! It's particularly at times like these that the clever cook needs to think up ways of stretching a meal. A well-stocked freezer helps, as do a microwave cooker, sandwich maker and, most of all, a good supply of staple foods, such as eggs, cheese and salad in the refrigerator. Encourage teenagers to make their own meals or snacks – such as toasted sandwiches, baps, omelettes or burgers.

Homemade soups are excellent fillers, economical to make and popular with all age groups, so a store of these 'on ice' will be very useful. To make soups even more substantial, add a handful of rice or pasta, lentils, split peas or pearl barley to thicken and to increase the nutritional content. Or add tiny made-in-minutes dumplings, float slices of toasted cheese or crisp-fried croûtons on top, or simply serve with slices of wholemeal bread or crusty rolls.

It's important to tempt children of all ages to experiment with new foods – they'll never know what they've been missing if they don't try! Fortunately most children love minced beef, and this can be dressed up in many different ways – as beefburgers, tasty bolognese sauce or lasagne filling, chilli con carne, and, of course, the ever-popular cottage pie. For convenience, make up a large batch of savoury mince mixture, then divide it up into either family-sized meals or smaller portions, as liked, with different flavourings according to individual tastes – curry, chilli, tomato and herb, etc. (see page 48) and freeze them away ready to take out and use as required.

PACKED LUNCHES

Nowadays it seems that more and more children are taking a packed lunch with them to school, and of course adults often find a tasty packed lunch convenient and economical to eat at work.

The first thing to bear in mind is that a packed lunch, whether it's to take to school, to work, on a fishing trip or for a picnic, should look and taste good and be a complete meal. Don't think of it simply as a filler between breakfast and the main meal of the day; bought snacks like doughnuts, crisps and cakes may satisfy the hunger for a time but will certainly not supply all the nutrition we need, whether at work or play. A packed lunch should be as healthy as a well-balanced meal prepared and eaten at home, and can be just as satisfying as a hot cooked meal.

With some advance planning you can achieve a combination of interesting flavours and textures which should include plenty of protein and other essential nutrients.

Scotch eggs, chicken drumsticks, cold sausages, cheese flans, meat pies and pasties are all rich in protein and if accompanied by a salad (packed in a margarine tub or yogurt carton) make substantial, appetizing meals.

Sandwiches should never be underestimated: popular and easy to make, they can be as simple or elaborate as liked, depending on personal preferences, and the same goes for baps and rolls. If sandwiches are required daily, it's sensible to make up batches in advance and keep them, wrapped in cling film, in the refrigerator overnight. Freezer owners can

either pack sandwiches individually or in stacks with the same filling, wrapped in freezer bags and labelled. Most sandwiches freeze well for up to 1 month, with the exception of those containing hard-boiled egg, which becomes rubbery when frozen, and salad foods such as tomatoes, lettuce, cress and cucumber, because of their high water content. Individually wrapped sandwiches, if removed from the freezer at breakfast time, will have thawed within 2-3 hours and will be ready for lunch.

The right kind of bread helps provide the fibre that is essential to the daily diet. Make the most of the exciting range of breads and rolls now so widely available: choose from mixed grain; granary; wholemeal; rye; poppy and sesame seed. Use two different types of bread of similar size to add flavour and interest to sandwiches, and try making double deckers, using three slices of bread, maybe two brown and one white, with two tasty layers of different filling in between.

When making sandwiches, always butter right up to the edges of the bread to prevent the fillings from seeping into the bread and making it soggy; use softened butter for easy spreading or, for economy (particularly if using a well-flavoured filling) use soft margarine instead of butter. For extra-tasty sandwiches, mix the butter or margarine with a little tomato purée or relish, fresh chopped herbs, mild curry powder or mustard, to taste. Fillings should be generous, but don't over-fill sandwiches or they become messy and difficult to eat. Choose fillings which contain plenty of protein (see chart, page 11), plus salad ingredients where possible, as well as relishes, chutneys and mayonnaise if liked. Whole tomatoes, chunks of cucumber, celery or carrot sticks, whole radishes or dill pickles can be conveniently packed in containers alongside sandwiches, rather than being included in the filling.

Whenever possible include a yogurt or a piece of fresh fruit in a packed lunch box. Be sparing with sweet things as these can become a habit and lead to weight problems later. You could occasionally add a small piece of homemade fruit cake or gingerbread; a muesli bar; a few dried prunes or apricots or some nuts and raisins. Finally pack the lunch box as neatly and attractively as possible (encourage the children to do their own) and remember to add a paper napkin for wiping fingers.

THE A B C OF COOKING

Generally speaking, most children can't wait to help Mum in the kitchen and love getting involved with cooking something for their tea. So whenever you've the time, do encourage them to do so, assuring them that practice makes perfect – this way they'll soon begin to understand and enjoy cooking for themselves. Make it fun by giving them simple tasks to begin with, gradually increasing their know-how as they get used to the idea. Give them a piece of spare pastry to 'play' with and help them make some little jam tarts with it, showing how to roll out and cut the pastry correctly and how to fill the cases with jam. Although the finished result may not be quite to your liking, the young cook will undoubtedly find them quite the nicest he or she's ever eaten and want to repeat the experience.

Another thing children find great fun to make is popcorn, where they start off with only a handful of corn and end up with a big bowlful. This makes an attractive – and economical – idea for a birthday party snack, too.

Whenever the children are helping you, be sure to keep an eye on them at all times; point out the dangers in the kitchen, such as a heated hob or oil in a deep-frier, and don't give them any jobs which involve food processors, sharp knives, graters and so on until they are old enough to handle these tools proficiently.

WASTE NOT, WANT NOT

Many of us are faced with the problem of what to do with the leftovers, once a cooking session is over. Here are a few suggestions for putting some of the more usual 'odds and ends' to good use.

Egg whites Can be used to make individual meringues or a large meringue shell to store away ready for a party, or a delicious meringue topping for pies, tartlets or rice pudding. Alternatively, stiffly whip an egg white and fold into a batter before coating fish fillets or fritters and frying – it will 'stretch' the batter and give a lovely light texture. Fold a stiffly whisked egg white into an omelette mixture to give a fluffy, soufflé-light texture.

A great idea for a party, or when running short of cream, is to stiffly whip an egg white and fold into 150 ml (¼ pint) whipped, whipping or double cream to make it go further. Lightly whip an egg white with a fork, brush liberally over a sweet pastry-topped pie and sprinkle with granulated sugar before baking, to give an attractive sugar-frosted glaze. To make a frothy jelly; whisk a stiffly whisked egg white into a partially set jelly and leave to set completely before serving.

Fold a stiffly whisked egg white into fruit purées, mousses and soufflés.

To freeze egg whites: Place in small containers without any additions and freeze for up to 6 months. Thaw for 1-2 hours at room temperature before using as required.
Egg yolks Can be used to make up several quantities of mayonnaise (ready for a fête or market stall) using 1 egg yolk to each 150 ml (¼ pint) of oil (see recipe, page 32). Add an egg yolk to a sweet or savoury sauce, just before the end of cooking, to add richness and extra nourishment.

Use an egg yolk for coating fish or Scotch eggs before bread-crumbing and frying.

Glaze breads, pies and pasties with a beaten egg yolk, thinning the consistency if necessary with a little milk or water. Beat an egg yolk into hot mashed potato to give colour as well as added nourishment, and if liked, pipe out swirls or rosettes of potato on to baking sheets and cook in a hot oven until lightly golden.

Add an extra yolk to 2 or 3 beaten eggs when making an omelette or scrambled eggs.

To freeze egg yolks: Mix ¼ teaspoon of salt or ½ teaspoon of caster sugar to every 2 yolks and freeze in small containers. Label with the number of yolks and whether salt or sugar was added. Thaw for 1-2 hours at room temperature before using as required in sweet or savoury dishes.
Puff and shortcrust pastry These trimmings can be re-rolled, cut into dainty shapes, using small biscuit cutters, glazed with milk or beaten egg (sprinkled, if liked, with poppy or sesame seeds) and baked in a hot oven until lightly golden. These can be stored successfully in an airtight tin for up to 2 weeks and only need refreshing quickly in a hot oven to crisp before serving. Sandwich them together with a

savoury or sweet filling and serve at teatime, or top with a spread for simple canapes to serve with drinks. Savoury pastry shapes also make an attractive garnish for casseroles and fish and vegetable dishes, while sweet ones can be used to decorate fruit mousses and custards.
Lemons, oranges and limes Freeze slices of these fruits to use for garnishing and decorating food, or for serving with drinks. The shells of halved citrus fruits (from which the juice has been extracted) can be frozen. These are useful for when grated rind is required; grate the rinds while still frozen. Alternatively, you could grate the rind before squeezing the juice out and then freeze the rind. Frozen grapefruit and orange half shells, with all the skin membranes and pith removed, make attractive 'serving dishes' for ice creams and sorbets.
Fresh herbs Sprigs can be frozen for up to 6 months. Wash whole sprigs, pat dry and place in small freezer bags. To chop before adding to a dish, simply rub the frozen sprigs (straight from the freezer) between the palms of hands – the leaves will crumble easily ready for use.

If preferred, wash and chop herbs (finely or coarsely, as liked) and two-thirds fill into ice cube trays. Top up with cold water and freeze until solid. Transfer cubes to a freezer bag and add as required, still frozen, to hot dishes like casseroles, soups, sauces and stews, or allow to thaw in a fine strainer for 15-20 minutes before using.
Bread Make crumbs of crusts and one-day-old slices of bread and freeze away, adding to them until you have a sufficient quantity for stuffing a chicken or Guard of Honour. Alternatively, use crumbs to coat Scotch eggs, pieces of fish or lamb cutlets, or use to make a few stuffing balls for serving with grilled meats.

Sprinkle a handful of buttered crumbs over a cauliflower or macaroni cheese before baking.

Stir a spoonful of breadcrumbs into a suet pudding mixture before baking or steaming to lighten the texture.

Make croûtons by cutting stale bread into neat cubes or triangles; shallow-fry until golden and serve with soups and casseroles. These keep successfully for up to 2 weeks, stored in an airtight tin.
Vegetables Add a handful of sweetcorn, peas or beans to soups, stews and casseroles; stir into savoury mince, macaroni cheese or cottage pie before baking. Use leftover peppers, courgettes and tomatoes to make a tasty vegetable and cheese quiche, or add to an omelette filling.

NUTRIENTS FOR HEALTH

NUTRIENT	SOURCES
Protein (to build and repair body tissues and for enzyme systems in the body)	Meats (lamb, pork, beef), poultry, fish, cheese, eggs, milk, nuts, bread, flour, cereals, dried peas and beans, potatoes
Carbohydrate (to provide energy – an excess is stored as fat)	Breads, cereals, sugary and starchy foods
Fat (to provide energy – an excess is stored as fat)	Butter, margarine, oil and all fats. Also found in meats, oily fish, cheeses, milk
Vitamin A (for healthy skin and eyes)	Butter, margarine, liver, kidney, milk, cheese, eggs, oily fish, green and orange vegetables and fruits, e.g. carrots, tomatoes, dried apricots
Vitamin B_1 (Thiamin) (for the release of energy from foods; a healthy appetite and nerves)	Milk, offal, pork, eggs, potatoes, peas, oranges, wholegrain cereals (and fortified cereals), flours (especially wholewheat)
Vitamin B_2 (Riboflavin) (as above)	Milk, cheese, eggs, beef, chicken, liver, kidney, yeast extract

NUTRIENT	SOURCES
Vitamin C (Ascorbic acid) (for healthy skin and connective tissue and to help the body absorb iron)	Potatoes (just under the skin – and chips have more than boiled potatoes), green vegetables, tomatoes, citrus and other fruits, especially blackcurrants and strawberries, rose hip syrup
Vitamin D (builds strong bones, nails and teeth and aids the absorption of calcium)	Mostly from sunshine, but following foods also important, particularly in winter when there is less sunshine: canned fish (sardines, pilchards and salmon), cheese of all kinds, butter and margarine, eggs, evaporated milk
Calcium (deposited from an early age – builds strong bones and teeth)	Milk, yogurt, cheese, eggs, bread, flours, green vegetables, canned fish (sardines and salmon) when the bones are eaten, hard water
Iron (for healthy red blood cells; aids transport of oxygen)	Liver, egg yolk, red meats, corned beef, cereal products, potatoes, green vegetables, cocoa powder, chocolate, dried fruits

MICROWAVE COOKERS

The microwave cooker can be an extremely useful appliance for family cooks, whether you are cooking complete meals in it, or just a part of one, or whether you are using it in conjunction with the freezer to thaw and reheat frozen foods. Throughout the recipes in this book, details are given of how to defrost or reheat frozen foods. The information is based on a cooker having a 650 watt output. Food may need to be cooked for a few minutes longer in a cooker with a lower output and vice versa in one with a higher output.

All the microwave information is for guidance only and reference should be made to your manufacturer's instruction/recipe book.

ONE

BREAKFAST BRUNCH AND ELEVENSES

Sunshine Health Drink *14*
Mocha Morning Toddy *14*
Creamy Yogurt Flips *14*
Tutti Frutti Muesli *15*
Oaty Sausage Cakes *15*
Cheesy Bacon Croissants *16*
Potato Fritters *17*
French Granary Toasts *17*
Wholewheat Date Muffins *18*
Hot Dog Brunch Rolls *18*
Milk Bread Rolls *19*
Smoked Haddock Scramble *20*
American Pancakes *20*
Banana Malties *20*
Baked Ham and Eggs in Tomatoes *20*
Mixed Fruit Jamboree *21*
Scottish Breakfast *22*

Sunshine Health Drink

SERVES 1

150 ml (¼ pint) fresh or
    unsweetened orange juice,
    chilled
150 ml (¼ pint) unsweetened
    pineapple or grapefruit juice,
    chilled
1 egg
1 tablespoon clear honey

PREPARATION TIME: *3-5 minutes*

When time is short this meal-in-a-glass makes a nourishing and refreshing start to the day.

1. Place the fruit juices, egg and honey in a blender goblet and blend for 30 seconds until thoroughly combined.
2. Pour into a glass or mug and serve at once.

Mocha Morning Toddy

SERVES 2

600 ml (1 pint) milk
50 g (2 oz) plain chocolate,
    broken into pieces
1½ teaspoons malted milk
    powder
1½ teaspoons instant coffee
a few drops of vanilla essence

TO DECORATE:
2 tablespoons double or
    whipping cream, lightly
    whipped (optional)
a little coarsely grated plain
    chocolate

PREPARATION TIME: *5 minutes*
COOKING TIME: *3 minutes*

1. Heat the milk until just at boiling point. Pour into a warmed blender goblet and add the chocolate, malted milk powder, coffee and vanilla essence. Blend for 30 seconds until the chocolate has melted and all the ingredients are thoroughly combined.
2. Pour into 2 mugs and top each with a spoonful of whipped cream, if using, and a sprinkling of grated chocolate. Serve at once.

Creamy Yogurt Flips

SERVES 2-3

150 ml (¼ pint) plain
    unsweetened yogurt
150 ml (¼ pint) fresh or
    unsweetened orange juice
1 medium banana, peeled
150 ml (¼ pint) top of the milk
    chilled
3 ice cubes
sugar, to taste (optional)

TO GARNISH:
sprigs of fresh mint (optional)

PREPARATION TIME: *3-5 minutes*

A wholesome drink that is made in minutes.

1. Place all the ingredients, including sugar if using, in a blender goblet and blend for 30 seconds until thoroughly combined.
2. Pour into 2 glasses and decorate with sprigs of mint, if using. Serve at once.

VARIATION:
Unsweetened pineapple or apple juice may be used instead of orange juice.

Clockwise from bottom left: Oaty Sausage Cakes; Tutti Frutti Muesli; Creamy Yogurt Flips; Mocha Morning Toddy. **Middle:** Sunshine Health Drink.

Tutti Frutti Muesli

MAKES 1.25 kg (2¾ lb)

450 g (1 lb) porridge oats
50 g (2 oz) natural wheat bran
100 g (4 oz) wheat flakes
100 g (4 oz) wheat germ
100 g (4 oz) dried apricots,
    chopped
75 g (3 oz) sunflower seeds
75 g (3 oz) hazelnuts, toasted
    and chopped
100 g (4 oz) sugar-rolled
    chopped dates
100 g (4 oz) seedless raisins or
    sultanas, halved if large

TO SERVE:
chopped fresh fruit (banana,
    apple, orange, strawberries
    or peaches)
plain unsweetened yogurt, milk
    or cream

PREPARATION TIME: *15 minutes*
COOKING TIME: *2 minutes*

This delicious muesli base can be stored in an airtight container for several weeks and makes a nutritious breakfast cereal or snack. It is particularly useful to take on a camping or caravanning holiday. All the ingredients are available from most health food shops and large supermarkets.

1. Put all the ingredients in a large bowl and stir well to mix. Transfer to an airtight container or jar. Ⓐ
2. Serve as required, topped with chopped fresh fruit, with yogurt, milk or cream.

VARIATION:
Just before serving add a little clear honey or brown sugar, if a sweeter flavour is liked.

Oaty Sausage Cakes

MAKES 8

450 g (1 lb) pork sausage meat
1 medium onion, peeled and
    finely chopped
3 heaped tablespoons plus 50 g
    (2 oz) porridge oats
¼-½ teaspoon dried mixed
    herbs
pinch of English mustard
    powder (optional)
¼ teaspoon salt
freshly ground black pepper
1 egg, beaten
4 tablespoons vegetable oil

PREPARATION TIME: *7 minutes*
COOKING TIME: *15 minutes*

1. Place the sausagemeat in a mixing bowl with the onion, 3 heaped tablespoons porridge oats, the herbs, mustard, if using, and salt and pepper. Mix well until thoroughly combined.
2. Divide the mixture into 8 equal portions. On a lightly floured board or work surface, form each into a 7.5 cm (3 inch) round. Ⓐ Ⓕ
3. Dip each sausage cake in beaten egg, then in the remaining 50 g (2 oz) porridge oats, to coat thoroughly.
4. Heat the oil in a frying pan, add the sausage cakes and fry over a moderate heat for about 15 minutes, turning frequently with a fish slice, until golden-brown and cooked through.
5. Drain on absorbent paper and serve hot with fried eggs and tomatoes.

Ⓐ Can be prepared the night before, covered in cling film and kept in the refrigerator.
Ⓕ Freeze at this stage, thaw overnight in the refrigerator, then coat just before using and cook for 20-25 minutes.
Ⓜ Or microwave on Defrost for 10-12 minutes. Stand for 10 minutes, then follow instructions from step 3.

Cheesy Bacon Croissants

MAKES 12

450 g (1 lb) strong plain white flour
½ teaspoon salt
15 g (½ oz) caster sugar
1 packet easy blend dried yeast (equivalent to 25 g (1 oz) fresh yeast)
250 ml (8 fl oz) milk
200 g (8 oz) butter, softened
1 egg, beaten

FILLING:

75 g (3 oz) streaky bacon rashers, rinded and chopped
25 g (1 oz) butter or hard margarine
15 g (½ oz) plain flour
150 ml (¼ pint) milk
2 teaspoons chopped fresh parsley
50 g (2 oz) Cheddar cheese, grated
salt
freshly ground black pepper

TO GLAZE:

1 egg, beaten
2 teaspoons cold water

PREPARATION TIME: *40 minutes, plus rising, proving and chilling*
COOKING TIME: *17-20 minutes*
OVEN: *200°C, 400°F, Gas Mark 6*

These savoury croissants freeze very well and can be conveniently reheated from frozen in minutes to make an unusually delicious breakfast or brunch treat. For a sweet version, try the Chocolate Spice variation. If using dried active baking yeast instead, follow the packet directions, as the method of using it is quite different from the easy blend variety.

1. Sift the flour with the salt into a mixing bowl. Add the sugar and yeast. Heat the milk with 50 g (2 oz) of the butter in a saucepan over a gentle heat until the butter has melted and the milk is tepid. Make a well in the centre of the flour and pour in the milk mixture with the egg. Using a wooden spoon, gradually draw the flour into the liquid, stirring vigorously to mix. Knead the dough for 5 minutes by hand in the bowl or for 2 minutes if using an electric mixer, fitted with a dough hook. Cover the bowl with cling film and leave at room temperature for about 1 hour or until doubled in bulk. Ⓐ

2. Meanwhile make the filling: put the bacon in a saucepan and fry without added fat over a moderate heat, for about 5 minutes, stirring frequently, until lightly browned. Add the butter or margarine to the pan and heat until melted, then stir in the flour and cook over a gentle heat, stirring constantly, for 1 minute. Remove the pan from the heat and gradually stir in the milk, then return to the heat and bring to the boil, stirring. Reduce the heat and simmer for 2 minutes, stirring constantly. Remove from the heat and stir in the parsley and cheese. Season to taste with salt and pepper. Set aside to cool.

3. Turn the risen dough on to a lightly floured board or work surface and knead gently for 2 minutes, or for 1 minute if using an electric mixer. Roll the dough into a 15×30 cm (6×12 inch) rectangle.

4. Using a sharp knife, lightly mark the rectangle into 3 equal sections and dot 2 of the sections with 75 g (3 oz) each of the remaining butter.

5. Fold the uncovered section of dough over the centre section and fold over the remaining section to cover the centre. Give the dough a quarter turn and roll out again into a 15×30 cm

(6×12 inch) rectangle.

6. Repeat the rolling, folding and turning of the dough three times, as in steps 4 and 5. Wrap the dough in cling film and chill in the refrigerator for 1 hour.

7. Roll the chilled dough into a 30×45 cm (12×18 inch) rectangle: cut in half lengthways and then cut each half into three 15 cm (6 inch) squares. Finally cut each square in half diagonally.

8. Spread a heaped teaspoonful of the cheese and bacon mixture over each triangle. Starting at the long edge, roll up fairly tightly. Place the croissants slightly apart on a lightly greased baking sheet and gently curl each one into a crescent shape. Cover the croissants lightly with cling film and leave to prove at room temperature for about 10 minutes, until doubled in size and puffy. Combine the egg and cold water for the glaze and brush each croissant with the mixture.

9. Bake in a preheated oven for about 17-20 minutes until golden-brown and cooked through. Transfer to a wire rack to cool slightly and serve warm. Ⓕ

Ⓐ Croissant dough can be made in advance and left to rise overnight in the refrigerator if placed in a large, lightly oiled polythene bag (tied loosely to allow room for expansion). Knead well to bring back to room temperature before using.
Ⓕ Freeze for up to 1 month. Reheat from frozen at 180°C, 350°F, Gas Mark 4 for 10-12 minutes. Cover with foil if necessary during this time to prevent over-browning.

VARIATION:
Chocolate Spice Croissants: Put 75 g (3 oz) plain grated chocolate, 50 g (2 oz) butter, 25 g (1 oz) soft brown sugar and ¼ teaspoon ground cinnamon in a bowl and mix well with a fork until thoroughly combined. Substitute this filling for the bacon and cheese filling and proceed from step 8.

Potato Fritters

MAKES 12

50 g (2 oz) plain flour
½ teaspoon salt
freshly ground black pepper
1 egg, beaten
3 tablespoons milk
750 g (1 ½ lb) potatoes, peeled
   and coarsely grated
6 tablespoons vegetable oil

PREPARATION TIME: *10-15 minutes*
COOKING TIME: *5-6 minutes*

These tasty potato fritters are delicious with bacon and eggs, mixed grills and fried fish. Smaller ones can be served with casseroles and goulashes.

1. Sift the flour with the salt and pepper into a mixing bowl and make a well in the centre. Pour in the egg and milk. Using a wooden spoon, gradually draw the flour into the liquid, stirring vigorously, until thoroughly mixed. Ⓐ
2. Wash and drain the grated potatoes, then stir into the flour mixture and mix well. Heat half the oil in a large frying pan and when it sizzles add 6 rounded tablespoons of the potato mixture, slightly apart. Flatten the potato fritters slightly with a fish slice and fry for 2-3 minutes until golden brown on the underside.
3. Carefully turn the fritters with a fish slice and cook for a further 2-3 minutes, turning once or twice, until golden-brown all over. Drain on absorbent paper and keep hot while frying the remaining potato mixture in the same way. Sprinkle with salt and serve hot.

Ⓐ Can be prepared several hours in advance, covered and kept chilled.

VARIATION:
Sweetcorn 'n' Potato Fritters: Use 450 g (1 lb) peeled grated potato and add 100 g (4oz) sweetcorn, drained if canned, thawed if frozen.

French Granary Toasts

4 thick slices granary bread
4 teaspoons tomato relish or
   tomato purée, for spreading
   (optional)
3 eggs, beaten
2 tablespoons milk
salt
freshly ground black pepper
2 tablespoons vegetable oil

PREPARATION TIME: *10 minutes*
COOKING TIME: *6 minutes*

1. Spread the granary bread slices with tomato relish or purée, if using. Whisk the eggs with the milk, salt and pepper and pour into a shallow dish. Soak the bread slices in the egg mixture and then transfer to a plate.
2. Heat the oil in a large frying pan until foaming. Add the bread slices and fry over a moderate heat for 3 minutes. Turn the bread slices, using a fish slice, and cook for a further 3 minutes until golden brown on both sides.
3. Remove the fried toasts from the pan and cut each into 4 triangles. Arrange on a heated serving dish and serve with crisply grilled bacon rashers and halved tomatoes.

VARIATION:
Saucy Citrus Toasts: Soak 4 granary bread slices without tomato relish or purée in the unseasoned egg and milk mixture, then fry as in step 2. Meanwhile, gently heat 4 tablespoons orange or lime jelly marmalade with 2 tablespoons golden syrup in a saucepan until melted and heated through. Spoon over the fried toasts and serve at once.

Left to right: Potato Fritters; Cheesy Bacon Croissants; French Granary Toasts.

Wholewheat Date Muffins

MAKES 12

100 g (4 oz) plain white flour
3 teaspoons baking powder
¼ teaspoon salt
100 g (4 oz) plain wholewheat flour
40 g (1½ oz) butter or hard margarine, diced
25 g (1 oz) soft dark brown sugar
50 g (2 oz) pressed cooking dates, chopped
25 g (1 oz) walnuts, chopped
150 ml (¼ pint) plain unsweetened yogurt
3 tablespoons milk

TO GLAZE:
a little beaten egg
15 g (½ oz) walnuts, finely chopped (optional)

PREPARATION TIME: *10 minutes*
COOKING TIME: *12-15 minutes*
OVEN: *220°C, 425°F, Gas Mark 7*

1. Sift the white flour, baking powder and salt into a mixing bowl. Stir in the wholewheat flour then add the butter or margarine and rub in with the fingertips until the mixture resembles fine breadcrumbs. Ⓐ
2. Stir in the sugar, dates and walnuts. Combine the yogurt with the milk and add all at once, mixing quickly with a round-bladed knife to form a soft dough.
3. Turn the dough on to a lightly floured board or work surface and knead very lightly until smooth. Lightly roll the dough into a round 2 cm (¾ inch) thick. Using a 6 cm (2½ inch) round cutter, cut out 8 rounds. Knead and roll the trimmings. Cut out 4 more rounds.
4. Place the muffins slightly apart on a lightly floured baking sheet. Brush the tops with a little beaten egg and sprinkle with walnuts, if using. Bake just above centre in a preheated oven for 12-15 minutes until well risen and golden brown. Ⓕ Serve warm with butter.

Ⓐ This mixture can be kept in a covered container in the refrigerator for up to 3 days. Ⓕ Freeze for up to 6 months. Thaw for 2 hours at room temperature to serve cold, or place on a baking sheet, cover with foil and reheat from frozen at 180°C, 350°F, Gas Mark 4 for 10 minutes. Ⓜ Or microwave, 6 at a time, on Defrost for 3-4 minutes, then stand for 10 minutes before serving cold.

VARIATION:
Use chopped dried bananas or raisins instead of dates.

Hot Dog Brunch Rolls

SERVES 6

3 tablespoons vegetable oil
1 small onion, peeled and grated
3 tablespoons tomato purée
2 tablespoons soft light brown sugar
2½ teaspoons mild burger mustard (optional)
6 frankfurters
6 Milk Bread Rolls (page 19), or bought hot dog rolls
a little butter, for spreading

PREPARATION TIME: *5 minutes, plus breadmaking*
COOKING TIME: *7 minutes*

Chipolatas can be used instead of frankfurters, in which case fry them first for 10 minutes, then drain off any fat from the pan before adding them to the tomato mixture in step 2.

1. Put the oil, onion, tomato purée, sugar and mustard, if using, into a bowl. Stir well to mix.
2. Place the frankfurters in a frying pan and spoon over the tomato mixture. Cook over a gentle heat for 7 minutes, stirring and turning the frankfurters constantly.
3. Meanwhile warm the rolls, if liked, then split them lengthways and spread with a little butter. Fill each roll with a frankfurter and some sauce. Serve hot, wrapped in paper napkins.

Milk Bread Rolls

MAKES 20 rolls

750 g (1½ lb) strong plain
   white flour
2 teaspoons salt
1 teaspoon caster sugar
25 g (1 oz) lard, diced
25 g (1 oz) hard margarine,
   diced
1 packet easy blend dried yeast
   (equivalent to 25 g (1 oz)
   fresh yeast)
150 ml (¼ pint) water
300 ml (½ pint) milk

PREPARATION TIME: *15 minutes,
plus rising and proving*
COOKING TIME: *20 minutes*
OVEN: *200°C, 400°F, Gas Mark 6*

A nutritious milk bread (with
good keeping qualities) that
the children will love. These
rolls are good for breakfast
or for brunch – see Hot Dog
Brunch Rolls (left). If using
dried active baking yeast
instead, follow the packet
directions, as the method of
using it is quite different
from the easy blend variety.

1. Sift the flour with the salt
and sugar into a mixing
bowl. Add the lard and
margarine and rub into the
flour with the fingertips,
until the mixture resembles
fine breadcrumbs. Stir in the
yeast and make a well in the
centre. Heat the water and
milk in a saucepan until tepid
and pour into the well. Using
a wooden spoon, gradually
draw the flour into the
liquid, stirring vigorously to
mix. Knead the dough by
hand until it leaves the sides
of the bowl clean.
2. Turn the dough on to a
floured board or work
surface and knead
thoroughly for 10 minutes by
hand or 2-3 minutes using an
electric mixer fitted with a
dough hook, until the dough
is firm, elastic and no longer
feels sticky.
3. Shape the dough into a
round ball and place in a
large lightly oiled polythene
bag: Tie loosely and leave in
a warm place for about 1
hour, until the dough is
doubled in size and springs
back when pressed with a
floured finger. Ⓐ
4. Turn the risen dough on
to a lightly floured board or
work surface and knead
vigorously for 5 minutes, or
for 2 minutes if using an
electric mixer. Take 50 g
(2 oz) pieces of dough and
form each piece into a roll
about 11 cm (4½ inches)
long. Place the rolls slightly
apart on a lightly floured
baking sheet. Using kitchen
scissors, snip crossways
along the top of each roll
about 4 times. Cover loosely
with cling film and leave to
prove for about 10 minutes
until puffy.
5. Brush with a glaze and
sprinkle with a topping if
liked (see Glazes and
Toppings below) and bake in
the centre of a preheated
oven for about 20 minutes
until golden-brown and
cooked through. Transfer to
a wire rack and serve warm
or cold. Ⓕ

Ⓐ The dough can be made in
advance and left to rise
overnight in the refrigerator
if placed in a large lightly
oiled polythene bag (tied
loosely to allow room for
expansion). Knead well to
bring back to room
temperature before using.
Ⓕ Freeze for 4-6 weeks. Place
frozen rolls on a baking
sheet, cover with foil and
reheat at 190°C, 375°F, Gas
Mark 5 for 15 minutes.
Ⓜ Or microwave, 6 at a time,
on Defrost for 2-3 minutes,
then stand for 5 minutes,
before heating, 6 at a time, on
Full/Maximum for 45
seconds to 1 minute.

GLAZES:
Each of the following glazes
gives a different result as
described.
1. Brush with melted butter
or a little oil for a soft crust.
2. Brush with salt water (1
teaspoon salt to 4
tablespoons water) for a
crisp crust.
3. Brush with milk for a
golden brown finish.
4. Brush with beaten egg or
egg yolk mixed with a little
creamy milk for a glossy
finish.

TOPPINGS:
A sprinkling of any of the
following can be used to give
an attractive finish and added
taste: poppy seeds, sesame
seeds, natural bran, cracked
wheat, rolled oats, dried
herbs.

Left to right: Milk Bread Rolls; Hot Dog
Brunch Rolls; Wholewheat Date
Muffins.

Smoked Haddock Scramble

225 g (8 oz) smoked haddock
300 ml (½ pint) milk
40 g (1½ oz) butter
4 eggs
2 teaspoons chopped fresh
    parsley
freshly ground black pepper
4 slices hot buttered toast

TO GARNISH:
parsley sprigs

PREPARATION TIME: *5 minutes*
COOKING TIME: *10 minutes*

1. Put the haddock in a wide saucepan or deep frying pan and pour in the milk. Cook over a gentle heat for 7 minutes or until cooked through. Strain and reserve the milk. Flake the haddock coarsely, discarding all skin and bones. Ⓐ
2. Melt the butter in a saucepan. Whisk the eggs with 4 tablespoons of the reserved milk, the parsley and plenty of pepper. Pour the mixture into the pan and cook over a gentle heat, stirring constantly, until the mixture just begins to set.
3. Add the flaked haddock and cook for a further 1-1½ minutes, stirring all the time, until the mixture is cooked but still soft and creamy. Remove at once from the heat and pile quickly on to the hot buttered toast. Garnish with parsley and serve straight away.

Ⓐ Can be prepared several hours in advance, covered with cling film and kept in a cool place. Bring back to room temperature before using.

VARIATION:
Substitute 100 g (4 oz) peeled prawns for the smoked haddock. Alternatively use 100 g (4 oz) haddock and 100 g (4 oz) grated Cheddar cheese.

Baked Ham and Eggs in Tomatoes

SERVES 3-4

6 large firm tomatoes, weighing
    450 g (1 lb)
10 g (¼ oz) butter
25 g (1 oz) sliced cooked ham,
    chopped
40 g (1½ oz) Cheddar cheese,
    finely grated
2 eggs
2 tablespoons milk
¼ teaspoon salt
freshly ground black pepper

PREPARATION TIME: *10 minutes*
COOKING TIME: *20-25 minutes*
OVEN: *180°C, 350°F, Gas Mark 4*

If your family enjoys the flavour of herbs, add some chopped parsley, mint or chives to the egg mixture when beating, or sprinkle with fresh chopped herbs just before cooking.

1. Cut a small slice off the stalk end of each tomato. Very carefully scoop out the tomato pulp and seeds and keep to use in a soup or casserole. Ⓐ
2. Arrange the tomato cases in a single layer in a greased shallow ovenproof dish. Mix the ham with 25 g (1 oz) of the cheese and spoon the mixture into the tomato cases. Beat the eggs with the milk and salt and pepper in a jug and carefully pour into the tomato cases. Sprinkle with the remaining cheese.
3. Cook in a preheated oven for 20-25 minutes until the filling has set and risen.

Ⓐ Can be prepared several hours in advance, covered with cling film and kept in a cool place.

American Pancakes

MAKES 16

25 g (1 oz) butter
2 tablespoons golden syrup
1 egg
150 ml (¼ pint) plain
    unsweetened yogurt
1 teaspoon bicarbonate of soda
5 tablespoons milk
100 g (4 oz) plain flour
2-3 tablespoons vegetable oil

TO SERVE:
50 g (2 oz) butter, softened
maple or golden syrup

PREPARATION TIME: *6 minutes*
COOKING TIME: *5 minutes*

These delicious pancakes – thicker and sweeter than crêpe-style pancakes – are often eaten for breakfast in the USA, when they are served with maple syrup and butter and often accompanied by crispy bacon rashers.

1. Heat the butter and golden syrup in a saucepan until the butter has melted. Beat the egg with the yogurt in a bowl. Blend the bicarbonate of soda with the milk and add with the flour to the yogurt mixture. Pour in the golden syrup mixture and stir well, using a wooden spoon, to make a smooth, fairly thick batter.
2. Heat 2 tablespoons of the oil in a large frying pan. Pour off any excess oil into a jug, to leave the pan only lightly greased. Drop tablespoonfuls of the batter into the frying pan, slightly apart, and fry over a moderate heat until the pancakes are golden-brown on the underside. Turn the pancakes with a fish slice and cook for a further 2-3 minutes until golden-brown all over. Remove from the pan and keep warm while frying the remaining batter in the same way.
3. Pile the pancakes into stacks of three with a knob of butter between each layer and serve hot with warmed maple syrup.

VARIATION:
Soured Cherry Cream: Heat a 450 g (1 lb) can of pitted black cherries in a saucepan. Strain, reserving the syrup, and mix the cherries with 150 ml (¼ pint) soured cream. Pile the hot pancakes into stacks of three, with a little cherry mixture between each layer, and spoon over the hot cherry syrup to serve.

Banana Malties

75 g (3 oz) butter
3 teaspoons soft dark brown
    sugar
½ teaspoon ground cinnamon
8 thick slices malt loaf
3 medium bananas, peeled and
    sliced

PREPARATION TIME: *5 minutes*
COOKING TIME: *7 minutes*

1. Put the butter, sugar and cinnamon in a bowl and beat with a wooden spoon until soft and creamy. Ⓐ Toast the malt loaf slices on one side only.
2. Spread the untoasted sides with half the butter mixture and top with banana slices. Dot with small pieces of the remaining butter mixture and grill under a preheated moderate grill for 5 minutes until sizzling. Serve hot.

Ⓐ Can be prepared several days in advance if covered and kept in a cool place.

Mixed Fruit Jamboree

1½ tablespoons clear honey
4 tablespoons water
1 tablespoon lemon juice
2 dessert apples (1 red and 1
   green)
2 medium oranges
1 grapefruit
75 g (3 oz) black grapes, halved
   and seeded

PREPARATION TIME: *15 minutes,
plus chilling*

This colourful fruit cocktail is
delicious alone or with plain
unsweetened yogurt.

1. Put the honey and water
in a small saucepan and heat
gently until the honey
dissolves. Remove from the
heat and add the lemon juice.
Pour into a glass serving
bowl and leave to cool.
2. Quarter and core but do
not peel the apples and cut
into slices. Add the apple
slices to the cooled honey
syrup.
3. Using a sharp knife, peel
away the skin, pith and
membranes from the
oranges and grapefruit,
holding the fruit over the
serving bowl to catch any
juice. Divide into segments
and, with any juice, add to the
serving bowl with the grapes.
Stir lightly to coat all the fruit
in syrup, cover the bowl and
chill for at least 1 hour. Ⓐ

Ⓐ Can be prepared the night
before required, if covered
and kept chilled.

VARIATION:
Just before serving the fruit
cocktail, sprinkle with
sunflower seeds or toasted
flaked almonds.

Clockwise from the top: American
Pancakes; Baked Ham and Eggs in
Tomatoes; Smoked Haddock
Scramble; Mixed Fruit Jamboree;
Banana Malties.

Mary Meredith's

Scottish Breakfast

═ MENU ═

PORRIDGE

HERRING FILLETS IN OATMEAL

KEDGEREE

OATCAKES

DUNDEE MARMALADE

Give the family a substantial, warming start to a cold winter's day with a traditional Scottish breakfast of porridge, smoked haddock kedgeree or fried herrings in oatmeal, and oatcakes with home-made marmalade.

Bacon is an all-time breakfast favourite, with its tantalizing aroma: in Scotland Ayrshire roll is popular; this is both back and streaky bacon rolled together and thinly sliced. For quick, crisp grilling use thinly cut rashers. The best way to grill bacon is to lay the rashers overlapping on the grill rack, covering the lean on one rasher with the fat of the next. This keeps the lean beautifully moist and succulent while crisping the rest.

For breakfast every day of the year I personally never tire of toast and marmalade. There are so many varieties to make at home when Seville oranges are in season. It's my first job after taking down the Christmas cards! Although Dundee marmalade is far and away my favourite I am probably biased as I was born just up the coast from Dundee.

Porridge

3 tablespoons medium oatmeal
¼ teaspoon salt
600 ml (1 pint) water

TO FINISH:
single cream

PREPARATION TIME: *1 minute, plus soaking overnight*

COOKING TIME: *10 minutes*

This porridge is how I like it myself, not too thick, but another tablespoon of oatmeal may be added if preferred. Serve with milk or single cream for a special treat, and brown sugar or syrup, condensed milk or even ice cream toppings.

1. Put the oatmeal, salt and water into a non-stick saucepan, cover and leave overnight.
2. In the morning stir the porridge over a gentle heat until it comes to the boil, then simmer, stirring occasionally, for 5 minutes.
3. Add a swirl of cream to each individual serving.

Herring Fillets in Oatmeal

4 herrings, cleaned and with backbone removed
6 tablespoons medium oatmeal
1 teaspoon salt
freshly ground black pepper
a little butter, for frying
1 tablespoon oil

TO GARNISH:
lemon wedges
parsley sprigs

PREPARATION TIME: *10 minutes*

COOKING TIME: *8-10 minutes*

These crisply fried flavoursome fillets of herring are quick to make provided the fishmonger has removed the backbone. Although any fishmonger will do this for you, herrings are easily boned at home.

1. Wash the herrings and dry them thoroughly with absorbent paper. Using sharp kitchen scissors cut each herring lengthways into 2 fillets. Cut off the fins.
2. Spread the oatmeal out on a large plate and mix with the salt and plenty of pepper. Coat each herring fillet in the seasoned oatmeal. Ｆ
3. Melt enough butter with the oil in a large frying pan to cover the base, add half the herring fillets skin side uppermost and fry over a moderately high heat for 3-4 minutes until lightly browned, then turn and fry for a further 3-4 minutes.
4. Remove the fried herring fillets with a fish slice, drain off any excess fat and keep warm in a heated serving dish while frying the remaining fillets in the same way. Garnish with lemon wedges and parsley. Serve at once.

TO BONE A HERRING:
1. Using a pair of sharp kitchen scissors, cut off the head then slit the herring the length of the belly and remove the guts, keeping any roes for frying. Cut off the fins and wash the inside thoroughly.
2. Open out the herring and lay it flat, bone side down, on a board or working surface. Using a heavy-bladed knife, press gently but firmly along the length of the backbone to loosen it.
3. Turn the herring over and, starting at the head end, carefully ease out the backbone with the smaller bones attached.

Ｆ Freeze before frying. Wrap the fillets individually for easy use. Thaw and fry as above, or cook from frozen for a little longer over a moderate heat.
Ⅿ Or microwave on Defrost for 6-8 minutes. Stand for 5 minutes before frying as above.

Clockwise from the bottom: Porridge; Herring Fillets in Oatmeal; Kedgeree.

Kedgeree

50 g (2 oz) butter
350 g (12 oz) smoked haddock
    fillets
150 ml (¼ pint) milk
4 eggs
225 g (8 oz) long-grain rice
salt
1.2 litres (2 pints) water
freshly ground white pepper
4 tablespoons chopped fresh
    parsley

TO GARNISH:
parsley sprigs

PREPARATION TIME: *7-10 minutes*

COOKING TIME: *20 minutes*

This is a moist, quick-to-make kedgeree which will keep hot for those extended breakfast times, without becoming dry.

1. Place the fish and the milk in a shallow pan and poach for 5-6 minutes or until the fish flakes easily when pierced with a sharp knife.
2. Meanwhile, hardboil the eggs, then cook the rice in a large saucepan of boiling, salted water for 12-15 minutes or until just tender. Drain well and stir in the butter.
3. Strain the cooking liquid from the fish into the rice. Flake the fish, discarding any bones or skin. Heat the rice through over a very gentle heat and season with plenty of pepper and a little salt if required. Lightly fork the fish into the rice and reheat, stirring gently to avoid breaking up the fish.
4. Shell the eggs. Finely chop 2 of them and stir into the kedgeree with the parsley. Pile the kedgeree into a warmed serving dish. Cut the remaining eggs into quarters and use to garnish the kedgeree with the parsley.

Oatcakes

SERVES 8

50 g (2 oz) plain flour
½ teaspoon bicarbonate of
 soda
½ teaspoon salt
100 g (4 oz) medium oatmeal
40 g (1½ oz) margarine or
 butter
2-3 tablespoons water

PREPARATION TIME: *10 minutes,
plus cooling*

COOKING TIME: *20 minutes*

OVEN: *180°C, 350°F, Gas Mark 4*

These traditional oatcakes are baked in the oven but can also be cooked on a moderately hot lightly floured girdle. They will curl at the edges so are cooked on one side only.

1. Sift the flour with the bicarbonate of soda and salt into a mixing bowl and stir in the oatmeal.
2. Put the margarine or butter and water into a small saucepan and heat gently until the fat is melted. Stir into the dry ingredients and knead to a smooth ball, adding an extra tablespoon of warm water to bind if necessary.
3. On a floured board or work surface, roll out the dough while still warm and pliable to a 25 cm (10 inch) round. Use a dinner plate of similar size to trim the edge neatly, if liked. Cut into 8 triangles using a large, sharp knife.
4. Using a fish slice, transfer the triangles to a lightly floured baking sheet. Bake for about 20 minutes in a preheated oven. Transfer the oatcakes to a wire tray and leave to cool completely. Store in an airtight tin.

Below: Oatcakes. **Right:** Dundee Marmalade.

Dundee Marmalade

MAKES 21 lb

2.25 kg (5 lb) Seville oranges
2 large sweet oranges
3 lemons
6.25 litres (11 pints) water
5 kg (11 lb) sugar
a knob of butter

PREPARATION TIME: *2 hours if cutting peel by hand; 45 minutes by mincer or food processor*

COOKING TIME: *about 2-2¼ hours*

A large preserving pan is needed to make this amount of marmalade. Half the quantity can be made in exactly the same way, but the final boiling will take less time; start testing after about 20 minutes.

1. Wipe the fruit with a damp cloth, score the skins into quarters and peel off.

Using a sharp knife, shred the peel pith side upwards to the required thickness. Alternatively, use a mincer or food processor.

2. Line a small bowl with a 20 cm (8 inch) square piece of muslin. Chop the fruit flesh and place the pips in the muslin. Tie the muslin tightly with string, leaving plenty of space for the boiling liquid to circulate through the pips.

3. Put the fruit peel, flesh and pips with the water in a preserving pan. Simmer for 1 or 1½ hours, depending on the thickness of the peel, until the peel is absolutely tender. (The peel will not soften after the sugar is added so it is important to cook it thoroughly at this stage.)

4. Remove the bag of pips, cool it on a plate, then squeeze all the juice from it into the marmalade. Add the sugar to the marmalade and stir over a gentle heat until it is dissolved. Bring to the boil and boil rapidly until the whole surface is bubbling vigorously. Boil for 30-45 minutes, stirring occasionally and at the same time moving the pan slightly to make sure that all of the base comes in contact with the heat.

5. Hang a sugar thermometer in the centre of the pan. The setting stage is reached at 112°C/242°F. If you do not have a sugar thermometer, for a simple test put a spoonful of marmalade on to a cold plate and leave to cool. Run your finger through it and if a wrinkle forms on the surface, the marmalade is ready.

6. Turn off the heat and stir

in the butter to clear any scum. Leave for 2-3 minutes to distribute the peel evenly, then ladle the marmalade into warm jars, filling them well up the necks.

7. Wipe the jars with a damp cloth while still warm, then cover them with waxed paper discs. Lightly moisten each transparent cover with a damp cloth and stretch it, damp side uppermost, over the jar top. Secure with an elastic band. Label carefully and store in a cool, dark, dry cupboard. The marmalade will probably thicken with keeping.

VARIATION:

Whisky Marmalade: Add 4 tablespoons whisky to the last 1 kg (2 lb) marmalade in the pan, bring briskly to the boil, then ladle into small jars and cover as in step 7.

Potato, Carrot and Barley Soup

SERVES 6

50 g (2 oz) butter or hard margarine
350 g (12 oz) potatoes, peeled and cut into 2.5 cm (1 inch) cubes
250 g (9 oz) carrots, scraped and thinly sliced
1 large onion, peeled and chopped
1 tablespoon plain flour
1.2 litres (2 pints) hot good chicken stock
½ teaspoon dried mixed herbs
salt
freshly ground black pepper
50 g (2 oz) pearl barley, soaked overnight in cold water, drained
300 ml (½ pint) milk

TO GARNISH:
croûtons of fried bread
a little chopped fresh parsley

PREPARATION TIME: *15 minutes, plus soaking overnight*
COOKING TIME: *40-45 minutes*

For best results do not add pearl barley until 30 minutes before serving as it will continue to swell and cause the soup to overthicken. To make croûtons, cut fresh or stale bread into neat cubes and fry in a little hot oil until golden brown. Drain on absorbent paper before serving.

1. Melt the butter or margarine in a large saucepan, add the potatoes, carrots and onion and fry gently over a gentle heat, stirring from time to time, for 5 minutes. Sprinkle in the flour and cook for 1 further minute, then add 900 ml (1½ pints) of the stock and bring to the boil, stirring.
2. Lower the heat, add the herbs and salt and pepper to taste, then cover and simmer gently for 30 minutes or until

the vegetables are tender. Allow to cool lightly, then place in a food processor or blender goblet and process for 30 seconds or until smooth. (Or pass the mixture through a sieve.) Ⓐ Ⓕ
3. Return the soup to the pan, stir in the remaining stock and the barley and bring to the boil. Lower the heat, cover and cook for a further 30 minutes, stirring occasionally, until the barley is tender.
4. Stir in the milk and taste and adjust the seasoning. Heat through gently. Serve the soup piping hot in warmed individual soup bowls, garnished with croûtons and parsley.

Ⓐ Can be prepared 2 days in advance and kept covered in a plastic or glass container in the refrigerator.
Ⓕ Reheat from frozen over a gentle heat, then follow instructions given in step 3.
Ⓜ Or microwave on Defrost for 20-25 minutes, breaking up gently as soon as possible, then follow instructions from step 3.

Creamy Corn and Chicken Chowder

SERVES 4-6

25 g (1 oz) butter or hard margarine
1 large onion, peeled and chopped
1 small red pepper, cored, seeded and diced
500 g (1¼ lb) potatoes, peeled and cut into dice
25 g (1 oz) plain flour
750 ml (1¼ pints) hot good chicken stock
175 g (6 oz) frozen sweetcorn, thawed
225 g (8 oz) cooked chicken, chopped
450 ml (¾ pint) milk
½ teaspoon salt
freshly ground white pepper
3 tablespoons chopped fresh parsley

PREPARATION TIME: *10 minutes*
COOKING TIME: *about 30 minutes*

1. Melt the butter or margarine in a large saucepan. Add the onion, red pepper and potatoes and fry over a moderate heat for 5 minutes, stirring from time to time.

2. Sprinkle in the flour and cook over a gentle heat for 1 minute. Gradually stir in the stock and bring to the boil, stirring, then lower the heat, cover and cook for 10 minutes. Ⓐ
3. Stir in the sweetcorn, chicken, milk, salt and pepper and parsley, then cover and simmer gently for a further 10 minutes until the potatoes are just tender. Taste and adjust the seasoning. Serve the chowder hot in warmed individual soup bowls, with crusty bread.

Ⓐ Can be prepared in the morning, covered with foil and kept in a cool place.

VARIATION:
Substitute diced ham, or peeled prawns (thawed if frozen) for the chicken.
  For a more creamy variation, substitute 150 ml (¼ pint) single cream for the same quantity of milk.

Tomato Cup Soup

SERVES 4-5

40 g (1½ oz) butter or hard margarine
100 g (4 oz) streaky bacon rashers, rinded, boned and chopped
2 large leeks, trimmed, washed and sliced
1 medium onion, peeled and sliced
1 garlic clove, peeled and crushed (optional)
750 g (1½ lb) ripe, firm tomatoes, quartered
1 tablespoon plain flour
600 ml (1 pint) hot chicken stock
1 tablespoon caster sugar
1 tablespoon tomato purée
salt
freshly ground black pepper
150 ml (¼ pint) single cream

TO GARNISH:
4 tablespoons single cream (optional)

PREPARATION TIME: *10 minutes*
COOKING TIME: *40 minutes*

When leeks are unavailable use 2 large onions, plus the onion given in the recipe. As tomatoes vary in sharpness during the year you may sometimes find it necessary to sweeten to taste with more caster sugar before serving.

1. Melt the butter or margarine in a large saucepan, add the bacon, leeks, onion and garlic, if using, and fry over a moderate heat for 5 minutes, stirring from time to time. Add the tomatoes and cook for a further 5 minutes, then sprinkle in the flour and cook for 1 further minute, stirring.
2. Gradually stir in the stock and bring to the boil, stirring. Lower the heat, then add the sugar, tomato purée and salt and pepper to taste. Cover and simmer gently for 25 minutes. Remove from the heat and allow to cool slightly, then place in a food processor or blender goblet and process for 30 seconds or until smooth. Pass the soup through a sieve. Ⓐ Ⓕ
3. Return the soup to the pan, stir in the cream and taste and adjust the seasoning. Reheat gently but do not allow to boil. Serve the soup in warmed mugs or cups with a swirl of cream on each, if liked.

Ⓐ Can be made 2 days in advance, if stored in a glass bowl, covered with cling film and kept chilled.
Ⓕ Reheat from frozen over a gentle heat, then follow instructions given in step 3.
Ⓜ Or microwave on Defrost for 15-20 minutes, breaking up gently as soon as possible, then continue with instructions in step 3.

Hot Cheesy Garlic Bread

SERVES 4-6

1 medium French loaf
100 g (4 oz) butter or hard margarine, softened
1 garlic clove, peeled and crushed
1½ tablespoons chopped fresh chives or parsley
100 g (4 oz) Red Leicester or Cheddar cheese, finely grated

PREPARATION TIME: *10 minutes*
COOKING TIME: *20 minutes*
OVEN: *190°C, 375°F, Gas Mark 5*

A tasty variation on garlic bread which makes a substantial snack on its own and an excellent accompaniment to a crisp summer salad or a bowl of piping hot soup.

1. Carefully cut the loaf into 2.5 cm (1 inch) thick slices, cutting almost through to the bottom crust but keeping the loaf whole. Using a wooden spoon, cream the butter or margarine with the garlic, chives or parsley and cheese in a bowl.
2. Spread the savoury butter on each side of each slice of bread and over the top of the loaf. Place the loaf on a large piece of kitchen foil and wrap the foil around the loaf to enclose it completely. Ⓐ Ⓕ
3. Place on a baking sheet and bake in a preheated oven for 15 minutes. Then carefully open up the foil and fold it back to expose the top of the loaf. Bake for a further 5 minutes. Cut into slices and serve hot.

Ⓐ Can be prepared a day in advance, well wrapped in cling film to prevent tainting other foods and kept in a cool place.
Ⓕ Thaw for 3 hours at room temperature and follow instructions given in step 3, or cook from frozen allowing another 5 minutes in the oven.

Top left: Potato, Carrot and Barley Soup; Creamy Corn and Chicken Chowder. **Above:** Tomato Cup Soup; Hot Cheesy Garlic Bread.

Crunchy Ham Roll-Ups

MAKES 8

2-3 teaspoons Mayonnaise
(page 32), or good quality
bought mayonnaise
100 g (4 oz) coleslaw
100 g (4 oz) cottage cheese
3 crisp lettuce leaves, finely
shredded
40 g (1½ oz) salted peanuts
salt
freshly ground black pepper
8 square slices cooked ham

TO GARNISH:
shredded lettuce
lemon slices

PREPARATION TIME: *10 minutes*

Arranged on a bed of
shredded lettuce and
garnished with lemon slices,
these stuffed ham rolls look
most attractive. Either serve
one per person as a starter or
two per person for a midday
meal.

1. Put the mayonnaise,
coleslaw, cottage cheese,
lettuce, peanuts and salt and
pepper to taste in a large
bowl and mix well together.
2. Place 2 teaspoonfuls of
the mixture on each ham
slice and roll up like a Swiss
roll.
3. Arrange the rolls on a bed
of shredded lettuce on a
serving dish and garnish with
lemon slices. Serve with
crusty bread.

VARIATION:
Vary the fillings with grated
Cheddar cheese; grated
carrot and a little finely
shredded red cabbage, or
full fat soft cheese with finely
chopped cucumber and red
or green pepper.

Top to bottom: Fisherman's Corn Pie;
Golden Beef Patties; Crunchy Ham
Roll-Ups.

Fisherman's Corn Pie

SERVES 4-6

1 kg (2 lb) old potatoes, peeled and cut into even-sized pieces
65 g (2½ oz) butter or hard margarine
100 g (4 oz) Cheddar cheese, finely grated
salt
freshly ground black pepper
450 g (1 lb) smoked haddock or cod fillets
450 ml (¾ pint) milk
25 g (1 oz) plain flour
100 g (4 oz) sweetcorn, canned and drained or frozen and thawed

---

PREPARATION TIME: *15 minutes*
COOKING TIME: *1 hour 10 minutes*
OVEN: *200°C, 400°F, Gas Mark 6*

---

1. Cook the potatoes in a saucepan of boiling, salted water for 20 minutes or until tender. Drain well, return to the pan and shake over a low heat to dry off. Add 25 g (1 oz) of the butter or margarine, half the cheese and salt and pepper to taste. Mash well with a potato masher or fork. Ⓐ
2. Meanwhile, place the fish in a large saucepan, add the milk, cover and cook over a gentle heat for 7 minutes. Strain, reserving the milk, and leave the fish to cool slightly. Flake the fish, discarding the skin and bones. Ⓐ
3. Melt the remaining butter or margarine in a saucepan. Sprinkle in the flour and cook for 1 minute, stirring, then remove from the heat. Make up the reserved milk to 450 ml (¾ pint) with extra milk or water, if necessary, and gradually stir into the pan. Return to the heat and bring to the boil, stirring, then lower the heat and simmer for 2 minutes, stirring all the time. Remove from the heat and stir in the remaining cheese, with the sweetcorn and flaked fish. Season to taste with salt and pepper and stir well to mix. Turn the mixture into a 1.2 litre (2 pint) ovenproof dish. Ⓐ
4. Cover the fish mixture with the mashed potato and mark attractively with a knife.
5. Cook in a preheated oven for 35-40 minutes until the topping is golden brown and the pie is heated through. Serve hot with a green vegetable.

Ⓐ The potatoes can be cooked and mashed several hours in advance, then left to cool, covered and kept in a cool place. Soften well with a wooden spoon before using.

The fish can be cooked and flaked the previous day, covered with cling film and kept chilled.

The fish and cheese sauce mixture can be prepared in the morning, covered with cling film and kept chilled.

VARIATIONS:
Add a few prawns to the fish sauce and use sliced green beans, broad beans, sliced carrots or peas instead of sweetcorn if preferred.

Golden Beef Patties

MAKES 4

1 tablespoon vegetable oil or beef dripping
225 g (8 oz) lean minced beef
1 small onion, peeled and chopped
1 small carrot, scraped and grated
1 celery stick, trimmed and chopped
½-1 teaspoon mild curry powder (optional)
1 tablespoon plain flour
4 tablespoons beef stock
2 teaspoons tomato purée
salt
freshly ground black pepper
1 × 400 g (14 oz) packet frozen puff pastry, thawed

TO GLAZE:
a little beaten egg

TO GARNISH:
tomato wedges
parsley sprigs

PREPARATION TIME: *12 minutes, plus cooling*
COOKING TIME: *about 55 minutes*
OVEN: *190°C, 375°F, Gas Mark 5*

Any left-over puff pastry can be re-rolled and cut into dainty shapes, then glazed with beaten egg and baked in a hot oven (220°C, 400°F, Gas Mark 6) for 7-10 minutes until golden brown. Use them to garnish hot soups, casseroles or fish dishes. Stored in an airtight container, they will keep for up to 3 weeks.

1. Heat the oil or dripping in a saucepan, add the minced beef, onion, carrot and celery and fry over a gentle heat for 5 minutes, stirring frequently. Stir in the curry powder, if using, and the flour and cook for 1 further minute. Gradually stir in the stock with the tomato purée and season to taste with salt and pepper. Bring to the boil, then lower the heat, cover and cook over a gentle heat for 20 minutes, stirring frequently. Taste and adjust the seasoning if necessary, then leave until cold (about 30 minutes). Ⓐ
2. Roll out the pastry on a lightly floured board or work surface to a 30×40 cm (12×16 inch) rectangle. Cut out 6 rounds using a 13 cm (5 inch) plate or saucer. Re-roll the trimmings and cut out 2 more rounds.
3. Spoon the mince mixture on to 4 of the pastry rounds, dividing it equally among them. Roll out the remaining 4 rounds 2.5 cm (1 inch) larger in diameter. Dampen the pastry edges and place over the mince mixture. Seal the pastry edges firmly. Knock up the pastry edges, using the back of a knife, and flute all the way round. Make a small hole in the centre of each patty Ⓐ and brush with beaten egg.
4. Place the patties on a dampened baking sheet and cook in a preheated oven for 25-30 minutes until well risen, golden brown and cooked through. Ⓕ Serve hot or cold, garnished with tomato and parsley.

Ⓐ Filling can be made the previous day, covered with cling film and kept chilled.

Patties can be prepared to this stage several hours before required, covered with cling film and kept chilled. Glaze with egg before cooking as in step 4.
Ⓕ Freeze for up to 3 months. Thaw at room temperature for 1-2 hours, then reheat at 180°C, 350°F, Gas Mark 4 for 15 minutes or until thoroughly heated through. Cover with foil if necessary to prevent overbrowning.

Mayonnaise

MAKES 150 ml (¼ pint)

1 egg yolk
½ teaspoon English mustard
  powder
½ teaspoon salt
freshly ground white pepper
½ teaspoon caster sugar
1 tablespoon lemon juice or
  white wine vinegar
150 ml (¼ pint) sunflower or
  corn oil

PREPARATION TIME: *7-10 minutes*

For best results have the egg yolk at room temperature before beginning the recipe. Mayonnaise can be kept successfully for up to 3 weeks in a screw-topped jar in the refrigerator.

1. Place the egg yolk in a clean dry bowl. Add the mustard powder, salt, pepper and sugar and blend well with a whisk or wooden spoon. Gradually blend in 1 teaspoon of the lemon juice.

2. Stand the bowl on a damp tea towel to keep it steady. Add the oil, drop by drop, from a jug, beating all the time until about a quarter of the oil has been absorbed. Gradually increase the addition of oil to a thin, steady stream, beating thoroughly all the time.
3. When the mayonnaise is thick and glossy and all the oil has been absorbed, stir in the remaining lemon juice. Spoon the mayonnaise into a

small bowl, cover with cling film and chill until required. Bring to room temperature before serving.

VARIATIONS:
Add any one of the following to a basic mayonnaise:
1 teaspoon curry powder; the finely grated rind of 1 small lemon; ¼ bunch of very finely chopped watercress; 1½ tablespoons tomato purée; 1 teaspoon Worcestershire sauce.

French Dressing

MAKES 150 ml (¼ pint)

6 tablespoons corn or
   sunflower oil
2 tablespoons malt or red wine
   vinegar
½ teaspoon caster sugar
¼ teaspoon English mustard
   powder (optional)
2 good pinches of salt
freshly ground black pepper
1 garlic clove, peeled and
   crushed (optional)

PREPARATION TIME: *5 minutes*

The dressing can be stored
for several months in the
refrigerator.

1. Place all ingredients in a
screw-topped jar and shake
vigorously until thoroughly
blended.
2. Always shake dressing
again vigorously before
using.

VARIATIONS:
Lemon Dressing: Add 2
tablespoons lemon juice
instead of vinegar and a little
finely grated lemon rind if
liked.
Herb Dressing: Add 1
tablespoon chopped fresh
chives, parsley, mint or basil.
Paprika Dressing: Add 1
teaspoon paprika pepper
instead of mustard.
Mustard Dressing: Increase
the quantity of English
mustard powder to 1
teaspoon, or add 1 teaspoon
Dijon or grainy Meaux
mustard.
   These flavoured French
Dressing variations should
be used within 1 week of
making.

Clockwise from the top: French
Dressing; Frankfurter Potato Salad
Deluxe; Saucy Liver and Mushroom
Pasta; Mayonnaise.

Saucy Liver and Mushroom Pasta

300 ml (½ pint) milk
350 g (12 oz) lamb's liver, cut
   into thin 5 mm × 5 cm
   (¼ × 2 inch) strips
50 g (2 oz) plain flour
¼ teaspoon salt
freshly ground black pepper
50 g (2 oz) butter
1½ tablespoons vegetable oil
2 large onions, peeled, halved
   and thinly sliced
100 g (4 oz) button
   mushrooms, wiped and
   thinly sliced
150 ml (¼ pint) hot chicken
   stock
1½ tablespoons tomato purée
225 g (8 oz) tagliatelle noodles
1½ tablespoons chopped fresh
   parsley

TO GARNISH:
chervil sprig

PREPARATION TIME: *10 minutes*
COOKING TIME: *20 minutes*

1. Put the milk and the strips
of liver in a shallow dish.
Turn the liver to soak in the
milk, then remove, reserving
the milk. Spread the flour out
on a plate, season with salt
and pepper and turn the liver
in the seasoned flour, to coat
thoroughly.
2. Heat 15 g (½ oz) of the
butter and ½ tablespoon of
the oil in a frying pan. Add
the liver strips and fry over a
moderate heat for 3 minutes,
stirring frequently. Remove
from the pan with a slotted
spoon and set aside on a
plate.
3. Add 25 g (1 oz) of the
butter and the remaining oil
to the pan, add the onions
and mushrooms and fry over
a gentle heat for 3 minutes,
stirring.
4. Stir in the stock, reserved
milk and tomato purée and

bring to the boil, stirring.
Lower the heat, add the liver,
cover the pan with a lid or
foil and cook over a gentle
heat for 12 minutes, stirring
frequently. Taste and adjust
the seasoning.
5. Meanwhile, cook the
tagliatelle noodles in a
saucepan of boiling, salted
water for 6-8 minutes until
tender. Drain well, rinse with
boiling water and drain well
again. Melt the remaining
butter in the rinsed out pan
and stir in the parsley. Add
the tagliatelle noodles and
toss to coat thoroughly in
melted butter.
6. Spoon the noodles on to a
warmed serving dish and
spoon the liver mixture in
the centre. Garnish with
chervil and serve at once.

Frankfurter Potato Salad Deluxe

1 kg (2 lb) small potatoes,
   scraped
salt
150 ml (¼ pint) French
   Dressing (opposite)
1 bunch of spring onions,
   trimmed and chopped
4 frankfurters, cut into 1 cm
   (½ inch) slices
1 head of fennel, trimmed,
   sliced and chopped
4 tablespoons Mayonnaise
   (page 32) or good quality
   bought mayonnaise
freshly ground black pepper
1 teaspoon mild Burger
   mustard (optional)
crisp lettuce leaves

TO GARNISH:
spring onion tops, chopped

PREPARATION TIME: *15 minutes,*
plus cooling
COOKING TIME: *about 12*
minutes

1. Cook the potatoes in a
large saucepan of boiling,
salted water for 10-12
minutes until just tender,
then drain. Take care not to
overcook, or the appearance
of the salad will be spoilt.
Using a knife and fork,
quickly cut the potatoes into
2 cm (¾ inch) cubes and
place in a salad bowl.
2. Pour the French Dressing
over the hot potatoes and
mix lightly to coat
thoroughly with dressing.
Leave for 30-40 minutes until
cold. Ⓐ
3. Meanwhile mix together
the spring onions,
frankfurters and fennel in a
bowl. Blend the mayonnaise
with salt and pepper to taste
and the mustard, if using.
Add to the frankfurter
mixture and stir well to mix.
4. Add the frankfurter
mixture to the cold potatoes
and mix lightly to combine

thoroughly. Line a serving
dish with crisp lettuce leaves
and pile the frankfurter
potato salad on top. Garnish
with spring onion tops.

Ⓐ Potatoes can be cooked
and mixed with French
Dressing several hours in
advance, covered with cling
film and kept in a cold place.

VARIATION:
Omit frankfurters and
mustard and add a 200 g
(7 oz) can of tuna, drained
and roughly flaked. Use 2-3
celery sticks, sliced, instead
of the fennel.

Chicken, Melon and Cress Salad

½ ripe honeydew melon, seeded, peeled and diced
450 g (1 lb) cooked boneless chicken, diced
1 red pepper, cored, seeded and cut into thin strips
100-175 g (4-6 oz) fresh beansprouts
salt
freshly ground white pepper
6-8 tablespoons Mayonnaise (page 32) or good quality bought mayonnaise
4 tablespoons single cream
3 teaspoons tomato purée
1 carton of mustard and cress

PREPARATION TIME: *10 minutes*

This salad is quick and simple to make and deliciously refreshing to eat.

1. Put the melon, chicken, red pepper and beansprouts into a large bowl and season to taste with salt and pepper.
2. Combine the mayonnaise, cream and tomato purée and pour over the chicken mixture. Mix lightly until all the ingredients are thoroughly coated.
3. Turn the mixture into a serving bowl and arrange the mustard and cress in an attractive border around the salad. Serve chilled with thin brown bread and butter.

VARIATION:
Shredded Chinese leaves or sliced celery can be used instead of fresh beansprouts.

Spinach Crunch Salad

SERVES 4-6

1½ tablespoons vegetable oil
1 garlic clove, peeled and crushed (optional)
2-3 slices brown or white bread, crusts removed and cut into neat cubes
225 g (8 oz) fresh young spinach, washed, stalks removed
2 medium courgettes, trimmed, quartered lengthways and sliced
1 medium onion, peeled, sliced and separated into rings
3 tablespoons raisins or sultanas
1 bunch of radishes, trimmed and quartered
100 g (4 oz) sliced salami, smoked sausage or ham, cut into strips
150 ml (¼ pint) French Dressing (page 33)

PREPARATION TIME: *10 minutes*
COOKING TIME: *4 minutes*

1. Heat the oil in a frying pan, add the garlic, if using, and the bread cubes and fry over a moderate heat until golden-brown, turning frequently. Drain on absorbent paper. Ⓐ
2. Dry the spinach thoroughly with absorbent paper and tear into bite-sized pieces. Place in a serving bowl.
3. Add the courgettes, onion rings, raisins, radishes and salami, smoked sausage or ham. Pour over the French Dressing and toss well until all the ingredients are well coated. Scatter the croûtons over the salad and serve immediately.

Ⓐ Can be prepared 3-4 days in advance if kept in an airtight container.

VARIATION:
When fresh spinach is unavailable use Chinese leaves, shredded red or white cabbage, or crisp lettuce as good crunchy alternatives.

Cottage Cheese Fruit Medley

SERVES 1-2

1 large orange
6 strawberries, hulled and sliced
½ red dessert apple, cored and sliced
1 slice fresh or canned pineapple, cut into cubes (optional)
1 small slice melon, about 175 g (6 oz), seeded, peeled and cut into cubes
225 g (8 oz) cottage cheese
1 tablespoon lemon juice
1 teaspoon clear honey
25 g (1 oz) walnuts, coarsely chopped

PREPARATION TIME: *10 minutes*

1. Using a sharp knife, peel away the skin and pith from the orange. Holding the orange over a plate to catch the juice, cut into segments, discarding all the membranes.
2. Arrange all the fruits on a small serving dish and pile the cottage cheese into the centre. Blend the lemon juice with the honey and any reserved orange juice, and spoon over the salad. Sprinkle the chopped walnuts over the top and serve chilled. Ⓐ

Ⓐ Can be prepared up to 3 hours in advance, covered with cling film and kept chilled.

Piperade Baps

1 tablespoon vegetable oil
50 g (2 oz) butter
1 large onion, peeled and chopped
1 garlic clove, peeled and crushed (optional)
1 medium green pepper, cored, seeded and cut into thin strips
4 rashers streaky bacon, rinded, boned and diced
4 eggs, beaten
1½ tablespoons cold water
salt
freshly ground black pepper
4 floury baps, warmed

PREPARATION TIME: *10 minutes*
COOKING TIME: *10 minutes*

This classic French open omelette makes a delicious and nutritious filling for baps or crusty rolls – and is also good served on its own or with a mixed salad.

1. Heat the oil and 15 g (½ oz) of the butter in a 20-23 cm (8-9 inch) frying pan. Add the onion, garlic, if using, the green pepper and bacon and fry over a gentle heat for about 5 minutes, stirring from time to time.
2. Meanwhile, whisk the eggs together with the water, and salt and pepper to taste. Pour into the onion mixture in the pan and stir lightly with a fork. Cook over a gentle heat for about 3 minutes, until the mixture is golden brown underneath.
3. Place the pan under a preheated hot grill for 2-3 minutes until the mixture is set on top. Turn on to a board and cut into quarters. Split the baps and spread with the remaining butter. Place an omelette quarter in each bap and serve at once.

Clockwise from bottom left: Chicken, Melon and Cress Salad; Piperade Baps; Spinach Crunch Salad; Cottage Cheese Fruit Medley.

Cornish Pasties

MAKES 8

PASTRY:
450 g (1 lb) plain white flour
¼ teaspoon salt
100 g (4 oz) hard margarine
100 g (4 oz) lard
150 ml (¼ pint) cold water

FILLING:
450 g (1 lb) braising steak,
    trimmed of fat and gristle and
    cut into thin strips
225 g (8 oz) potatoes, peeled
    and chipped into thin flakes
175 g (6 oz) swede, peeled and
    chipped into thin flakes
2 medium onions, peeled and
    finely chopped
salt
freshly ground black pepper
25 g (1 oz) butter

TO GLAZE:
a little beaten egg, mixed with a
    little milk

TO GARNISH:
lettuce leaves
tomato wedges

PREPARATION TIME: *45-55
minutes*
COOKING TIME: *1 hour*
OVEN: *190°C, 375°F, Gas Mark 5*

1. Make the pastry: sift the flour with the salt into a mixing bowl, add the margarine and lard and rub into the flour with the fingertips, until the mixture resembles coarse breadcrumbs. Add the water and mix to form a soft dough, using a round-bladed knife. Knead gently on a lightly floured work surface until free from cracks. Chill while preparing the filling. Ⓐ
2. Put the meat, potatoes, swede and onions into a bowl and season well with salt and pepper. Stir to mix.
3. Divide the pastry into 8. Roll out each piece on a lightly floured board or work surface to an 18 cm (7 inch) round and using an 18 cm (7 inch) plate as a guide, trim round each.
4. Spoon equal portions of the filling on to the centre of each pastry round. Divide the butter into 8 and place on each portion of filling, then dampen the pastry edges and draw up both sides to meet on top of the filling, taking care not to stretch the pastry. Seal the edges firmly and form a 1 cm (½ inch) high edge on top of each pasty. Crimp the edge decoratively with the fingertips, folding and tucking the edge under, to give a 'rope' effect down the length of each pasty. Place the pasties on a lightly greased baking sheet. Ⓐ
5. Make a small hole at the side of each join and brush each pasty with beaten egg and milk. Place in a preheated oven and bake for 1 hour or until golden brown and cooked through. (Cover with foil if necessary to prevent over-browning.) To test if the vegetables are tender, insert a fine metal skewer or wooden cocktail stick into the hole in each pasty. Serve hot or cold, garnished with lettuce and tomato. Ⓕ

Ⓐ The pastry can be made 2-3 days in advance, wrapped in cling film and stored in the refrigerator.
    The pasties can be prepared 3-4 hours before required, then covered with cling film and kept chilled.
Ⓕ Thaw for several hours at room temperature then cover with foil and heat through in a preheated oven (180°C, 350°, Gas Mark 4) for 15 minutes.
Ⓜ Or microwave, 4 at a time, on Defrost for 8-12 minutes. Stand for 20-30 minutes before heating in conventional oven as above.

Chunky Pan-Fried Sandwiches

8 medium-thick slices white or
    wholemeal bread, crusts
    removed, if liked
4 slices cooked ham
1 medium onion, peeled, thinly
    sliced and separated into
    rings
100 g (4 oz) Cheddar cheese,
    thinly sliced
50 g (2 oz) butter, softened

TO GARNISH:
watercress sprigs

PREPARATION TIME: *5 minutes*
COOKING TIME: *6-7 minutes*

You don't have to own a sandwich toaster to make these lovely melted cheese and ham sandwiches – they can be made just as easily in a frying pan.

1. Place 4 bread slices on a board and cover each one with a slice of ham. Top with onion rings to taste and then cover with slices of cheese. Top with the remaining bread slices and press down lightly. Ⓐ
2. Spread a little butter on

the outer sides of each sandwich. Heat a large frying pan over moderate heat, without added fat. Add two of the sandwiches and fry over a gentle heat for 2-3 minutes until golden brown on the undersides.

3. Using a fish slice, carefully turn the sandwiches and fry for a further 3-4 minutes, pressing the sandwiches down with the fish slice until golden brown on both sides. Keep warm while frying the

remaining sandwiches in the same way. Cut each sandwich into 4 triangles and serve immediately, garnished with watercress sprigs.

Ⓐ The sandwiches can be made a day in advance, wrapped in cling film and kept in a cool place.

VARIATIONS:
Tuna Tomato Special: fill the sandwiches with 1×200 g (7 oz) can tuna in oil, drained and flaked, combined with

50 g (2 oz) Edam cheese, finely grated and 1½ tablespoons tomato relish, with 2 tomatoes, thinly sliced. Fry the sandwiches in the same way.
Bacon, Cheese and Pineapple: fill the sandwiches with 8 streaky bacon rashers, rinded, boned and fried, 1×225 g (8 oz) can pineapple rings, drained and halved and 100 g (4 oz) Cheddar cheese, grated. Fry the sandwiches in the same way.

Souffléd Ham Rarebits

4 slices bread, crusts removed if liked
100 g (4 oz) Red Leicester cheese, thinly sliced
4 thin slices cooked ham
4 eggs, separated
½ tablespoon milk
salt
freshly ground black pepper

TO GARNISH:
parsley sprigs

PREPARATION TIME: *10 minutes*
COOKING TIME: *15-20 minutes*
OVEN: *180°C, 350°F, Gas Mark 4*

These tasty rarebits are quick to prepare. The soufflé topping, piled high on the ham and cheese, makes an impressive snack meal which children will love.

1. Toast the bread slices on one side only. Arrange, toasted sides down, on a baking sheet. Top each bread slice with slices of cheese and a slice of ham.
2. Beat the egg yolks with the milk and salt and pepper to taste. Whisk the egg whites until stiff peaks form, then gently fold into the egg yolk mixture, using a large metal spoon.
3. Spoon a portion of the egg mixture over each rarebit. Bake in a preheated oven for 15-20 minutes until the soufflé topping is set and golden brown. Serve immediately, garnished with parsley sprigs.

VARIATION:
Spread untoasted sides of bread with a little French mustard if liked before adding the ham, cheese and egg topping.

Left to right: Cornish Pasties; Souffléd Ham Rarebits; Crunchy Pan-Fried Sandwiches.

Apple Salad Cups

4 large red dessert apples
1 tablespoon lemon juice
1 small banana, peeled,
  quartered and sliced
50 g (2 oz) sultanas
25 g (1 oz) flaked almonds,
  chopped
3 tablespoon diced melon
  (optional)
150 ml (¼ pint) black cherry
  yogurt

PREPARATION TIME: *20 minutes*

Encourage children to eat more fruit by serving these pretty little individual fruit, yogurt and nut salads.

1. Cut a thin slice off each apple at the flower end. Using a serrated grapefruit knife or small sharp knife, carefully scoop out the apple flesh, cutting to within 5 mm (¼ inch) of the edge of each apple. Discard the cores. Cut the apple flesh into small dice and place in a bowl.
2. Brush the insides of the apple shells with lemon juice and sprinkle the remainder over the diced apple. Toss well to prevent the apple from discolouring. Ⓐ
3. Add the banana, sultanas, almonds and melon, if using, to the apple. Stir in the yogurt and lightly mix together. Spoon the fruit mixture into the apple shells and serve immediately.

Ⓐ The Apple Salad Cups can be prepared up to 1 hour in advance, covered with cling film and kept in a cool place.

VARIATION:
Use a ripe peach, stoned and chopped, instead of the banana, when in season.

Peachy Almond Meringues

SERVES 4-6

---

4 ripe peaches, peeled and
  halved
10 g (¼ oz) butter
8 maraschino or glacé cherries
3 egg whites
75 g (3 oz) ground almonds
75 g (3 oz) soft light brown
  sugar

PREPARATION TIME: *10 minutes*

COOKING TIME: *15 minutes*

OVEN: *190°C, 375°F, Gas Mark 5*

---

1. Arrange the peach halves cut side up in a buttered shallow ovenproof dish. Place a cherry in the middle of each peach half.
2. Whisk the egg whites until stiff peaks form. Using a large metal spoon, lightly and carefully fold the ground almonds and sugar into the whisked egg whites.
3. Spoon the almond meringue over the peach halves. Bake in a preheated oven for 15 minutes or until the meringue is set and golden brown. Serve hot with ice cream.

VARIATIONS:
Canned peach halves can be used instead of fresh peaches; pat dry on absorbent paper before placing in the dish. Heat the peach syrup from the can in a small saucepan and hand separately in a jug with the Peachy Almond Meringues.

The almond meringue can be sprinkled with flaked almonds or chopped mixed nuts before baking.

Buttered Bananas with Pineapple Cream Sauce

4 medium bananas, peeled and
  halved lengthways
2 tablespoons soft light brown
  sugar
40 g (1 ½ oz) butter
150 ml (¼ pint) unsweetened
  pineapple juice
150 ml (¼ pint) single cream

TO DECORATE:
1 tablespoon chopped mixed
  nuts

PREPARATION TIME: *5 minutes*
COOKING TIME: *7 minutes*

A deliciously rich dessert
made in a matter of moments
from a few simple
ingredients.

1. Roll the bananas in the
sugar. Melt the butter in a
large frying pan until
foaming, then add the
bananas and fry over a
moderate heat, for about 3-4
minutes, turning
occasionally, until the sugar
begins to caramelize.
Carefully transfer the
bananas to a warmed serving
dish and keep warm.
2. Pour the pineapple juice
into the pan, bring to the boil
and boil for 2 minutes,
stirring constantly. Stir in the
cream and boil for a further 5
minutes or until the sauce is
thickened and smooth.
Spoon the hot sauce over the
bananas and sprinkle with
nuts. Serve hot.

Yogurt Fruit Whip

SERVES 6

15 g (½ oz) powdered gelatine
150 ml (¼ pint) fresh or
  unsweetened orange juice, at
  room temperature
2 teaspoons caster sugar
300 ml (½ pint) low-fat
  rhubarb yogurt, at room
  temperature
2 egg whites

TO DECORATE:
strips of thinly pared orange
  rind (optional)

PREPARATION TIME: *10-15
minutes, plus setting*
COOKING TIME: *2 minutes*

A delicately flavoured, light
dessert to enjoy after a rich
main course. Remove from
the refrigerator 30 minutes
before serving, to appreciate
the subtle flavour.

1. Sprinkle the gelatine over
2 tablespoons of the orange
juice in a small heatproof
bowl and leave to soften for
10 minutes until spongy.
Stand the bowl in a saucepan
of simmering water and stir
until the gelatine dissolves.
Stir in the sugar, then
remove from the heat and
leave to cool for about 6
minutes; do not allow to set.
2. Place the remaining
orange juice, yogurt and
cooled liquid gelatine in a
blender goblet and blend for
30 seconds until thoroughly
combined and smooth. Pour
the mixture into a bowl and
leave for about 20-30
minutes until just beginning
to set around the edges.
3. Whisk the egg whites
until stiff peaks form. Using a
large metal spoon, lightly
fold them into the yogurt
mixture until well
incorporated. Spoon the
mixture into a serving bowl
and leave for 2-3 hours to set
in the refrigerator. Decorate
with strips of orange rind, if
liked, and serve with dainty
sweet biscuits.

VARIATION:
Plain unsweetened yogurt or
another flavour, such as
raspberry or strawberry, can
replace the rhubarb yogurt.

Left to right: Apple Salad Cups;
Peachy Almond Meringues; Buttered
Bananas with Pineapple Cream Sauce;
Yogurt Fruit Whip.

Choc-Orange Rice Creams

1 tablespoon cornflour
600 ml (1 pint) milk
50 g (2 oz) pudding rice
100 g (4 oz) plain chocolate,
 finely chopped
1 tablespoon soft light brown
 sugar
a few drops of vanilla essence
150 ml (¼ pint) single cream
2 medium oranges

PREPARATION TIME: *7 minutes*
COOKING TIME: *35 minutes*

This is delicious hot or cold. The orange segments can be omitted if liked.

1. Blend the cornflour with a little of the milk in a cup, to make a smooth paste. Put the remaining milk in a saucepan and bring to the boil. Add the rice, stir well, then cover and cook over a gentle heat for 30 minutes, stirring occasionally.
2. Stir the blended cornflour into the rice mixture. Bring to the boil and cook for 2 minutes, stirring all the time. Remove from the heat and stir in the chopped chocolate, sugar, vanilla essence and cream.
3. Using a sharp knife, peel away the skin and pith from the oranges. Holding an orange over the pan, carefully cut into segments, discarding all the membranes. Segment the other orange in the same way.
4. Spoon the hot rice mixture into 4 individual serving dishes and top with orange segments. Serve hot or cold.

Peaches and Cream Flan

SERVES 6

15 g (½ oz) butter
100 g (4 oz) digestive biscuits,
 finely crushed
1 × 400 g (14 oz) can peach
 slices, drained
300 ml (½ pint) soured cream
25 g (1 oz) caster sugar
a little freshly grated nutmeg
 (optional)

TO DECORATE:
150 ml (¼ pint) whipping
 cream, whipped

PREPARATION TIME: *7 minutes*
COOKING TIME: *30 minutes*
OVEN: *180°C, 350°F, Gas Mark 4*

1. Grease a 23 cm (9 inch) ovenproof flan dish with the butter. Press the finely crushed biscuits into the base of the flan dish. Ⓐ
2. Put the peach slices, soured cream and sugar into a food processor or blender goblet and process for 30 seconds until the mixture is smooth and thoroughly combined. Ⓐ
3. Pour the mixture into the dish, smooth the surface. Sprinkle with nutmeg, if using. Bake in a preheated oven for 30 minutes.
4. Leave to cool, then chill before serving, decorated with cream.

Ⓐ The biscuit base can be made a day in advance, then wrapped in cling film.
 The filling can be prepared several hours in advance, covered with cling film and kept cool.

VARIATIONS:
Use canned, drained strawberries or raspberries instead of the peaches and omit the nutmeg.

Choc-Orange Rice Creams; Peaches and Cream Flan.

Left to right: Speedy Blackcurrant Sponge Pie; Raspberry Whirls; Orange Apricot Fool.

Orange Apricot Fool

SERVES 8

175 g (6 oz) dried apricots,
    soaked overnight in 150 ml
    (¼ pint) cold water
150 ml (¼ pint) fresh or
    unsweetened orange juice
50 g (2 oz) caster sugar
1 × 425 g (15 oz) can custard
150 ml (¼ pint) whipping
    cream, whipped
1 egg white, beaten

PREPARATION TIME: *10 minutes,
plus soaking overnight and
cooling*
COOKING TIME: *30 minutes*

1. Put the apricots with the soaking water into a saucepan. Add the orange juice and sugar and bring to the boil. Lower the heat, cover and simmer gently for 30 minutes until tender. Allow to cool slightly. Ⓐ
2. Pour the mixture into a food processor or blender goblet and process for 30 seconds to make a smooth purée (or pass the mixture through a sieve). Ⓐ
3. Mix the custard into the apricot purée. Using a large metal spoon, lightly fold in the cream, then the beaten egg white. Spoon the mixture into a serving dish and serve chilled with dainty sweet biscuits.

Ⓐ The apricots can be cooked and puréed up to 2 days in advance, covered with cling film and kept in the refrigerator.

Speedy Blackcurrant Sponge Pie

SERVES 8

10 g (¼ oz) butter
450 g (1 lb) blackcurrants,
    topped and tailed if fresh,
    thawed if frozen
75 g (3 oz) granulated sugar
100 g (4 oz) soft margarine
100 g (4 oz) soft light brown
    sugar
2 eggs
100 g (4 oz) self-raising flour,
    sifted
1 teaspoon baking powder
25 g (1 oz) flaked almonds

PREPARATION TIME: *10 minutes*
COOKING TIME: *40-45 minutes*
OVEN: *180°C, 350°F, Gas Mark 4*

1. Grease a 23 cm (9 inch) fluted ceramic flan dish (or similar dish) with the butter. Mix the blackcurrants with granulated sugar and place in the dish. Ⓐ
2. Put the margarine, brown sugar, eggs, flour and baking powder into a mixing bowl.

Using a wooden spoon, beat vigorously for about 2 minutes until soft and creamy. If using an electric mixer, cream for only 1 minute.
3. Spread the mixture over the blackcurrants, smooth the surface and sprinkle with the almonds. Bake in a preheated oven for 40-45 minutes until the sponge topping is well risen, golden brown and cooked through. If necessary, cover with foil during baking to prevent over-browning. Serve hot or cold with vanilla icecream, custard or cream. Ⓕ

Ⓐ Can be prepared the previous day, covered with cling film and kept chilled.
Ⓕ Freeze for up to 2 months. Thaw overnight in the refrigerator and serve cold.
Ⓜ Or microwave on Defrost for 10-15 minutes. Stand for 20 minutes before serving.

Raspberry Whirls

225 g (8 oz) raspberries,
    thawed and drained if frozen
50 g (2 oz) caster sugar
1 egg white
150 ml (¼ pint) whipping
    cream, whipped

TO DECORATE:
65 ml (2½ fl oz) whipping
    cream, whipped
whole raspberries (optional)

PREPARATION TIME: *10 minutes*

This dessert is delicious with fresh or frozen fruit.

1. Mash the raspberries and sugar together in a bowl. Whisk the egg white until stiff peaks form, then lightly fold into the raspberry mixture, using a large metal spoon.
2. Lightly fold in the cream and turn the mixture into 4 individual serving dishes. Decorate with swirls of whipped cream and raspberries, if using.

Packed Lunches

Spicy Chicken Samosas

MAKES 12

2 tablespoons vegetable oil
1 medium onion, peeled and chopped
150 g (6 oz) cooked chicken, chopped
1½-2 teaspoons mild curry powder
50 g (2 oz) frozen peas, thawed
100 g (4 oz) cooked potato, mashed or diced
2 teaspoons lemon juice
a good pinch of salt
350 g (12 oz) plain flour
75 g (3 oz) butter, diced
8 tablespoons tepid milk
vegetable oil, for deep frying

PREPARATION TIME: *30-35 minutes*

COOKING TIME: *20 minutes*

Samosas are delicious hot or cold (however if you are going to eat them hot allow to cool slightly before serving). Adults will enjoy these accompanied by mango chutney and a side dish of plain unsweetened yogurt mixed with grated cucumber or a tomato and onion salad.

1. Heat the oil in a frying pan, add the onion and fry over a gentle heat for 2 minutes. Add the chicken, curry powder and peas and cook for a further 3 minutes. Stir in the potato, lemon juice and salt to taste and cook for a further 3 minutes. Leave to cool while making the pastry. Ⓐ
2. Sift the flour with the salt into a mixing bowl, add the butter and rub in with the fingertips until the mixture resembles fine breadcrumbs. Add the milk and mix to a stiff dough, using a round-bladed knife. Knead gently until free from cracks.
3. Divide the dough into 6 equal pieces. Knead each piece and roll out on a lightly floured board or work surface to a 15 cm (6 inch) circle. Cut each round in half.
4. Spoon a portion of the filling mixture on to each pastry semi-circle, dividing it equally among them. Dampen the pastry edges and fold over, pressing the edges firmly together to seal, and forming triangular-shaped pasties. Make sure that all the edges are thoroughly sealed. Ⓐ
5. Heat the oil in a deep fat fryer to 180°-190°C/350°-375°F or until a stale bread cube browns in 30 seconds. Fry the samosas, a few at a time, for 5-6 minutes, turning occasionally, until golden brown and heated through. Drain on absorbent paper and keep hot while cooking the remainder in the same way. Serve hot or cold.

Ⓐ The filling can be prepared up to 2 days in advance and stored in an airtight container in the refrigerator.

The samosas can be made 1 day in advance, then wrapped in cling film and kept chilled in the refrigerator.

VARIATIONS:
Use cooked minced beef or lamb in place of chicken.

French Bread Wonders

MAKES 3

1 short French loaf
50-75 g (2-3 oz) butter, softened
4 slices cooked ham
1 tablespoon chutney or sweet pickle (optional)
75 g (3 oz) Emmenthal or Cheddar cheese, grated
2 large tomatoes, thinly sliced
a few watercress sprigs
salt
freshly ground black pepper
100 g (4 oz) smooth liver pâté
crisp lettuce leaves
7.5 cm (3 inch) piece of cucumber, thinly sliced
1 tablespoon mayonnaise

PREPARATION TIME: *15 minutes*

1. Cut the French loaf horizontally into 3 slices. Spread the top and bottom slices with butter on the cut side only and spread the centre slice on both sides.
2. Place the bottom slice on a board and cover with the ham slices. Spread with the chutney, if using, and sprinkle with the cheese.
3. Cover with tomato slices and watercress sprigs and season with salt and pepper.
4. Place the centre bread slice on top and spread with the pâté. Top with lettuce leaves and cucumber slices. Top with mayonnaise and cover with the top slice.
5. Press down firmly, then carefully cut into 3 equal portions. Tie each portion together with clean, fine string at either end. Wrap in cling film before packing into lunchboxes.

VARIATIONS:
Try different fillings for the French loaf; sliced tongue, corned beef or cold chicken; peeled prawns or smoked mackerel; cream cheese, egg mayonnaise or coleslaw.

Granary Roll Fillers

MAKES 4

4 granary rolls
100 g (4 oz) full fat soft cheese
1 tablespoon chopped fresh chives
7.5 cm (3 inch) piece of cucumber, halved lengthways and thinly sliced
25 g (1 oz) butter, softened
2 hard-boiled eggs, shelled
1½ tablespoons mayonnaise
salt
freshly ground black pepper
a little mustard and cress

PREPARATION TIME: *15 minutes*

COOKING TIME: *10 minutes*

1. Using a sharp knife, carefully make 2 vertical cuts in each roll, taking care not to cut right through the bottom crust, to give 2 'pockets' in each roll for fillings.
2. Mix the full fat soft cheese with the chives and spread into one 'pocket' in each roll. Arrange halved cucumber slices in each cheese-filled pocket, protruding slightly above the top crust.
3. Spread the remaining 'pocket' in each roll with the butter. Mash the hard-boiled eggs, stir in the mayonnaise and add salt and pepper to taste and use to fill the buttered 'pockets'. Arrange a little mustard and cress along each egg-filled pocket. Wrap the rolls in cling film before packing into lunch boxes.

Left to right: French Bread Wonders; Spicy Chicken Samosas; Granary Roll Fillers; Salami Crunch Specials.

Salami Crunch Specials

MAKES 2

50 g (2 oz) butter, softened
50 g (2 oz) full fat soft cheese
6 slices crusty white or brown
 bread
6 thin slices of salami, rinded
50 g (2 oz) coleslaw
a little mustard and cress
crisp lettuce leaves
1 large tomato, thinly sliced
salt
freshly ground black pepper

PREPARATION TIME: *10-15 minutes*

Wrap these double decker sandwiches in cling film and pack into lunchboxes, with sticks of celery, spring onions, radishes and tomatoes.

1. In a bowl, thoroughly combine the butter and full fat soft cheese, using a wooden spoon. Spread 4 of the bread slices with the mixture on one side only, and spread the remaining 2 slices on both sides.
2. Place 2 of the bread slices spread on one side on a board and cover each one with slices of salami. Top with coleslaw and a little mustard and cress.
3. Cover each with the bread slices spread on both sides. Place lettuce leaves on each one and top with slices of tomato. Sprinkle with salt and pepper and cover with the remaining bread slices buttered on one side. Press down firmly, then cut each into quarters to serve.

VARIATIONS:
Beef and Celeriac: Use 2 slices of roast beef, 50 g (2 oz) grated celeriac or 2 celery sticks, chopped, mixed with 1½ tablespoons mayonnaise and slices of cucumber and onion rings for the filling. Make up the sandwiches in the same way.
Raisin, Peanut and Banana: Use 4 tablespoons crunchy peanut butter, 50 g (2 oz) full fat soft cheese, 1 banana, peeled and sliced, 2 tablespoons seedless raisins and 2 bacon rashers, rinded, grilled and crumbled for the filling. Make up the sandwiches in the same way but using the peanut butter to spread instead of butter.

Giant Pinwheel Puffs

MAKES 10

1 × 200 g (7 oz) can tuna in oil, drained and finely flaked
4 tablespoons tomato or Burger relish
salt
freshly ground black pepper
1 × 400 g (14 oz) packet frozen puff pastry, thawed
75 g (3 oz) Cheddar cheese, finely grated

TO GLAZE:
a little beaten egg

PREPARATION TIME: *15 minutes*
COOKING TIME: *25 minutes*
OVEN: *190°C, 375°F, Gas Mark 5*

Easy to make and fun to eat, these tasty pinwheel puffs are good served hot or cold.

1. Put the tuna, relish and salt and pepper into a bowl and stir thoroughly to mix.
2. Roll out the pastry on a lightly floured board or work surface to a 45 × 30 cm (18 × 12 inch) rectangle. Spread the tuna mixture over the pastry to within 5 mm (¼ inch) of the edges. Sprinkle with the cheese and flatten lightly with the fingertips.
3. Starting from a short edge, roll up the pastry to form a neat roll, dampening the second short pastry edge with water and sealing the join well. Brush the roll all over with beaten egg.
4. Cut the roll into 10 equal slices and arrange them slightly apart on a dampened baking sheet. Flatten each one slightly with a palette knife or fish slice. Place in a preheated oven and bake for 25 minutes or until well risen, golden brown and cooked through. (Cover with foil if necessary to prevent over-browning.) Serve hot or cold. F

Cheesy Scotch Eggs

MAKES 4

225 g (8 oz) pork sausage meat
1 small onion, peeled and finely chopped
25 g (1 oz) grated Parmesan cheese
salt
freshly ground black pepper
4 hard-boiled eggs, shelled
a little plain flour
1 egg, beaten
4 tablespoons golden breadcrumbs
½ teaspoon dried mixed herbs (optional)
vegetable oil, for deep frying

PREPARATION TIME: *15 minutes, plus cooling*
COOKING TIME: *6 minutes*

1. Put the sausage meat, onion, cheese and salt and pepper to taste in a bowl. Mix together well until thoroughly combined.
2. Divide the sausage meat mixture into 4 equal pieces and shape into flat 10 cm (4 inch) rounds on a well-floured board.
3. Roll the hard-boiled eggs in the flour, to coat thoroughly. Wrap each egg in a sausage meat round, pressing the edges firmly together so that the egg is completely enclosed. Smooth over the joins.
4. Put the beaten egg in a flat dish. Mix the bread crumbs with the herbs, if using, and spread out on a plate. Dip each Scotch egg in beaten egg, then roll in the breadcrumbs, pressing them firmly with the palms of the hands. A
5. Heat the oil in a deep fat fryer to 180°-190°C/350°-375°F or until a stale bread cube browns in 30 seconds. Fry the Scotch eggs for 6 minutes until golden brown and cooked through. Drain on absorbent paper and leave for about 1 hour to cool completely. Serve cold with salad, or wrap in cling film before packing into lunch-boxes.

A The Scotch eggs can be made several hours in advance, covered with cling film and kept in the refrigerator.

E Freeze for up to 1 month. Thaw for 1½ hours at room temperature before heating through in a preheated oven 180°C, 350°F, Gas Mark 4 for 8-10 minutes
M Or microwave, 5 at a time, on Defrost for 4-6 minutes. Stand for 10 minutes, before

heating through in conventional oven as described above.

VARIATION:
Replace the tuna with 2 cans of sardines in oil, drained and finely flaked or 150 g (6 oz) smooth liver pâté.

Wholemeal Cheese and Onion Scones

MAKES 8

½ tablespoon vegetable oil
1 small onion, peeled and finely chopped
100 g (4 oz) self-raising white flour
2 teaspoons baking powder
¼ teaspoon salt
100 g (4 oz) plain wholewheat flour
50 g (2 oz) hard margarine, diced
15 g (½ oz) grated Parmesan cheese
75 g (3 oz) Cheddar cheese, finely grated
150 ml (¼ pint) milk

TO GLAZE:
a little beaten egg

PREPARATION TIME: *10 minutes*
COOKING TIME: *12-15 minutes*
OVEN: *220°C, 425°F, Gas Mark 7*

These scones are delicious served warm or cold, split and buttered. Although at their nicest eaten freshly baked, they are also good toasted, buttered and served warm the following day.

1. Heat the oil in a frying pan, add the onion and fry over a gentle heat for 3 minutes. Remove the onion with a slotted spoon, drain on absorbent paper and leave to cool. A
2. Sift the self-raising flour with the baking powder and salt into a mixing bowl. Stir in the wholewheat flour. Add the margarine and rub in with the fingertips until the mixture resembles fine breadcrumbs. Add the Parmesan cheese, 50 g (2 oz) of the Cheddar cheese and the onion. Stir well to mix. A
3. Add the milk, all at once, and mix quickly to form a soft dough, using a round-bladed knife. Turn the dough

on to a floured board or work surface and knead very gently until free from cracks. Either pat out with the fingertips or gently roll out the dough to an 18 cm (7 inch) round.
4. Brush the surface with the beaten egg and sprinkle with the remaining Cheddar cheese. Using a sharp knife, cut the scone round into 4 and then 4 again, to make 8 wedges.
5. Place the scones on a lightly floured baking sheet and cook just above the centre of a preheated oven for 12-15 minutes until well risen and golden brown. E Serve warm or cold, split and buttered.

A The onion can be cooked the previous day, then covered with cling film and kept in a cool place.
    The dry scone mixture can be prepared several hours in advance and stored in an airtight container in the refrigerator.
E Freeze for up to 1 month. Place on a baking sheet, cover with foil and reheat from frozen at 180°C, 350°F, Gas Mark 4 for 8 minutes.
M Or microwave on Defrost for 3-4 minutes. Stand for 2 minutes before heating on Maximum (Full) for 1-1½ minutes.

Clockwise from the bottom: Cheesy Scotch Eggs; Giant Pinwheel Puffs; Wholemeal Cheese and Onion Scones.

High Butter Shorties

MAKES 26

225 g (8 oz) butter, softened
50 g (2 oz) caster sugar
½ teaspoon vanilla essence
225 g (8 oz) plain flour, sifted
7 blanched almonds
3 glacé cherries, halved
50 g (2 oz) plain chocolate,
    broken into pieces

PREPARATION TIME: *15 minutes, plus cooling*

COOKING TIME: *10-12 minutes*

OVEN: *190°C, 375°F, Gas Mark 5*

This recipe makes a selection of rich butter biscuits. The mixture is piped into different shapes – some are chocolate-dipped fingers and others are stars decorated with almonds and cherries.

1. Put the softened butter and sugar in a bowl and cream with a wooden spoon until light and fluffy. Mix in the vanilla essence and the flour to form a soft mixture.
2. Place the mixture in a piping bag fitted with a large star tube and pipe thirteen 7.5 cm (3 inch) finger lengths on to a greased baking sheet. Place in a preheated oven and bake for 10 minutes until pale golden and cooked through. Transfer to a wire rack and leave to cool completely (about 15 minutes). Ⓐ
3. Meanwhile pipe the remaining mixture into 13 stars on a greased baking sheet. Top 7 of these with a blanched almond and the remaining 6 with a halved glacé cherry. Bake in a preheated moderate oven for 12 minutes, until pale golden and cooked through. Transfer to a wire rack and leave to cool completely (about 30 minutes). Ⓐ
4. Place chocolate pieces in a heatproof basin over a saucepan of hot but not boiling water until melted (do not stir chocolate). Dip the ends of the finger biscuits in melted chocolate and leave to set for about 45 minutes on a wire rack before serving. Ⓐ

Ⓐ The biscuits can be stored for up to 2 weeks in an airtight container.

Sticky Fruit and Nut Bars

MAKES 24

175 g (6 oz) hard margarine
75 g (3 oz) granulated sugar
75 g (3 oz) soft dark brown
   sugar
2 tablespoons black treacle
2 tablespoons golden syrup
1½ teaspoons bicarbonate of
   soda
175 g (6 oz) plain flour, sifted
50 g (2 oz) chopped mixed
   nuts
50 g (2 oz) sultanas
225 g (8 oz) porridge oats

PREPARATION TIME: *10 minutes*
COOKING TIME: *12-15 minutes*
OVEN: *180°C, 350°F, Gas Mark 4*

1. Grease a shallow
28 × 18 cm (11 × 7 inch)
baking tin. Put the
margarine, sugars, treacle
and half the golden syrup in a
saucepan and stir over a low
heat until the margarine has
melted.
2. Add the bicarbonate of
soda to the treacle mixture,
then stir in the flour, nuts,
sultanas and oats and stir
well to mix.
3. Turn the mixture into the
prepared tin, smooth the
surface and bake in a
preheated oven for 12
minutes or until rich golden
brown and cooked through.
Remove from the oven and
brush immediately with the
remaining golden syrup.
Leave to cool for 5 minutes,
then cut into 24 fingers with a
sharp knife. Leave to cool
completely in the tin. Store
in an airtight container for up
to 3 weeks.

In tuck box: High Butter Shorties; Tuck
Box Cake. **On plate:** Sticky Fruit and
Nut Bars; Apple Sultana Bran Loaf;
High Butter Shorties.

Tuck Box Cake

MAKES ONE 1 kg (2 lb) CAKE

75 g (3 oz) soft margarine
175 g (6 oz) caster sugar
3 eggs, beaten
3 medium bananas
100 g (4 oz) glacé cherries,
   rinsed, dried and quartered
225 g (8 oz) self-raising flour
1 tablespoon demerara sugar

PREPARATION TIME: *15 minutes,
plus cooling*
COOKING TIME: *1 hour - 1 hour
10 minutes*
OVEN: *180°C, 350°F, Gas Mark 4*

This cake can be stored in an
airtight tin for up to one
week. To prevent glacé
cherries from sinking to the
bottom of the cake, wash
them to remove the sticky
syrup and dry them
thoroughly before adding to
the cake mixture.

1. Grease a 1 kg (2 lb) loaf
tin and line with greased
greaseproof paper. Put the
margarine and sugar in a
mixing bowl and cream with
a wooden spoon until light
and fluffy. Gradually add the
beaten eggs, beating well
after each addition.
2. Peel and mash the
bananas until smooth, then
add to the mixture and stir
well to mix. Chop half the
cherries and stir into the
mixture. Sift the flour over
the mixture and fold in
lightly, using a large metal
spoon.
3. Turn the mixture into the
prepared tin and smooth the
surface. Arrange the
remaining glacé cherries on
top of the cake and sprinkle
with the demerara sugar.
4. Place in a preheated oven
and bake for 1 hour to 1 hour
10 minutes until the cake is
well risen, golden brown
and cooked through. To test
if the cake is cooked, insert a
fine metal skewer or wooden

cocktail stick into the centre
of the cake. If it comes out
clean, the cake is cooked; if
not, return to the oven and
retest after 5 minutes. Cover
the top of the cake with
greaseproof paper or foil
during cooking, if necessary,
to prevent over-browning.
Turn on to a wire rack to cool
completely (about 1½
hours). F Remove the lining
paper and serve thinly sliced.
The slices can be buttered, if
preferred.

F Thaw for several hours at
room temperature before
serving sliced and buttered.
M Or microwave on Defrost
for 5-8 minutes. Stand for 15
minutes before serving as
described above.

VARIATIONS:
Replace the glacé cherries
with the same quantity of
chopped almonds, walnuts
or sultanas.

Apple Sultana Bran Loaf

MAKES ONE 1 kg (2 lb) LOAF

75 g (3 oz) soft margarine
175 g (6 oz) caster sugar
3 eggs, beaten
250 g (9 oz) self-raising flour
½ teaspoon baking powder
¼ teaspoon finely grated lemon
   rind
225 g (8 oz) dessert apples,
   peeled, cored and coarsely
   grated
1 tablespoon lemon juice
40 g (1½ oz) bran
65 g (2½ oz) sultanas
2 tablespoons milk

PREPARATION TIME: *20 minutes*
COOKING TIME: *1 hour*
OVEN: *190°C, 375°F, Gas Mark 5*

A nutritious loaf that keeps
well for up to 4 days,
wrapped in greaseproof
paper and foil. The best

dessert apples to use are
Granny Smiths or Cox's
Orange Pippins.

1. Grease a 1 kg (2 lb) loaf
tin and line with greased
greaseproof paper. Put the
margarine and sugar in a
mixing bowl and cream until
light and fluffy. Gradually
add the beaten eggs, beating
well after each addition.
2. Sift the flour with the
baking powder over the
mixture and fold in lightly,
using a large metal spoon.
Stir in the lemon rind, grated
apple, lemon juice, bran,
sultanas and milk and mix
well to form a soft dropping
consistency.
3. Turn the mixture into the
prepared tin and smooth the
surface. Place in a preheated
oven and bake for 1 hour or

until the loaf is well risen,
golden brown and cooked
through. (Cover with foil
during cooking if necessary
to prevent over-browning.)
To test if it is cooked, insert a
fine metal skewer, or
wooden cocktail stick into
the centre of the loaf. If it
comes out clean, the loaf is
cooked; if not, return to the
oven and retest after 5
minutes.
4. Turn on to a wire rack to
cool. F Remove the lining
paper and serve sliced and
buttered, if liked.

F Freeze for up to 1 month.
Thaw for several hours at
room temperature before
serving.
M Or microwave on Defrost
for 5-8 minutes. Stand for 15
minutes before serving.

Sonia Allison's
'Twin Sets'

═ MENU ═

BATCH MINCE

CHILLI CON CARNE

SPAGHETTI BOLOGNESE SAUCE

OATMEAL MINCE WITH VEGETABLES

MILD CURRY MINCE

---

*T*ake a batch of mince, divide it into four and use it as a base to prepare a selection of delicious family dishes for the freezer in next to no time. This way, you can forget all about cooking on busy days.

Batch Mince

SERVES 16-20

1.75 kg (4 lb) lean minced beef
450 g (1 lb) onions, peeled and chopped
100 g (4 oz) celery sticks, thinly sliced
900 ml (1½ pints) boiling water
3 teaspoons salt

PREPARATION TIME: *20 minutes*

COOKING TIME: *40 minutes*

1. Place the mince in a large saucepan and fry without added fat over a moderately high heat, stirring from time to time, for about 12 minutes or until the meat has lost its pinkness.
2. Add the onions and celery and fry for a further 7 minutes, stirring from time to time.
3. Stir in the water with the salt. Return to the boil, stirring all the time. Lower the heat, cover and simmer gently for 40 minutes. Divide the mince equally between 4 medium-sized saucepans. ☒

☒ Freeze in 450 g (1 lb) batches for up to 6 months. Thaw overnight in the refrigerator or for 3-4 hours at room temperature.

The 4 variations which follow should not be refrozen if made from already frozen and thawed mince. If made from hot Batch Mince, freeze and thaw as above. Reheat in saucepan until very hot.

Ⓜ Or microwave the frozen 450 g (1 lb) batches on Defrost for 12-15 minutes separating with a fork as soon as possible. Stand for 10 minutes before finishing.

Chilli Con Carne

SERVES 4-5

¼ portion of the cooked mince
2 tablespoons tomato purée
1 × 425 g (15 oz) can red
  kidney beans, drained
2 teaspoons chilli seasoning
1 teaspoon salt
¼ teaspoon garlic or onion
  powder
1 tablespoon cornflour
150 ml (¼ pint) cold water

PREPARATION TIME: *10 minutes*
COOKING TIME: *30 minutes*

1. Bring the mince in the pan just to the boil. Stir in the tomato purée, kidney beans, chilli seasoning, salt and garlic powder.
2. In a small bowl, blend the cornflour with 2 tablespoons of the water, to make a smooth paste. Mix in the remaining water, then stir into the mince mixture.
3. Return to the boil, stirring all the time. Cover and simmer gently for 30 minutes, stirring from time to time to prevent the mixture from sticking. Taste and adjust the seasoning if necessary.
4. Serve the Chilli Con Carne with freshly cooked rice, allowing 40 g (1½ oz) raw weight per serving.

Chilli Con Carne; Batch Mince.

Spaghetti Bolognese Sauce

SERVES 4-5

¼ portion of the cooked mince
1 green pepper, cored, seeded and diced
1 × 400 g (14 oz) can tomatoes
2 tablespoons tomatoe purée
1 teaspoon mixed herbs
1 teaspoon salt
½ teaspoon freshly ground black pepper
1 tablespoon cornflour
150 ml (¼ pint) cold water

PREPARATION TIME: *10 minutes*
COOKING TIME: *30 minutes*

1. Bring the mince in the pan just to the boil. Add the green pepper, tomatoes, tomato purée, herbs, salt and pepper.
2. In a small bowl, blend the cornflour with 2 tablespoons of the water, to make a smooth paste. Mix in the remaining water, then stir into the mince mixture.
3. Return to the boil, stirring all the time and breaking up the tomatoes against the sides of the pan with a wooden spoon.

4. Lower the heat, cover and simmer gently for 30 minutes, stirring from time to time to prevent the mixture from sticking. Taste and adjust the seasoning if necessary.
5. Spoon the Bolognese sauce over plates of freshly-cooked spaghetti, allowing 40-50 g (1½-2 oz) raw weight per serving. Serve grated Cheddar or Parmesan cheese in a separate dish for sprinkling over the top of the sauce.

Left to right: Oatmeal Mince with Vegetables; Spaghetti Bolognese Sauce; Mild Curry Mince.

Oatmeal Mince with Vegetables

SERVES 5-6

¼ portion of the cooked mince
1 small parsnip, scraped and coarsely grated
2 carrots, scraped and coarsely grated
1 large leek, trimmed and thinly sliced
50 g (2 oz) porridge oats
300 ml (½ pint) boiling water
1 beef gravy cube, crumbled

PREPARATION TIME: *12 minutes*

COOKING TIME: *30 minutes*

1. Bring the mince in the pan just to the boil. Add the vegetables, porridge oats and water.
2. Add the gravy cube, stir well and cook over a moderate heat, stirring all the time, until the mixture begins to bubble.
3. Lower the heat, cover and simmer gently for 30 minutes, stirring from time to time to prevent the mixture from sticking. Taste and adjust the seasoning if necessary. Serve with baked jacket potatoes or creamed potatoes and a green vegetable, such as cabbage, spring greens or Brussels sprouts.

Mild Curry Mince

SERVES 4-5

¼ portion of the cooked mince
3 tablespoons mild curry powder
2 tablespoons mango chutney
25 g (1 oz) seedless raisins
1 large dessert apple, about 100 g (4 oz), peeled and coarsely grated
2 tablespoons smooth peanut butter
1 tablespoon desiccated coconut
1 teaspoon salt
1 tablespoon cornflour
150 ml (¼ pint) cold water

TO GARNISH:
lime twists

PREPARATION TIME: *10 minutes*

COOKING TIME: *30 minutes*

1. Bring the mince in the pan just to the boil. Stir in the curry powder, mango chutney, raisins, apple, peanut butter, coconut and salt.
2. In a small bowl, blend the cornflour with 2 tablespoons of the water, to make a smooth paste. Mix in the remaining water, then stir into the mince mixture.
3. Return to the boil, stirring all the time, cover and simmer gently for 30 minutes, stirring once or twice to prevent the mixture from sticking. Taste and adjust the seasoning if necessary.
4. Garnish wih lime twists and serve with freshly cooked rice, allowing 40 g (1½ oz) raw weight per serving.

Cream Cheese Éclairs

MAKES 15

65 g (2½ oz) plain flour
pinch of salt
150 ml (¼ pint) water
45 g (1¾ oz) butter
2 eggs, beaten
1 tablespoon sesame seeds or
    poppy seeds (optional)
225 g (8 oz) full fat soft cheese
100 g (4 oz) piece of
    cucumber, unpeeled and
    finely chopped
2 tablespoons chopped chives
    or spring onion tops
1 tablespoon mayonnaise
salt
freshly ground black pepper

TO GARNISH:
watercress sprigs

PREPARATION TIME: *15 minutes,
plus cooling*
COOKING TIME: *about 35
minutes*
OVEN: *200°C, 400°F, Gas Mark 6*

1. Sift the flour with the salt on to a sheet of greaseproof paper. Put the water and butter into a saucepan and heat gently without boiling, until the butter has melted. Bring rapidly to the boil, then remove from the heat and immediately add the flour, all at once. Using a wooden spoon, stir vigorously until all the flour is absorbed and the mixture is smooth.
2. Return the pan to a moderate heat and beat with a wooden spoon for 15-30 seconds until the dough forms a ball and leaves the sides of the pan clean. (Do not overbeat at this stage or the dough will become oily.)
3. Remove from the heat and allow to cool slightly. Gradually add the beaten egg, a spoonful at a time, beating well after each addition to form a glossy dough, which is thick enough to hold its shape but is not stiff.
4. Transfer the choux pastry to a piping bag fitted with a 1 cm (½ inch) plain nozzle and pipe 15×7.5 cm (3 inch) lengths, about 5 cm (2 inches) apart, on a lightly greased baking sheet, neatly trimming off the ends with a wet sharp knife. Sprinkle with sesame seeds or poppy seeds, if using.
5. Bake the éclairs in a preheated oven for 30 minutes, or until crisp and golden brown. Remove from the oven and slit along the side of each éclair to allow the steam to escape. Return to the oven for a further 2 minutes, then transfer to a wire rack and leave to cool completely. Ⓐ Ⓕ
6. In a bowl, thoroughly mix together the cheese, cucumber, chives or spring onion tops, mayonnaise and salt and pepper to taste. Ⓐ Using a small teaspoon or the point of a small knife, fill each éclair with the cheese mixture. Serve within 30 minutes of filling, garnished with watercress sprigs.

Ⓐ The éclairs can be made up to 1 week in advance, if kept in an airtight tin and stored in a cool place. To crisp and refresh before serving, place on a baking sheet at 180°C, 350°F, Gas Mark 4 for 3-4 minutes. Cool completely before filling.

The cheese filling can be made in the morning, covered with cling film and kept chilled. Allow to come to room temperature and mix well with a fork to soften before using.
Ⓕ Freeze for up to 3 months. Arrange frozen éclairs on a baking sheet and reheat at 180°C, 350°F, Gas Mark 4 for 6-8 minutes. Cool completely before filling.
Ⓜ Or microwave, 5 at a time, on Defrost for 1-2 minutes. Stand for 10 minutes before filling.

VARIATIONS:
Replace the cucumber with 50-75 g (2-3 oz) chopped peeled prawns.

Raspberry Éclairs: Mash 100 g (4 oz) fresh or frozen (thawed) raspberries and mix with 150 ml (¼ pint) sweetened, whipped whipping cream. Use this mixture to fill the éclairs. To ice: sift 175 g (6 oz) icing sugar into a bowl, add 3-4 teaspoons water and mix until smooth. Add a few drops of pink food colouring and mix until evenly blended. Dip the tops of the filled éclairs into the icing and leave to set for 30 minutes before serving.

Chocolate Éclairs: Whip 200 ml (7 fl oz) whipping cream until stiff and sweeten with a little sieved icing sugar to taste. Use this mixture to fill the éclairs. To ice: melt, without stirring, 50 g (2 oz) plain chocolate, broken into small pieces, and 15 g (½ oz) butter in a heatproof bowl, set over a saucepan of hot, not boiling, water. Stir 3 tablespoons warm water and a few drops of vanilla essence into the melted chocolate. Leave the bowl over the pan of hot water and gradually stir in 175 g (6 oz) sifted icing sugar, until smooth. Dip the tops of the filled éclairs in the chocolate mixture, stirring occasionally to keep it smooth and prevent a thin skin forming. Sprinkle the iced éclairs with toasted chopped almonds, if liked, and leave to set for 30 minutes before serving.

Tomato Cups Monaco

MAKES 6

6 medium-sized firm tomatoes,
    total weight 750 g (1½ lb)
1 × 90 g (3½ oz) can tuna,
    drained and finely flaked
2 hard-boiled eggs, shelled and
    chopped
4 cm (1½ inch) piece of
    cucumber, chopped
3 tablespoons mayonnaise
salt
freshly ground black pepper
6 small crisp lettuce leaves

TO GARNISH:
chervil sprigs

PREPARATION TIME: *15 minutes*

Individual tuna and egg mayonnaise salads, served in tomato shells, make an attractive and nutritious teatime dish, served with brown bread and butter.

1. Cut a slice off the top of each tomato and reserve. Using a teaspoon, carefully scoop out the flesh from the tomatoes Ⓐ and discard.
2. In a bowl combine the tuna, chopped hard-boiled eggs, cucumber, mayonnaise and salt and pepper to taste, stir lightly but well to mix.
3. Spoon into the tomato cups. Place the reserved tomato slices on top as 'lids'. Arrange the tomato cups on the lettuce leaves on a serving plate. Garnish with chervil and serve chilled.

Ⓐ The tomato cups can be prepared in the morning, covered with cling film and kept in the refrigerator.

VARIATION:
Replace tuna with salmon, crab or chopped prawns.

Tomato Cups Monaco; Cream Cheese Éclairs.

Cock-a-Leekie Flan

SERVES 6-8

225 g (8 oz) plain flour
½ teaspoon salt
50 g (2 oz) lard, diced
75 g (3 oz) butter or hard
  margarine, diced
50 g (2 oz) Cheddar cheese,
  finely grated
3 teaspoons cold water
1 egg yolk
2 medium leeks, trimmed and
  cut into 5 mm (¼ inch) slices
4 rashers streaky bacon, rinded,
  boned and chopped
3 eggs
150 ml (¼ pint) single cream
¼ teaspoon dried thyme or
  dried mixed herbs
salt
freshly ground black pepper
100 g (4 oz) cooked chicken,
  skin removed and diced

TO GARNISH:
watercress sprigs
radishes

PREPARATION TIME: *20 minutes*

COOKING TIME: *1 hour 5 minutes*

OVEN: *200°C, 400°F, Gas Mark 6*

1. Sift the flour with the salt into a mixing bowl. Add the lard and 50 g (2 oz) of the butter or margarine and rub in until the mixture resembles fine breadcrumbs. Add the cheese and stir well to mix. Stir in the water and egg yolk to make a fairly firm dough. Knead gently until free from cracks.
2. Roll out the pastry on a lightly floured board or work surface to a 30 cm (12 inch) round and use to line a 25 cm (10 inch) loose-bottomed flan tin set on a baking sheet. Line the tin carefully with the pastry, removing excess to give a neat edge. Prick the base all over with a fork. Ⓐ
3. Line with a large round of greaseproof paper or foil and fill with baking beans.

Bake in a preheated oven for 15 minutes. Remove the paper and beans and return to the oven for a further 5-10 minutes until the pastry is dry and light golden-brown. Remove from oven. Ⓐ Ⓕ
4. Melt the remaining 25 g (1 oz) butter or margarine in a pan. Add the leeks and bacon and cook gently for 10 minutes, stirring often. Put the eggs and cream into a bowl and whisk until well blended. Stir in the thyme or mixed herbs. Season to taste with salt and pepper.
5. Spoon the leek and bacon mixture evenly into the flan case and add the chicken. Pour over the egg mixture and bake in a preheated oven for 30 minutes until the filling is set and a light golden-brown. Ⓕ Garnish with watercress and radishes. Serve hot or cold.

Ⓐ The flan tin can be lined with pastry in the morning, covered with cling film and kept chilled. The flan case can be baked blind a week in advance, then stored in an airtight tin.
Ⓕ After baking blind, freeze the flan case for up to 1 month. Thaw at room temperature for 1 hour before proceeding from step 4. The baked filled flan can be frozen for up to 1 month. Thaw for 1½-2 hours at room temperature, then reheat on a baking sheet at 180°C, 350°C, Gas Mark 4 for 15-20 minutes, covering with foil if necessary to prevent over-browning.
Ⓜ Or microwave flan case on Defrost for 2-3 minutes, then stand for 5 minutes before continuing as from step 4. Microwave filled flan case for 10-12 minutes on Defrost, then stand for 15 minutes before heating in a conventional oven as above.

Ham and Mushroom Vol-au-vents

MAKES 12

1 × 400 g (14 oz) packet frozen
  puff pastry, thawed
a little beaten egg
50 g (2 oz) butter or hard
  margarine
100 g (4 oz) button
  mushrooms, wiped and finely
  chopped
1 small onion, peeled and finely
  chopped
40 g (1½ oz) plain flour
175 ml (6 fl oz) milk
100 g (4 oz) cooked ham, finely
  chopped
3 tablespoons single cream
½-1 tablespoon chopped fresh
  parsley
salt
freshly ground black pepper

PREPARATION TIME: *30 minutes*

COOKING TIME: *about 50 minutes*

OVEN: *200°C, 400°F, Gas Mark 6*

You could use frozen vol-au-vent cases, thawed, for this recipe. These come in packets of 36, so you could either take out 12 or treble the filling quantities for a party.

1. Roll out the pastry on a lightly floured board or work surface to a 40 × 28 cm (16 × 11 inch) rectangle. Using a floured plain 7.5 cm (3 inch) round cutter, cut out 16 pastry rounds. Re-roll the pastry trimmings and cut out a further 8 rounds, to make 24 in all.
2. Transfer 12 to a dampened baking sheet, spaced apart, and brush the surfaces with beaten egg.
3. Using a floured 5 cm (2 inch) plain round cutter, cut out and reserve the centres of the remaining 12

pastry rounds. Turn over the pastry rings and place them over the 12 pastry rounds on the baking sheet. Press lightly to seal the rings on to the bases. Place the reserved pastry circles, cut from the centres, on a separate dampened baking sheet. Leave the vol-au-vents and pastry circles for the 'lids' to rest in the refrigerator for 15 minutes. Ⓐ

4. Glaze the rings on the vol-au-vents with beaten egg. Place just above the centre of a preheated oven and bake for 25 minutes until well risen and golden brown.

5. Glaze the pastry lids with beaten egg and bake in a preheated oven for about 10 minutes until golden brown.

6. While the vol-au-vent cases are still warm, scoop out a little of the soft pastry inside using a teaspoon. Ⓐ Ⓕ

7. To make the filling, melt the butter or margarine in a saucepan, add the mushrooms and onion and cook over a gentle heat for 5 minutes. Stir in the flour and cook for 1 minute. Remove from the heat and gradually stir in milk, then return to the heat and bring to the boil, stirring constantly. Lower the heat and cook for 2 minutes, stirring all the time.

8. Remove from the heat and stir in the ham, cream, parsley and salt and pepper to taste; cook over a gentle heat, stirring often, for 5 minutes. Ⓐ

9. Spoon the hot filling into the vol-au-vent cases and top with the pastry lids. Place on a baking sheet and reheat in the oven for 5 minutes. Serve hot on lettuce leaves.

Ⓐ The vol-au-vent cases can be prepared in the morning, covered with cling film and kept in the refrigerator.

Vol-au-vent cases can be baked 3 days in advance and stored in an airtight container. Reheat at 180°C, 350°F, Gas Mark 4 for 5 minutes before adding the hot filling.

The sauce can be prepared in the morning, covered with cling film and kept in the refrigerator. Reheat gently, thinning the consistency slightly with a little extra milk if necessary.

Ⓕ Freeze for up to 6 months. Reheat from frozen at 180°C, 350°F, Gas Mark 4 for 6-7 minutes before adding the hot filling.

Ⓜ Or microwave, 6 at a time, on Defrost. Stand for 5 minutes before filling.

VARIATIONS:
Replace ham with chopped, cooked chicken or prawns.

Ham and Mushroom Vol-au-vents; Cock-a-Leekie Flan.

Golden Fishy Cakes

MAKES 8

225 g (8 oz) cod fillets
150 ml (¼ pint) milk
150 ml (¼ pint) water
450 g (1 lb) potatoes (peeled
    weight), cut into even-sized
    pieces
25 g (1 oz) butter or hard
    margarine
1-2 tablespoons tomato purée
1 tablespoon chopped fresh
    parsley
1 × 215 g (7½ oz) can pink
    salmon, drained and finely
    flaked
salt
freshly ground black pepper
1 tablespoon plain flour
1 egg (size 1) beaten
75 g (3 oz) golden
    breadcrumbs
oil, for shallow frying

TO GARNISH:
8 lemon butterflies
8 capers

PREPARATION TIME: *30 minutes,
plus resting*

COOKING TIME: *30 minutes*

The garnish really makes
these 'fishy' cakes! Place a
lemon butterfly at one end of
each oval-shaped fish cake to
form the 'tail fin' and a caper
at the other end to form the
fish 'eye'.

1. Place the cod fillets, milk
and water in a wide saucepan
and cook over a gentle heat
for 10 minutes. Strain and
leave the fish to cool, then
flake finely, discarding the
skin and bones.
2. Meanwhile cook the
potatoes in a saucepan of
boiling, salted water for 15-
20 minutes or until tender.
Drain well, return the
potatoes to the pan and dry
off over a moderate heat,
shaking the pan frequently.
Mash well and stir in the
butter or margarine, tomato
purée to taste and the parsley.

3. Stir the flaked cod and
salmon into the potato
mixture, season to taste with
salt and pepper and stir well
to mix. Ⓐ
4. On a lightly floured board
or work surface, shape the
mixture into 8 oval cakes,
about 2 cm (¾ inch) thick.
Dip first in the flour, then in
the beaten egg, to coat
thoroughly. Coat the fish
cakes in breadcrumbs,
pressing them on firmly with
the palm of the hand. Leave
to rest in the refrigerator for
30 minutes. Ⓐ Ⓕ
5. Heat the oil to a depth of
5 mm (¼ inch) in a large
frying pan, add the fish cakes
and fry over a moderate heat
for 10 minutes, turning once
with a fish slice, until golden
brown all over. Drain on
absorbent paper and arrange
on a warmed serving plate.
Garnish each one with a
lemon butterfly at one end
and a caper at the other.
Serve straightaway with
chips and peas.

Ⓐ The fish and potato
mixture can be prepared in
the morning, covered with
cling film and kept chilled.
Fish cakes can be shaped in
the morning, covered with
cling film and kept chilled.
Ⓕ Freeze for up to 1 month.
Thaw for 1 hour at room
temperature before frying in
hot shallow oil, over a
moderate heat, for 6-7
minutes on each side until
cooked through and golden
brown. Drain on absorbent
paper.
Ⓜ Or microwave on Defrost
for 8-10 minutes, then stand
for 10 minutes before frying
as above.

Clockwise from bottom left: Golden
Fishy Cakes; Potato Scone Surprises;
Crumpets Pizza-Style.

Crumpets Pizza-Style

MAKES 8

65 g (2½ oz) butter or hard
   margarine
1 small onion, peeled and finely
   chopped
50 g (2 oz) button mushrooms,
   wiped and thinly sliced
50 g (2 oz) streaky bacon
   rashers, rinded, boned and
   chopped
15 g (½ oz) plain flour
120 ml (4 fl oz) milk
75 g (3 oz) Cheddar cheese,
   grated
1 good pinch of dried mixed
   herbs (optional)
salt
freshly ground black pepper
8 crumpets
1 tablespoon tomato relish
2 medium tomatoes, thinly
   sliced

PREPARATION TIME: *10 minutes*
COOKING TIME: *15-20 minutes*

1. Melt 15 g (½ oz) of the butter or margarine in a saucepan, add the onion, mushrooms and bacon and cook over a gentle heat for 5 minutes. Stir in the flour and cook for 1 minute. Remove from the heat and gradually stir in the milk, then return to the heat and bring to the boil, stirring. Lower the heat and cook for 2 minutes, stirring all the time. Add 40 g (1½ oz) of the grated cheese, herbs, if using, and salt and pepper to taste; keep hot. A
2. Meanwhile toast the crumpets lightly on both sides. Dice the remaining butter or margarine, combine with the tomato relish and spread over the hot crumpets. Spoon over the hot cheese mixture and arrange tomato slices on top.
3. Sprinkle with the remaining cheese and cook under a preheated medium-hot grill until the topping is golden brown and sizzling. Serve at once.

A Can be prepared in the morning, covered and kept in a cool place. Reheat gently until piping hot before proceeding from step 2.

VARIATION:
Split, toasted muffins or thick slices of toast can be used instead of crumpets for this substantial teatime snack. Replace the bacon with thinly sliced pepperoni sausage or cooked and chopped chipolatas and add a little chopped green or red pepper to the mixture, with the onion.

Potato Scone Surprises

500 g (1¼ lb) potatoes (peeled
   weight), cut into even-sized
   pieces
1 medium onion, peeled and
   finely chopped
salt
freshly ground black pepper
175 g (6 oz) plain flour
225 g (8 oz) minute steak or
   quick-frying steak, finely
   chopped or minced
25 g (1 oz) butter, cut into 4
   equal pieces
a little beaten egg, to glaze and
   seal

PREPARATION TIME: *25 minutes*
COOKING TIME: *1 hour 5 minutes*
OVEN: *190°C, 375°F, Gas Mark 5*

Leftover mashed potato can be used to make these tasty beef-filled scones. However the mixture should not be too moist, otherwise the scones will lose their shape during cooking.

1. Cook the potatoes in a saucepan of boiling, salted water for 15-20 minutes or until tender. Drain well, return the potatoes to the pan and dry off over a moderate heat, shaking the pan frequently. Mash well until smooth, then leave to cool slightly.
2. Add half the chopped onion and season to taste with salt and pepper. Work in the flour, kneading well until thoroughly combined. A
3. Mix the steak with the remaining chopped onion and season to taste with salt and pepper.
4. Divide the potato mixture into 8 equal portions. On a well-floured board or work surface, pat out 4 portions into 13 cm (5 inch) rounds. Divide the meat mixture into 4 equal portions and place on the 4 potato rounds. Flatten out slightly to within 1 cm (½ inch) of the potato edges. Place a piece of butter in the centre of each and brush the edges with a little beaten egg.
5. Pat out the remaining 4 potato portions to form 15 cm (6 inch) rounds and place over the meat filling. Press the edges together firmly, to seal. Mark the edges with a fork and make a hole in the top of each. Using a fish slice, carefully transfer the scones to a well-greased roasting tin and glaze each with beaten egg. Place in a preheated oven and cook for 40-45 minutes until golden brown and cooked through. Serve hot.

A The mashed potato mixture can be prepared the previous day, covered with cling film and kept in the refrigerator. Knead well until smooth before using.

Vitality Salad Platter

SERVES 4-6

175 g (6 oz) long-grain brown rice
150 ml (¼ pint) French Dressing (page 33)
50 g (2 oz) sultanas
1 red dessert apple, cored and diced
½ tablespoon lemon juice
2 celery sticks, trimmed and chopped
7.5 cm (3 inch) piece of cucumber, diced
1 red or green pepper, seeded, cored and cut into thin strips
1 small onion, peeled and sliced and separated into rings
1 bunch of radishes, trimmed and left whole
4 medium tomatoes, cut into wedges
3 hard-boiled eggs, shelled and sliced

PREPARATION TIME: *15 minutes*
COOKING TIME: *30 minutes*

Rich in nutrients and fibre, brown rice has a lovely nutty flavour and chewy texture. It is also far easier to cook successfully than the white 'polished' type because the brown husk, enclosing the white starchy grain, prevents the rice from sticking together during cooking.

1.   Cook the rice in a saucepan of boiling, salted water for 30 minutes or until tender. Drain well and place in a bowl. Shake or whisk the French Dressing vigorously and pour over the warm rice; toss well and leave to cool.
2.   Add the sultanas, apple tossed in lemon juice, celery and cucumber and stir well to mix. Turn the mixture into the centre of a serving plate.
3.   Arrange the remaining ingredients round the rice salad. Serve with crusty bread and butter.

Farmhouse Scone Ring

MAKES 10 scones

225 g (8 oz) self-raising flour
½ teaspoon baking powder
¼ teaspoon salt
40 g (1½ oz) hard margarine, diced
100 g (4 oz) Cheddar cheese, finely grated
1 small onion, peeled and finely chopped
25 g (1 oz) salted peanuts, finely chopped
6 tablespoons milk
a little milk, to glaze

TO GARNISH:
cherry tomatoes

PREPARATION TIME: *10 minutes*
COOKING TIME: *15 minutes*
OVEN: *220°C, 425°F, Gas Mark 7*

These tasty scones, cooked in an overlapping ring shape, look especially attractive when the centre is filled with miniature tomatoes.

1.   Sift the flour with the baking powder and salt into a mixing bowl. Add the margarine and rub in until the mixture resembles fine breadcrumbs. Stir in 75 g (3 oz) of the cheese, the onion and the peanuts and mix well. Ⓐ
2.   Stir in the milk, all at once, and mix to form a fairly soft dough, using a round-bladed knife. Knead lightly until free from cracks.
3.   Roll out the dough on a lightly floured board or work surface to a 2.5 cm (1 inch) thickness. Using a floured 5 cm (2 inch) plain round cutter, cut out 6 rounds. Re-knead and re-roll the trimmings and cut out a further 4 rounds.
4.   On a lightly floured baking sheet, arrange the scone rounds slightly overlapping into a neat 18 cm (7 inch) ring. Brush the tops with milk and sprinkle with the remaining cheese.
5.   Bake in a preheated oven for 15 minutes until well risen, golden brown and cooked through. Ⓕ Serve warm or cold, split and buttered, garnished with tomatoes.

Ⓐ The dry scone mix can be prepared 1 day in advance, covered with cling film and kept in the refrigerator.
Ⓕ Freeze for up to 3 months. Reheat from frozen at 180°C, 350°F, Gas Mark 4 for 8-10 minutes, covering with foil if necessary to prevent overbrowning.
Ⓜ Or microwave on Defrost for 6 minutes. To serve warm, heat on Full/Maximum for 2-3 minutes.

Creamy Custard Horns

MAKES 8

3 egg yolks
50 g (2 oz) caster sugar
25 g (1 oz) plain flour
150 ml (¼ pint) milk
150 ml (¼ pint) single cream
15 g (½ oz) butter, diced
a few drops of vanilla essence
1 × 215 g (7½ oz) packet frozen puff pastry, thawed
a little beaten egg
4 heaped teaspoons strawberry or raspberry jam

TO DECORATE:
4 fresh strawberries

PREPARATION TIME: *15 minutes*
COOKING TIME: *20 minutes*
OVEN: *220°C, 425°F, Gas Mark 7*

Cream horn tins are readily available from most large departmental stores and cook shops.

1. Put the egg yolks and sugar in a bowl and beat with a wooden spoon until smooth. Stir in the flour and mix well.
2. Heat the milk and cream in a saucepan until hot but not boiling, and gradually stir into the egg yolk mixture. Return the mixture to the pan and bring to the boil over a low heat, stirring all the time with a wooden spoon. Cook very gently for 2 minutes, stirring all the time. Remove from the heat and beat in the butter and vanilla

essence to taste, until the butter has melted. Pour into a bowl and leave to cool for 30 minutes, covered with dampened greaseproof paper to prevent a skin forming. Ⓐ
3. Roll out the pastry on a lightly floured board or work surface to a 10×60 cm (4×24 inch) rectangle, and trim the edges. Brush all over with beaten egg and cut lengthways into eight 1×60 cm (½×24 inch) strips.
4. Wind each pastry strip, egg side uppermost, around a cream horn tin, starting at the pointed end and overlapping the pastry by 5 mm (¼ inch) at each turn.

Place the cornets, with the pastry end underneath, on a dampened baking sheet and cook in a preheated oven for 10-12 minutes until the pastry is golden brown and cooked through. While the pastry cornets are still warm, gently twist each one from its tin, holding the tin with a cloth. Return the pastry cornets to the oven for a further 2 minutes. Transfer to a wire rack and leave to cool completely. Ⓐ Ⓕ
5. Place the custard in a piping bag fitted with a 1 cm (½ inch) plain nozzle. Spoon ½ teaspoon jam into the pointed end of each cornet and pipe in the custard, to fill the cornets. Smooth over the

ends with a damp knife and decorate each one with a strawberry. Serve immediately.

Ⓐ The custard can be prepared in the morning, covered with dampened greaseproof paper and kept in the refrigerator.

The pastry cornets can be baked 5 days in advance and stored in an airtight tin. Reheat the cornets on a baking sheet in a preheated oven 180°C, 350°F, Gas Mark 4 for 3-4 minutes to crisp and refresh. Cool completely before filling.
Ⓕ Freeze for up to 3 months. Reheat from frozen at 180°C, 350°F, Gas Mark 4 for 8-10 minutes to crisp and refresh. Cover with foil during reheating if necessary to prevent overbrowning. Cool completely before filling.
Ⓜ Or microwave, 8 at a time, thin end pointing inwards on a roasting rack or on kitchen paper, for 2-4 minutes. Stand for 10 minutes before filling.

VARIATION:
Fill the pastry horns with sweetened whipped cream instead of custard and decorate each one with a fresh strawberry.
Cheese and Liver Pâté: Beat together 75 g (3 oz) smooth liver pâté, 75 g (3 oz) full fat soft cheese and 1-2 tablespoons single cream or mayonnaise until thoroughly combined. Pipe the mixture into the pastry cornets and garnish each one with a slice of stuffed olive or a small parsley sprig.

Left to right: Vitality Salad Platter; Farmhouse Scone Ring; Creamy Custard Horns.

Lemon Cream Swiss Roll

MAKES a 33×23 cm (13×9 inch) Swiss Roll

75 g (3 oz) soft margarine
200 g (7 oz) caster sugar
3 eggs
175 g (6 oz) self-raising flour, sifted
½ teaspoon finely grated lemon rind
150 ml (¼ pint) whipping cream
2 tablespoons lemon curd
1 tablespoon toasted, chopped mixed nuts (optional)
1 tablespoon icing sugar, sifted, for dredging

PREPARATION TIME: *20 minutes, plus cooling*

COOKING TIME: *12-15 minutes*

OVEN: *190°C, 375°F, Gas Mark 5*

This is a quick, easy and foolproof Swiss roll, which is best eaten the day it is baked.

1. Grease a 33×23 cm (13×9 inch) Swiss roll tin and line the base and sides with greaseproof paper.
2. Put the margarine, 175 g (6 oz) of the sugar, eggs, flour and lemon rind in a mixing bowl and beat well with a wooden spoon for 2-3 minutes, or with an electric mixer for 1 minute.
3. Turn the mixture into the prepared Swiss roll tin and spread out evenly. Bake in a preheated oven for 12-15 minutes or until well risen, light golden and cooked through. To test, press lightly in the centre with the little finger; if the sponge springs back it is done, if your finger leaves an impression bake for a further few minutes.
4. Meanwhile have ready on a work surface, a large sheet of greaseproof paper, placed over a dampened tea towel. Dredge the greaseproof paper evenly with the remaining sugar.
5. Turn the sponge out on to the sugared paper. Quickly, but carefully, remove the lining paper and trim the edges neatly.
6. Working quickly, roll up the Swiss roll, starting with a short end and using the greaseproof paper to help you form a neat roll. Wrap closely in the greaseproof paper to hold in shape and leave to cool completely. Ⓐ
7. Whip the cream until soft peaks form, then add the lemon curd and whisk again until thick and evenly mixed.
8. Unroll the Swiss roll and spread evenly with the lemon cream mixture. Sprinkle with chopped nuts if using, and re-roll neatly. Sprinkle with icing sugar and serve cut into chunky slices.

Ⓐ The Swiss roll can be made in the morning, wrapped in the greaseproof paper and kept at room temperature.

VARIATION:
The lemon curd can be replaced with raspberry jam.

Left to right: Lemon Cream Swiss Roll; Chocolate Oaty Flapjacks; Blancmange Surprise.

Blancmange Surprise

SERVES 4-6

75 g (3 oz) cornflour
3 tablespoons sugar
900 ml (1½ pints) milk
300 ml (½ pint) single cream
6 tablespoons strawberry jam,
  with any whole strawberries
  cut into small pieces
50 g (2 oz) butter, diced
a few drops of red food
  colouring

TO DECORATE:
100-175 g (4-6 oz) fresh
  strawberries, hulled

PREPARATION TIME: *7 minutes,*
plus setting

COOKING TIME: *5 minutes*

1. Blend the cornflour with the sugar and 8 tablespoons of the milk in a bowl to make a smooth paste. Bring the remaining milk to the boil in a saucepan. Pour on to the cornflour mixture, stirring constantly.
2. Return to the pan and stir in the cream. Bring slowly to the boil, stirring all the time with a wooden spoon, then lower the heat and simmer gently for 2 minutes, stirring all the time until thickened and smooth. Remove from the heat and stir in the strawberry jam, butter and add a few drops of food colouring, stirring all the time until the jam and butter have melted and the mixture is evenly coloured to your liking.
3. Pour the mixture into a wetted 1.2 litre (2 pint) ring mould and leave to set for 3 hours, or overnight in the refrigerator. Ⓐ

4. To unmould, dampen a serving plate (this enables you to centralize blancmange on plate once it has been turned out). Dip the base of the mould into hot water for a few seconds and place the serving plate over the mould. Invert the mould and give a firm shake, holding both the plate and mould securely with both hands. Remove the mould carefully and fill the centre of the blancmange with strawberries. Ⓐ Leave the blancmange to set overnight in the refrigerator.

VARIATION:
Use sieved raspberry jam in place of strawberry jam and fill the centre of the blancmange with fresh raspberries.

Chocolate Oaty Flapjacks

MAKES 12

100 g (4 oz) hard margarine
4 tablespoons golden syrup
50 g (2 oz) demerara sugar
225 g (8 oz) porridge oats
½ teaspoon finely grated
  orange rind (optional)

TOPPING:
75 g (3 oz) plain chocolate,
  broken into pieces
15 g (½ oz) desiccated
  coconut

PREPARATION TIME: *7 minutes,*
plus cooling

COOKING TIME: *15 minutes*

OVEN: *180°C, 350°F, Gas Mark 4*

These delicious flapjacks are sure to be a popular birthday tea treat.

1. Grease the base and sides of a 20 cm (8 inch) round sandwich cake tin. Put the margarine, golden syrup and sugar in a saucepan and heat gently until melted. Remove from the heat.
2. Stir in the oats and orange rind, if using, and mix well. Turn into the prepared tin and spread out evenly. Ⓐ
3. Bake in a preheated oven for 15 minutes until lightly golden.
4. Meanwhile, prepare the topping, melt the chocolate without stirring in a heatproof bowl set over a saucepan of hot, not boiling, water. Spread the melted chocolate over the hot baked flapjack mixture in the tin and sprinkle with desiccated coconut. Cut into 12 wedges and leave to cool in the tin for 1 hour. Store the flapjacks in an airtight tin.

Ⓐ The flapjack mixture can be prepared in the morning, covered with cling film and kept at room temperature.

Marzipan Spice Teabread

MAKES a 1 kg (2 lb) LOAF

450 g (1 lb) strong plain white
  flour
½ teaspoon salt
1 tablespoon caster sugar
50 g (2 oz) butter, diced
1 packet easy blend dried yeast
  (equivalent to 25 g (1 oz)
  fresh yeast)
75 g (3 oz) mixed dried fruit
200 ml (7 fl oz) tepid milk
1 egg, beaten

FILLING:
100 g (4 oz) ground almonds
100 g (4 oz) soft light brown
  sugar
1 teaspoon ground cinnamon
1 egg beaten

TO GLAZE:
6 tablespoons icing sugar, sifted
1 tablespoon lemon juice

PREPARATION TIME: *15 minutes,
plus cooling*

COOKING TIME: *40 minutes*

OVEN: *200°C, 400°C, Gas Mark 6*

This easy-to-make teabread
is filled like a Swiss roll with
a mouthwatering almond,
sugar and spice mixture that
looks most attractive when
the loaf is sliced. The tea
bread is best eaten the day it
is baked, with butter.

1. Sift the flour with the salt
and sugar into a large mixing
bowl. Rub in the butter with
the fingertips until the
mixture resembles fine
breadcrumbs. Add the yeast
and dried fruit and stir well
to mix.
2. Add the milk and egg and
mix to form a soft dough,
using a wooden spoon. Turn
the dough on to a lightly
floured board or work
surface and knead by hand
for about 10 minutes until
the dough is smooth and
elastic. (Or mix for 2-3
minutes in an electric mixer
fitted with a dough hook.)

3. Shape the dough into a
round ball, place in a large
lightly oiled polythene bag
and tie loosely. Leave in a
warm place to rise for about
1 hour until the dough is
doubled in size and springs
back when pressed with a
floured finger. Ⓐ
4. To make the filling, mix
all the filling ingredients in a
bowl until thoroughly
blended. Ⓐ
5. Turn the risen dough on
to a lightly floured board or
work surface and knead for 1
minute. Roll the dough out to
a rectangle, with the width
equal to the length of a 1 kg
(2 lb) loaf tin, and 30 cm
(12 inches) long.
6. Spread the filling over the
dough to within 1 cm
(½ inch) of the edges. Roll
up the dough, like a Swiss
roll, starting from a short
edge. Place, join side down,
in a greased 1 kg (2 lb) loaf
tin and ease the dough into
the corners. Cover with
lightly oiled cling film and
leave to prove for about 30
minutes until doubled in size
and almost reaching the top
of the tin.
7. Place in a preheated oven
and bake for 40 minutes or
until golden brown and
cooked through. (Cover with
foil during cooking if
necessary to prevent over-
browning.)
8. Turn the loaf out of the tin
on to a wire rack. Mix the
icing sugar with the lemon
juice and brush over the top
and sides of the hot loaf. Ⓕ
Leave to cool slightly before
serving warm or cold, sliced
and buttered.

Ⓐ The dough can be made in
advance and left to rise
overnight in the refrigerator
in a large, lightly oiled
polythene bag (tied loosely
to allow room for
expansion). Knead well to

bring back to room
temperature before using.
  The filling can be made
several hours in advance,
covered with cling film and
kept in a cool place.
Ⓕ When cold, freeze for up
to 1 month. Thaw for 3-4

hours at room temperature
to serve cold, or toast chunky
slices and serve hot with
butter.
Ⓜ Or microwave on Defrost
for 4-6 minutes, then stand
for 15 minutes before
serving.

Top to bottom: American Carrot Cake; Marzipan Spice Teabread; Fudge Brownies.

American Carrot Cake

MAKES a 20 cm (8 inch) ROUND CAKE

225 g (8 oz) self-raising flour
2 teaspoons baking powder
1 teaspoon ground cinnamon
¼ teaspoon salt
150 g (5 oz) soft dark brown sugar
75 g (3 oz) walnuts, chopped
175 g (6 oz) carrots, grated
2 tablespoons desiccated coconut
1½ teaspoons vanilla essence
2 eggs, beaten
150 ml (¼ pint) corn oil
2 tablespoons milk

FROSTING:
75 g (3 oz) full fat soft cheese
50 g (2 oz) butter, softened
a few drops of vanilla essence
175 g (6 oz) icing sugar, sifted

PREPARATION TIME: *15 minutes, plus cooling*

COOKING TIME: *1 hour*

OVEN: *180°C, 350°F, Gas Mark 4*

A deliciously moist cake with a light, fluffy cream cheese and sugar frosting.

1. Grease a deep 20 cm (8 inch) round cake tin and line the base with greased greaseproof paper.
2. Sift the flour with the baking powder, cinnamon and salt into a mixing bowl. Add the sugar, nuts, grated carrot and desiccated coconut; stir well to mix.
3. Make a well in the centre and add the vanilla essence, eggs, oil and milk. Beat well with a wooden spoon for about 30 seconds until thoroughly blended.
4. Turn the mixture into the prepared tin and smooth the surface. Bake in a preheated oven for 1 hour or until well risen, golden brown and cooked through. To test, insert a fine warm skewer into the centre of cake; if when removed the skewer is clean, the cake is cooked, if not, return to the oven and bake for a further few minutes before testing again.
5. Leave the cake to cool in the tin for 15 minutes before turning out on to a wire rack. Remove the lining paper and leave for about 2 hours to cool completely. Ⓐ
6. To make the frosting, put the cheese, butter and vanilla essence to taste into a bowl and beat well with a wooden spoon until soft and creamy. Gradually add the icing sugar, beating well after each addition. Spread the mixture over the cold cake and rough up with a fork. Ⓕ

Ⓐ The cake can be baked up to 1 week in advance, and stored in an airtight tin.
Ⓕ Freeze for up to 2 months. Thaw for 3-4 hours at room temperature before serving.

Fudge Brownies

MAKES 12

100 g (4 oz) butter or hard margarine, softened
225 g (8 oz) dark soft brown sugar
1 teaspoon vanilla essence
2 eggs, beaten
50 g (2 oz) plain flour
25 g (1 oz) cocoa powder
½ teaspoon baking powder
100 g (4 oz) walnuts, chopped
1 tablespoon milk

TOPPING AND DECORATION:
100 g (4 oz) plain chocolate, broken into pieces
15 g (½ oz) butter
100 g (4 oz) icing sugar, sifted
2 tablespoons warm water
12 walnut halves

PREPARATION TIME: *20 minutes, plus cooling*

COOKING TIME: *30-35 minutes*

OVEN: *180°C, 350°F, Gas Mark 4*

1. Grease an 18×28 cm (7×11 inch) oblong cake tin and line the base with greased greaseproof paper.
2. In a bowl beat the butter or margarine with the sugar and vanilla essence until soft and creamy. Gradually add the beaten eggs, beating well after each addition.
3. Sift the flour with the cocoa and baking powder on to the creamed mixture, add the walnuts and milk and fold in gently but thoroughly, using a large metal spoon. Turn the mixture into the prepared tin and smooth the surface.
4. Bake in a preheated oven for 30-35 minutes until well risen and cooked through. Turn on to a wire rack and leave to cool. Ⓐ
5. Melt the chocolate and butter, without stirring, in a heatproof bowl set over a saucepan of hot, not boiling, water. Remove from the heat and gradually stir in the icing sugar and water to make a thick coating consistency. Use the chocolate topping at once, spooned evenly over the cooked cake and swirled with a knife.
6. Cut into 12 squares and decorate each with a walnut half. Ⓕ

Ⓐ The brownies can be made 2 days in advance and stored in an airtight tin before continuing with step 5.
Ⓕ Freeze for up to 3 months. Thaw for 2-3 hours at room temperature.
Ⓜ Or microwave on Defrost for 7-10 minutes, then stand for 30 minutes before serving.

Blackcurrant Kuchen

SERVES 10-12

PASTRY:
175 g (6 oz) plain flour
3 egg yolks
150 g (5 oz) caster sugar
good pinch of salt
50 g (2 oz) ground hazelnuts
100 g (4 oz) butter or
  margarine

FILLING AND TOPPING:
3 egg whites
75 g (3 oz) caster sugar
75 g (3 oz) soft light brown
  sugar
100 g (4 oz) ground hazelnuts
225 g (8 oz) fresh or frozen
  (thawed) blackcurrants,
  topped and tailed

PREPARATION TIME: *20 minutes, plus cooling*

COOKING TIME: *1 hour 45 minutes*

OVEN: *200°C, 400°F, Gas Mark 6;*

THEN: *120°C, 250°F, Gas Mark ½*

A rich hazelnut pastry base, topped with a delicious fruit and nut meringue. Use a blender or a food processor to grind the hazelnuts quickly and finely.

1. Place a 25 cm (10 inch) loose-bottomed fluted flan tin on a baking sheet.
2. To make the pastry, put the sifted flour, egg yolks, sugar, salt, hazelnuts and butter or margarine altogether in a bowl and knead by hand to form a smooth dough.
3. Press the hazelnut pastry on to the base of the flan tin. Place in a preheated oven and bake for 30 minutes until golden brown. (Cover with foil if necessary during cooking to prevent overbrowning.) Remove from the oven and leave to cool. Ⓐ
4. Whisk the egg whites stiffly, then whisk in the caster sugar and brown sugar and continue whisking until very stiff and glossy. Gently fold in the ground hazelnuts and blackcurrants, using a large metal spoon.
5. Spread the meringue over the pastry in the tin and peak with a fork. Reduce the oven temperature and bake for a further 1½ hours or until the meringue topping is light gold and crisp on the surface. Leave to cool in the tin for several hours, then carefully remove the flan ring and leave the Blackcurrant Kuchen on the flan tin base. Serve cut into wedges, with cream.

Ⓐ The pastry can be baked the previous day, covered with cling film and kept in an airtight tin.

VARIATION:
Use redcurrants or a mixture of redcurrants and blackcurrants, or raspberries or blackberries, instead of blackcurrants.

Top to bottom: Nutty Brown Sugar Meringues; Apple Slice Cake; Blackcurrant Kuchen.

Nutty Brown Sugar Meringues

MAKES 10

2 egg whites
100 g (4 oz) soft light brown sugar
25 g (1 oz) chopped mixed nuts
150 ml (¼ pint) whipping cream
1 teaspoon icing sugar
a few drops of vanilla essence

PREPARATION TIME: *10-15 minutes, plus cooling*

COOKING TIME: *6-8 hours, or overnight*

OVEN: *110°C, 225°F, Gas Mark ¼*

Meringues keep well for several weeks, stored in a polythene bag in an airtight tin, and are a useful standby for tea or a dessert when unexpected guests arrive.

1. Line a baking sheet with non-stick silicone paper or lightly greased greaseproof paper.
2. Whisk the egg whites in a bowl until stiff. Sprinkle over 50 g (2 oz) of the sugar and whisk again until very stiff and glossy.
3. Lightly fold in the remaining sugar, using a large metal spoon. Put the mixture into a piping bag fitted with a large star tube, and pipe 20 star-shapes on to the prepared baking sheet. Sprinkle with nuts.
4. Bake the meringues in a preheated very low oven for 6-8 hours, or overnight, until completely dried out. Transfer to a wire rack to cool for 15 minutes only, then store in polythene bags in an airtight tin until required. Ⓐ
5. Whip the cream with the icing sugar and vanilla essence to taste until stiff peaks form. Use to sandwich the meringues together in pairs. Serve within 30 minutes of assembling.

Ⓐ The meringue shells can be kept successfully for up to 6 weeks. Store as described.

VARIATIONS:
White Meringues: Use caster sugar instead of soft light brown sugar.
Choc and Nut Meringues: Mix whipped cream (without icing sugar and vanilla essence) with 1½-2 tablespoons of chocolate hazelnut spread and use to sandwich the meringues together.
Pineapple Cream Meringues: Cut 5 pineapple rings in half (to give 10 thin rings) and sandwich between cream and meringues.

Apple Slice Cake

SERVES 12

2 crisp dessert apples peeled, cored and thinly sliced
1 tablespoon lemon juice
100 g (4 oz) full fat soft cheese
25 g (1 oz) butter or hard margarine, softened
100 g (4 oz) soft light brown sugar
2 eggs, beaten
½ teaspoon finely grated lemon rind
100 g (4 oz) self-raising flour
1 teaspoon baking powder
1 tablespoon demerara sugar

PREPARATION TIME: *30 minutes*

COOKING TIME: *50 minutes*

OVEN: *180°C, 350°F, Gas Mark 4*

Serve this dual-purpose cake warm as a pudding with custard, or cold at teatime with whipped cream. Granny Smith or Russet apples are ideal.

1. Grease a 18×28 cm (7×11 inch) oblong cake tin and line the base with greased greaseproof paper.
2. Sprinkle the apple slices with lemon juice and reserve.
3. In a bowl, beat the cheese with the butter or margarine and sugar until light and fluffy. Add the egg, a little at a time, beating well after each addition to give a runny batter consistency. Stir in the lemon rind. Ⓐ
4. Sift the flour with the baking powder on to the cheese mixture and fold in gently, using a large metal spoon. Turn the mixture into the prepared tin and smooth the surface. Press the apple slices, core sides down, in three rows lengthways along the cake mixture. Sprinkle the surface evenly with the demerara sugar.
5. Place the cake in a preheated oven and bake for 50 minutes until the topping is golden brown and the apples are tender. (Cover with foil after 30 minutes cooking time to prevent overbrowning.) Ⓕ
6. Serve the apple slice hot or cold, cut into squares, with custard, scoops of ice cream or spoonfuls of whipped cream.

Ⓐ The apples and batter mixture can be prepared in the morning, covered with cling film and kept at room temperature.
Ⓕ Freeze for up to 3 months. Thaw for 3-4 hours at room temperature before serving cold.
Ⓜ Or microwave on Defrost for 8-12 minutes, then stand for 30 minutes before serving.

Butterscotch Meringue Pie

SERVES 8-10

175 g (6 oz) soft margarine
pinch of salt
1½ tablespoons cold water
275 g (10 oz) plain flour
75 g (3 oz) butter
175 g (6 oz) soft dark brown
  sugar
200 ml (7 fl oz) boiling water
3 tablespoons cornflour
450 ml (¾ pint) milk
2 eggs, separated
75 g (3 oz) caster sugar

PREPARATION TIME: *30 minutes, plus cooling*

COOKING TIME: *1 hour 5 minutes*

OVEN: *200°C, 400°F, Gas Mark 6;*

THEN: *150°C, 300°F, Gas Mark 2*

1. Put the margarine with the salt, water and 2 tablespoons of the flour into a bowl and mix vigorously with a fork for 30 seconds until thoroughly blended. Add the remaining flour and continue mixing with a fork to form a fairly firm dough. Knead gently until free from cracks. Wrap in cling film and chill in the refrigerator for at least 15 minutes before using. Ⓐ
2. Roll out the pastry on a lightly floured board or work surface to a 30 cm (12 inch) round and use to line a 25 cm (10 inch) loose-bottomed fluted flan tin, set on a baking sheet. Gently ease the pastry into the tin and press on to the base and up the sides, pressing firmly into the flutes but taking care not to stretch the pastry. Fold the excess pastry over the edge of the tin and run a rolling pin firmly over the top to cut through the pastry and give a neat edge.
3. Prick the pastry base all over with a fork.
4. Line with a large round of greaseproof paper or foil and fill with baking beans. Bake in a preheated oven for 15 minutes. Remove the paper and beans and return to the oven for a further 5-10 minutes until the pastry is dry and light golden-brown. Remove from the oven and leave to cool. Ⓐ Ⓕ
5. Melt the butter in a heavy-based saucepan until just turning light golden and foaming. Add the sugar and stir well, then remove from the heat. Add the boiling water and stir well.
6. Blend the cornflour with a little of the milk, to make a smooth paste. Put the remaining milk in a saucepan, and stir in the blended cornflour and the butter and sugar mixture. Place over a gentle heat and bring to the boil, stirring all the time with a wooden spoon. Lower the heat and simmer for 1 minute, stirring all the time. Remove from the heat and allow to cool slightly.
7. Pour half the mixture on to the egg yolks in a bowl, beating well all the time, then return this to the mixture in pan and cook over a very gentle heat for 2 minutes, stirring all the time. Remove from the heat and pour into the prepared flan case. Leave for 1 hour to cool completely. Ⓐ
8. Whisk the egg whites until stiff, sprinkle over 40 g (1½ oz) of the sugar and whisk again until very stiff and glossy. Lightly fold in the remaining sugar, using a large metal spoon. Spoon the meringue evenly over the cold filling in the pastry case and peak, using the flat side of a knife.
9. Reduce the oven temperature and bake the flan for 30 minutes until the meringue is set and lightly browned. Leave to cool for 2 hours before serving cold, cut into slices.

Ⓐ The pastry can be prepared the previous day, covered with cling film and kept chilled.

The flan case can be baked a week in advance and stored in an airtight tin, before filling.

The filled flan case can be prepared in the morning and kept at room temperature before proceeding from step 8.

Ⓕ Freeze for up to 6 months. Thaw the pastry flan case for 1½ hours at room temperature before proceeding from step 5.

Ⓜ Or microwave on Defrost for 2-3 minutes, then stand for 5 minutes before proceeding from step 5.

Flaky Cream Slices; Butterscotch Meringue Pie.

Flaky Cream Slices

MAKES 10

1 × 215 g (7½ oz) packet
   frozen puff pastry, thawed
150 ml (¼ pint) whipping
   cream
3 teaspoons icing sugar, sifted
a few drops of vanilla essence
225 g (8 oz) strawberries,
   hulled and halved

PREPARATION TIME: *15 minutes,
plus resting and cooling*
COOKING TIME: *8-10 minutes*
OVEN: *230°C, 450°F, Gas Mark 8*

Flaky layers of golden pastry,
sandwiched together with
fruit and cream make a
delicious teatime or birthday
treat.

1. Cut the pastry in half
lengthways and place one
strip on top of the other. Roll
out pastry on a lightly floured
board or work surface to
50 × 10 cm (20 × 4 inch)
rectangle.
2. Cut the pastry crossways
into ten 5 × 10 cm (2 × 4 inch)
pieces. Place these on a
dampened baking sheet and
set aside for 15 minutes.
3. Bake in a preheated oven

for 8-10 minutes until golden
brown and cooked through.
Remove from the oven,
carefully transfer to a wire
rack and leave to cool
completely. Ⓐ
4. Carefully split each pastry
rectangle in half, to give 2
layers. In a bowl, whip the
cream with 1 teaspoon of the
icing sugar and vanilla
essence to taste, until stiff.
Spread the 10 pastry bases
with whipped cream and
arrange the strawberry
halves on top. Add the
remaining pastry layers and
dredge with the remaining
icing sugar.

Ⓐ Can be prepared 5 days in
advance, then stored in an
airtight tin. Reheat the pastry
rectangles at 180°C, 350°F,
Gas Mark 4 for 5 minutes to
refresh and crisp. Cool
completely before splitting
and filling.

VARIATION:
If fresh fruit is not available,
replace with strawberry jam
and decorate with a little
reserved whipped cream.
   Vary the flavour of jam
used: try blackberry, apricot,
raspberry or black cherry as
liked.

Fluffy Lemon Cloud

SERVES 4-5

2 teaspoons powdered gelatine
4 tablespoons lemon juice
75 g (3 oz) caster sugar
3 eggs, separated
½ teaspoon finely grated lemon rind
150 ml (¼ pint) whipping cream

PREPARATION TIME: *10 minutes, plus setting*
COOKING TIME: *2 minutes*

1. Sprinkle the gelatine over the lemon juice in a small heatproof bowl and leave to soften for 10 minutes. Stand the bowl in a pan of gently simmering water and stir with a wooden spoon until the gelatine dissolves. Remove from the heat and leave to cool for about 5 minutes, but do not allow the mixture to set.
2. Put the sugar, egg yolks and lemon rind into a bowl and whisk for about 1 minute with an electric hand whisk, until the mixture is creamy, thick and standing in soft peaks. Stir in the cooled gelatine mixture.
3. Whisk the egg whites until stiff. Whisk the cream until soft peaks form. Gently fold the egg whites and cream into the egg yolk and lemon mixture. Turn into a glass serving dish. Chill in the refrigerator for at least 1 hour, until set. Serve chilled.

Choc-o-Nut Gâteau

MAKES a 20 cm (8 inch) round cake

CAKE:
100 g (4 oz) plain chocolate, broken into pieces
100 g (4 oz) unsalted butter
4 eggs, separated
100 g (4 oz) caster sugar
25 g (1 oz) plain flour, sifted
50 g (2 oz) ground almonds
25 g (1 oz) fresh white breadcrumbs

BUTTERCREAM:
100 g (4 oz) unsalted butter
175 g (6 oz) icing sugar, sifted
a few drops of almond essence (optional)
1 teaspoon cold water

FROSTING:
175 g (6 oz) caster sugar
1 egg white
2 teaspoons hot water
pinch of cream of tartar

TO DECORATE:
12 toasted, blanched almonds
6 glacé cherries, halved
1 tablespoon caster sugar

PREPARATION TIME: *25 minutes, plus cooling and setting*
COOKING TIME: *1¼ hours*
OVEN: *180°C, 350°F, Gas Mark 4*

A special occasion cake for a birthday or anniversary celebration.

1. Grease a deep 20 cm (8 inch) round cake tin and line the base and sides with greased greaseproof paper.
2. Melt the chocolate and butter without stirring in a heatproof bowl set over a saucepan of hot, not boiling water. Leave to cool but do not allow to set.
3. Meanwhile, place the egg yolks and sugar in a heatproof bowl over a pan of gently simmering water (do not allow the base of the bowl to touch the water). Whisk until the mixture is light and fluffy and leaves a trail from the whisk. Remove from the heat and gradually whisk in the cool, melted chocolate mixture.
4. Stir in the flour, almonds and breadcrumbs. Whisk the egg whites until stiff and gently fold into the mixture, using a large metal spoon.
5. Turn the mixture into the prepared tin and bake in a preheated oven for 1¼ hours or until the cake is well risen and cooked through. A fine warmed skewer inserted into the centre of the cake should come out clean; if not, bake for a further few minutes before testing again. Turn out on to a wire rack, remove the lining paper and leave to cool for 1½-2 hours. Ⓐ
6. To make the buttercream, beat the butter in a bowl until soft and creamy, then gradually mix in the icing sugar, beating well after each addition. Beat in the almond essence, if using, with the water. Ⓐ
7. Split the cold cake into 3 equal layers and place the bottom layer on a serving plate. Spread with half the buttercream. Cover with the centre layer and spread with the remaining buttercream. Top with the final layer. Ⓕ
8. To make the frosting, place all the ingredients into a heatproof bowl and set over a saucepan of boiling water which has just been removed from the heat. Whisk with a rotary beater or electric hand whisk until the mixture thickens and forms soft peaks. Quickly spread the frosting over the top and sides of the cake, swirling with a knife. Leave to set for 10 minutes, then decorate with a border of almonds and glacé cherries rolled in caster sugar. Leave to set for 2 hours before serving.

Ⓐ The cake and buttercream can be prepared the previous day: store the cake in an airtight tin and the buttercream in a covered container in the refrigerator. Beat the buttercream well to soften, before using.
Ⓕ Freeze for up to 2 months. Thaw for 3-4 hours at room temperature before proceeding from step 8.
Ⓜ Or microwave on Defrost for 2-5 minutes, keeping a careful eye on the buttercream. Stand for 30 minutes before proceeding from step 8.

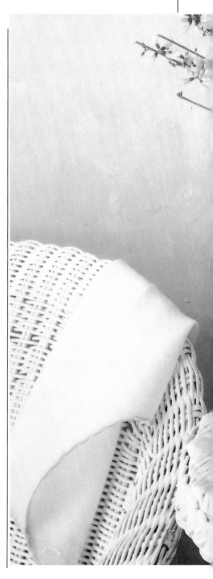

Farmhouse Sultana Cherry Cake

MAKES a 1 kg (2 lb) loaf-shaped cake

225 g (8 oz) plain flour
1½ teaspoons baking powder
175 g (6 oz) soft margarine
175 g (6 oz) caster sugar
2 eggs
75 g (3 oz) glacé cherries, washed, dried and quartered
75 g (3 oz) sultanas
1 tablespoon milk
8 sugar lumps, roughly crushed, to decorate (optional)

PREPARATION TIME: *10 minutes, plus cooling*

COOKING TIME: *1¼-1½ hours*

OVEN: *160°C, 325°F, Gas Mark 3*

1. Grease a 1 kg (2 lb) loaf tin and line the base and sides with greased greaseproof paper.
2. Sift the flour with the baking powder into a mixing bowl. Add the margarine, sugar and eggs and beat well for 2-3 minutes with a wooden spoon, or for 1 minute in an electric mixer, until thoroughly mixed.
3. Stir in the cherries, sultanas and milk, then turn the mixture into the prepared tin. Smooth the surface with a spoon and sprinkle with the crushed sugar lumps, if using.

4. Place in a preheated oven and cook for 1¼-1½ hours until well risen, golden brown and cooked through. To test: insert a fine warmed skewer into the centre of the cake; if when removed the skewer is clean, the cake is cooked; if not, return to the oven and bake for a further few minutes before testing again.
5. Turn the cake out of the tin on to a wire rack, remove the lining paper and leave for 1½-2 hours to cool completely. E When cold, wrap up the cake in greaseproof paper and store in an airtight tin.

E Freeze for up to 3 months. Thaw for 2-3 hours at room temperature.
M Or microwave on Defrost for 5-8 minutes, then stand for 15 minutes before serving.

VARIATION:
Add ½ teaspoon finely grated orange or lemon rind to the mixture.

Clockwise from the top: Choc-o-Nut Gâteau; Farmhouse Sultana Cherry Cake; Fluffy Lemon Cloud.

Aunt Lucy's Lardy Cake

MAKES 16 slices

450 g (1 lb) strong plain white flour
1 teaspoon salt
200 g (7 oz) lard, finely diced
1 packet of easy blend dried yeast (equivalent to 25 g (1 oz) fresh yeast)
150 ml (¼ pint) tepid milk
150 ml (¼ pint) tepid water
175 g (6 oz) caster sugar
1 teaspoon mixed spice
175 g (6 oz) sultanas

TO GLAZE:
4 tablespoons granulated sugar
4 tablespoons water

PREPARATION TIME: *20 minutes, plus proving and cooling*

COOKING TIME: *about 45 minutes*

OVEN: *190°C, 375°F, Gas Mark 5*

If using dried active baking yeast instead of the easy blend dried yeast, follow packet directions carefully as the method of using is quite different.

1. Sift the flour with the salt into a mixing bowl. Rub in 25 g (1 oz) of the lard until the mixture resembles fine breadcrumbs. Stir in the easy blend dried yeast.
2. Stir in the milk and water and mix to a soft dough by hand. Turn on to a lightly floured board or work surface and knead well for about 10 minutes, until smooth and elastic. (Or mix for 2-3 minutes in an electric mixer fitted with a dough hook.)
3. Place in a large, lightly oiled polythene bag and tie loosely. Leave in a warm place for about 1 hour to rise until doubled in size. Ⓐ
4. Turn the risen dough on to a lightly floured board or work surface and knead for 1 minute. Roll out to a 32×20 cm (14×8 inch) rectangle and mark crossways into 3 equal sections. Dot the top two sections with 50 g (2 oz) of the lard. Mix the caster sugar with the mixed spice and sprinkle 50 g (2 oz) of the mixture over the lard, then sprinkle with 50 g (2 oz) of the sultanas. Roll lightly with a rolling pin, to flatten.
5. Fold the uncovered bottom section of dough over the centre section, then fold the top section over this. Give the dough a quarter turn, then repeat the rolling; covering with lard, spiced sugar and sultanas; folding and turning twice more.
6. Roll out the dough to fit a greased 23×28 cm (9×11 inch) roasting tin. Line the tin with the dough, pressing it into the corners. Cover with lightly oiled polythene and leave to prove for about 1 hour, until doubled in size. Using a sharp knife, cut a lattice design on top of the dough.
7. Bake in a preheated oven for 30 minutes until golden brown. Invert the lardy cake on to a preheated baking sheet and return to the oven for a further 10 minutes until golden brown all over.
8. Meanwhile, make the glaze: dissolve the sugar in the water in a saucepan, then bring to the boil and boil rapidly for 3 minutes. Turn the hot cake right way up on a serving plate and immediately brush over the sugar glaze. Cut into 12 slices and serve warm or cold Ⓕ

Ⓐ The Lardy Cake dough can be made in advance and left to rise overnight in the refrigerator in a large, lightly oiled polythene bag, tied loosely to allow room for expansion. Knead well to bring back to room temperature before using.
Ⓕ Freeze for up to 1 month. Reheat from frozen at 180°C, 350°F, Gas Mark 4 for 12-15 minutes. (Cover with foil if necessary during reheating to prevent overbrowning.)
Ⓜ Or microwave on Defrost for 6-8 minutes. Stand for 10 minutes before serving.

Creamy Blackberry Fool

SERVES 6

450 g (1 lb) fresh or frozen (thawed) blackberries
100 g (4 oz) caster sugar
25 g (1 oz) butter
300 ml (½ pint) whipping cream
2 individual jam-filled Swiss rolls, sliced (optional)

PREPARATION TIME: *12 minutes, plus cooling and chilling*

COOKING TIME: *15 minutes*

1. Put the blackberries into a saucepan with the sugar and butter. Cover and cook over a gentle heat for about 15 minutes until the blackberries are tender. Remove from the heat and allow to cool slightly.
2. Pass the contents of the pan through a sieve into a bowl, pressing well with the back of a wooden spoon to extract as much juice and pulp as possible; discard all the seeds. Leave to cool completely. Ⓐ

3. Whip the cream until stiff and gently fold in the strained blackberry syrup, using a spatula to mix until evenly blended.
4. Place slices of Swiss roll in a glass serving dish, if using, and spoon the blackberry mixture on top. Chill in the refrigerator for at least 1 hour before serving.

Ⓐ The blackberry purée can be prepared several hours in advance.

VARIATION:

Gooseberry Fool: Replace the blackberries with fresh or frozen (thawed) gooseberries, topped and tailed, and cook for 20 minutes or until tender. Cool slightly, then place in a blender goblet and blend for 30-60 seconds until smooth. Then proceed from step 3.

Glazed Peach Tart

SERVES 6

PASTRY:
200 g (7 oz) plain flour
pinch of salt
75 g (3 oz) butter or hard margarine, diced
20 g (¾ oz) caster sugar
1 egg, beaten

FILLING:
3 eggs
1 ½ teaspoons vanilla essence
2 tablespoons caster sugar
450 ml (¾ pint) milk
a little freshly grated nutmeg (optional)

TOPPING:
1 × 425 g (15 oz) can peach slices, drained, with syrup reserved
1 teaspoon arrowroot

PREPARATION TIME: *15 minutes, plus cooling*

COOKING TIME: *about 35 minutes*

OVEN: *180°C, 350°F, Gas Mark 4*

1. To make the pastry, sift the flour with the salt into a mixing bowl. Add the butter or margarine and rub in with the fingertips until the mixture resembles fine breadcrumbs. Stir in the sugar. Reserve 2 teaspoons of the beaten egg for glazing the tart; add the remainder to the bowl and mix to form a firm dough, using a round-bladed knife. Knead gently until free from cracks.
2. Roll out the pastry on a lightly floured board or work surface to a 25 cm (10 inch) round and use to line a 20 cm (8 inch) pie dish 4 cm (1½ inches) deep. Trim the pastry edge with a sharp knife and decorate the border by pinching the pastry between the little finger of one hand and the thumb and forefinger of the other. Chill in the refrigerator while preparing the filling.
3. To make the filling, beat the eggs with the vanilla essence and sugar in a bowl. Heat the milk until tepid and pour on to the egg and sugar mixture, stirring well. Strain into the prepared pastry case and sprinkle with freshly grated nutmeg, if using. Glaze the pastry border with the reserved beaten egg.
4. Place the tart on a preheated baking sheet and cook in a preheated oven for 35 minutes or until the custard filling is just set. Remove from the oven and leave to cool for 2 hours. Ⓐ
5. Arrange the peach slices over the custard filling, in rows radiating from the centre.
6. In a small saucepan, blend the arrowroot with 1 tablespoon of the reserved peach syrup. Add the remaining syrup and bring slowly to the boil, stirring all the time. Lower the heat and simmer for 2 minutes, stirring, until thickened and clear. Remove from the heat and cool slightly, then spoon the glaze over the peach slices. Chill in the refrigerator for 20 minutes or until set before serving. Ⓐ

Ⓐ The tart and custard filling can be kept in the refrigerator for up to 2 days. The glazed tart will also keep for up to 2 days in the refrigerator, covered with cling film.

Left to right: Aunt Lucy's Lardy Cake; Glazed Peach Tart; Creamy Blackberry Fool.

Rose Elliot's

Children's Tea Party

═══ MENU ═══

CHEESE STRAWS

INDIVIDUAL PIZZAS

EGG PIN WHEELS

FUNNY FACE CUP CAKES

CHOCOLATE ICE CREAM

SPACE ADVENTURE NOVELTY CAKE

Most children are highly conventional when it comes to food and are anxious about trying things which look different from tried and tested favourites. So in this menu, I've aimed to provide food which is reassuringly familiar, but presented in an interesting way.

Since this will probably be the last meal which the children will eat before bed, I've included two quite substantial savoury items: individual pizzas, based on a scone mixture, and egg pinwheels, an interesting version of good old egg sandwiches.

Although I do not give my children many sugary foods normally, I make an exception for a party. I have suggested using 85% wholewheat flour, which you can get from health shops, for the cakes and pizzas, because that is my preference, but you could substitute an ordinary self-raising flour if you prefer.

Cheese Straws

MAKES about 100

225 g (8 oz) plain wholewheat flour
50 g (2 oz) grated hard cheese
50 g (2 oz) butter, diced

PREPARATION TIME: *15 minutes*
COOKING TIME: *10 minutes*
OVEN: *200°C, 400°F, Gas Mark 6*

The wholewheat flour gives a delicious nutty flavour to these easy-to-make, crisp and crunchy savoury straws that are a popular teatime treat. This quantity will serve about 10.

1. Dust a baking sheet lightly with a little wholewheat flour.
2. Put the flour, cheese and butter into a bowl. Rub the mixture with the fingertips until well combined. Add a little water to make a dough.
3. Turn the dough out on to a lightly-floured board or work surface and knead lightly. Roll out to a rectangle about 20 × 40 cm (8 × 16 inches) and 6 mm (¼ in) thick. Cut across into 3 equal pieces, then down into strips about 6 mm (¼ in) wide. Using a fish slice, transfer the strips in batches to the baking sheet, then space them out.
4. Bake in a preheated oven for 8-10 minutes, until the straws are golden brown. Cool for a few seconds on the baking sheet, then transfer to a wire tray to cool completely. Ⓕ

Ⓕ Freeze for up to 4 weeks. To serve, place on a wire tray and allow to thaw (15-20 minutes).
Ⓜ Or microwave 12 at a time on Defrost for 1-2 minutes. Stand for 5 minutes before serving.

Individual Pizzas

MAKES 10

225 g (8 oz) self-raising 85% wholemeal flour
2 teaspoons baking powder
1 teaspoon salt
50 g (2 oz) soft margarine
120 ml (4 fl oz) milk

FOR THE TOPPING:
2 medium onions, peeled and chopped
2 tablespoons oil
2 tablespoons tomato purée
salt
freshly ground black pepper
50-75 g (2-3 oz) finely grated cheese
2 teaspoons oregano (optional)

TO GARNISH:
sliced stuffed olives (optional)

PREPARATION TIME: *25 minutes*
COOKING TIME: *25 minutes*
OVEN: *220°C, 425°F, Gas Mark 7*

1. Lightly brush 1 large or 2 small baking sheets with cooking oil.
2. Sift the flour, baking powder and salt into a mixing bowl, adding any residue of bran from the sieve too. Rub in the margarine with your fingertips until the mixture resembles breadcrumbs, then pour in the milk and mix to a smooth dough.

Cover the bowl with clingfilm and leave to one side while you prepare the topping.
3. Fry the onions gently in the oil, in a covered saucepan, for 10 minutes, until soft but not browned. Remove from the heat and stir in the tomato purée and season with salt and pepper to taste.
4. Turn the prepared dough out on to a lightly-floured work surface and knead for 1 minute. Roll it out to a thickness of 8 mm (⅓ inch), then use a plain 7.5 cm (3 inch) cutter to cut out 12 rounds, re-rolling trimmings as necessary.
5. Place the rounds on to the prepared baking sheets. Spoon the onion mixture on top, dividing it between the pizzas and spreading it to the edges. Sprinkle with grated cheese and oregano, if using. Garnish with a few slices of olive, if using.
6. Bake in a preheated oven for 15 minutes. Ⓐ Serve warm.

Ⓐ Pizzas can be baked in advance, then covered with foil and reheated in a moderate oven, 180°C, 350°F, Gas Mark 4, for about 10 minutes.

Egg Pin Wheels

MAKES 30

2 hard-boiled eggs
15 g (½ oz butter)
1 tablespoon salad cream
salt
freshly ground black pepper
6 slices from a large sliced
 wholewheat loaf
butter, for spreading

PREPARATION TIME: *15 minutes*
COOKING TIME: *10 minutes, for eggs*

1. First make the filling. Put the eggs into a bowl and, using a fork, mash until fairly smooth. Add the butter, salad cream and salt and pepper, then beat to a fairly smooth paste.
2. Put the slices of bread on a board and roll with a rolling pin to flatten slightly. Cut off the crusts and butter the bread.
3. Spread with filling, then roll up each slice from one of the short edges. Press the roll together gently but firmly. Slice each roll into about 5 pieces and arrange on a serving dish. Ⓐ

Ⓐ Can be made up to 2 hours in advance, covered tightly with clingfilm and stored in a cool place.

Clockwise from top right: Cheese Straws; Individual Pizzas; Egg Pin Wheels.

Funny Face Cup Cakes

MAKES 18

100 g (4 oz) soft margarine
100 g (4 oz) caster sugar
2 eggs
165 g (5½ oz) self-raising flour
15 g (½ oz) cocoa
2-3 teaspoons milk

FOR ICING AND DECORATION:
225 g (8 oz) icing sugar
3-4 tablespoons warm water
few drops of green and red food
    colouring
2 chocolate flakes
2 chocolate sugar strands
assorted sweets, glacé cherries

PREPARATION TIME: *30 minutes*
COOKING TIME: *20 minutes*
OVEN: *160°C, 325°F, Gas Mark 3*

1. Place 18 paper cakes cases on a baking sheet.
2. Put the margarine, sugar and eggs into a mixing bowl. Sift in the flour and cocoa. Beat with a wooden spoon or electric mixer for 1-2 minutes, until smooth and glossy. Add a little milk, as necessary, until the mixture drops heavily from the spoon tapped against the bowl.
3. Divide the mixture between the cake cases. Bake in a preheated oven for 20 minutes, until firm in the centre. Remove and transfer to a wire tray to cool. F
4. Sift the icing sugar into a bowl. Mix with enough warm water to make a smooth, thick consistency. Transfer half the mixture to another bowl. Add a few drops of green colouring to one bowl and colour the other pink with a little red colouring.
5. Ice half the cakes with pink icing and the remainder with green. Use crushed chocolate flake or sugar strands around the top edge to represent hair. Decorate with sweets to represent eyes, noses, and ears; use small pieces of cherry or red jelly sweets for mouths.

F Freeze for up to 4 weeks. To serve, stand cakes on wire tray for about 1 hour, until thawed, then ice and decorate as described.
M Or microwave 6 at a time on Defrost for 1-2 minutes. Stand for 5 minutes before icing and decorating as described.

Chocolate Ice Cream

SERVES 12

1½ tablespoons cornflour
1.25 litres (2¼ pints) milk
175 g (6 oz) plain chocolate
3 tablespoons caster sugar
450 ml (¾ pint) whipping
    cream

PREPARATION TIME: *20 minutes,*
plus freezing and standing
COOKING TIME: *5-10 minutes*

This is a refreshing, not-too-rich ice cream that children love. It freezes hard, so take it out of the refrigerator in good time, to allow it to soften a little before serving.

1. Turn the refrigerator to its coldest setting or use freezer at normal setting.
2. Put the cornflour into a small bowl and blend to a paste with a little of the milk.

Leave to one side.
3. Break up the chocolate, place in a large saucepan with the rest of the milk and sugar. Bring to the boil. Pour a little boiling milk over the cornflour mixture, blend, then pour into the saucepan with the rest of the milk. Stir for 2-3 minutes, until slightly thickened.
4. Remove from the heat, cool slightly, then liquidize with the cream. Turn the mixture into a polythene container. Freeze until 2 cm (1 inch) of the mixture is solid around the edges, then beat. Return the mixture to the refrigerator and freeze until solid.
5. Remove from the refrigerator or freezer and allow to stand at room temperature 30-40 minutes before serving.

Space Adventure Novelty Cake

MAKES one cake 24 cm (9½ inches) square

6 eggs
175 g (6 oz) caster sugar
175 g (6 oz) plain flour, sifted
75 g (3 oz) butter, melted and cooled

FOR FILLING AND DECORATION:
175 g (6 oz) unsalted butter
350 g (12 oz) icing sugar
3 tablespoons hot water
'Star Wars' figures, space men, small spacecraft; silver ribbon to tie round cake (optional)

PREPARATION TIME: *1½ hours*
COOKING TIME: *35-55 minutes*
OVEN: *180°C, 350°F, Gas Mark 4*

1. Line a 24 cm (9½ inch) square cake tin with greased greaseproof paper.
2. Put the eggs and sugar into a bowl set over a pan of steaming water and whisk for 20-25 minutes until the mixture is very thick and leaves a trail which remains for several seconds. If you have a table or electric hand mixer, this can be used without hot water and will take about 15 minutes.
3. Remove the bowl from the heat, if using. Using a metal spoon, fold in the flour and melted butter alternately, a little at a time.
4. Turn the mixture into the prepared tin and level the top. Bake in a preheated oven, without opening the door, for 40-45 minutes. The cake should have shrunk from the sides of the tin and spring back when touched lightly in the centre.
5. Remove from the oven and allow to stand on wire tray for 5 minutes before turning out. Leave until completely cold, then remove the greaseproof paper Ⓕ and split cake in half using a sharp knife.

6. To make the icing, beat the butter and icing sugar together until light and creamy. Add the hot water and beat again. Sandwich the halves of the cake together with a quarter of the icing. Coat the sides with another quarter, and spread the remainder over the top, making pits and peaks to resemble a lunar landscape. Arrange the space figures on top. Allow the icing to set, then tie the ribbon, if using, around the cake.

Ⓕ Freeze for up to 4 weeks. Stand cake on a wire tray for about 2 hours, until thawed, then split in half and ice as in step 6.
Ⓜ Or microwave on Defrost for 4-6 minutes. Stand for 30 minutes, then split in half and ice as in step 6.

VARIATIONS:
This recipe for a basic novelty cake can easily be adapted according to the interests of the child concerned. Colour the icing with a little green food colouring and decorate with plastic farm animals, trees and hedges or with ponies in a paddock; or colour the icing yellow and decorate with a wigwam or ranch and cowboys and indians. Other ideas are to colour the icing pale blue, make wave-like swirls on top and decorate with sailing boats, or to ice the cake smoothly in white and top with ice skaters or ballet dancers.

Space Adventure Novelty Cake; Chocolate Ice Cream; Funny Face Cup Cakes.

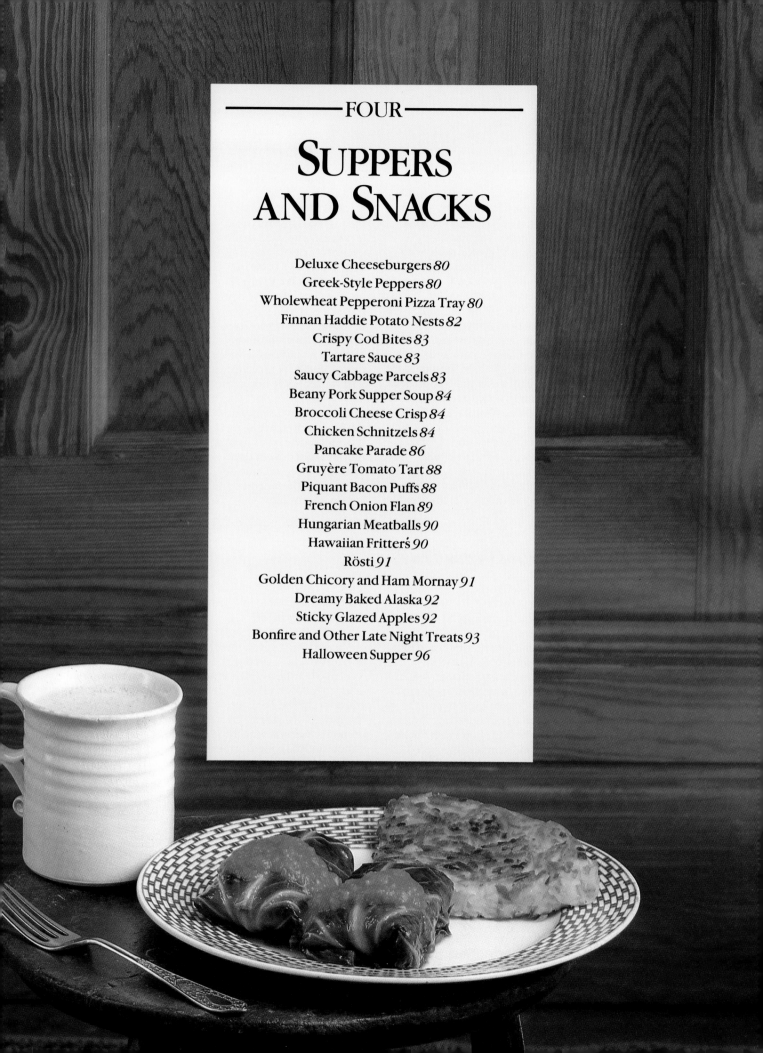

FOUR

SUPPERS AND SNACKS

Greek-Style Peppers

3 tablespoons vegetable oil
1 small onion, peeled and finely chopped
1 garlic clove, peeled and crushed (optional)
1 celery stick, trimmed and finely chopped
100 g (4 oz) long-grain brown rice
1 × 225 g (8 oz) can tomatoes
100-175 g (4-6 oz) cooked lamb, minced
200 ml (7 fl oz) chicken stock
¼ teaspoon dried oregano
1 bay leaf (optional)
salt
freshly ground black pepper
4 squat green or red peppers
50 g (2 oz) Cheddar cheese, finely grated

PREPARATION TIME: *15 minutes*
COOKING TIME: *about 1 ½ hours*
OVEN: *180°C, 350°F, Gas Mark 4*

1. Heat 2 tablespoons of the oil in a saucepan, add the onion, garlic, if using, and celery and fry over a gentle heat for 2 minutes. Add the rice and fry, stirring, for a further 3 minutes.
2. Add the tomatoes with their juice, breaking them up with a wooden spoon. Stir in lamb, stock, oregano, bayleaf (if using) and salt and pepper to taste. Stir well to mix.
3. Bring the mixture to the boil, then cover and simmer gently for 40-50 minutes or until the liquid is absorbed and the rice is tender. Discard the bayleaf. Ⓐ
4. Cut a 1 cm (½ inch) slice off the stalk end of each pepper and reserve for 'lids'. Core and seed the peppers, then blanch them with the 'lids' in a saucepan of boiling water for 2 minutes. Drain well, plunge into cold water for 5 minutes, then drain well again.
5. Stuff each pepper with the rice and lamb mixture, arrange in a greased shallow ovenproof dish and sprinkle with the cheese. Place the lids in position and brush each pepper lightly with the remaining oil. Ⓐ
6. Cover loosely with foil and cook in a preheated oven for 20 minutes. Remove the foil and cook for a further 25 minutes. Serve hot.

Ⓐ The savoury rice mixture can be prepared in the morning, covered with cling film and kept in a cool place. The stuffed peppers can be prepared in the morning and kept in a cool place.

Wholewheat Pepperoni Pizza Tray

SERVES 10

3 medium onions, peeled
1 garlic clove, peeled
3 tablespoons vegetable oil
1 × 800 g (1 lb 12 oz) can tomatoes
1 tablespoon tomato purée
½ teaspoon dried mixed herbs
salt
freshly ground black pepper
225 g (8 oz) plain wholewheat flour
100 g (4 oz) self-raising flour
1 ½ teaspoons baking powder
½ teaspoon salt
175 g (6 oz) hard margarine
150 ml (¼ pint) milk, plus 1 tablespoon milk
100 g (4 oz) button mushrooms, wiped
175 g (6 oz) Mozzarella cheese
75 g (3 oz) pepperoni (salami sticks), thinly sliced

PREPARATION TIME: *25 minutes*
COOKING TIME: *50-60 minutes*
OVEN: *190°C, 375°F, Gas Mark 5*

1. Slice the onions and crush the garlic. Add with the oil to a frying pan and cook over a gentle heat for 5 minutes, until soft and lightly coloured. Stir in the tomatoes with their juice, breaking them up. Stir in the tomato purée, herbs, and salt and pepper to taste. Bring to the boil, then lower the heat and simmer, uncovered, for 15 minutes. Remove from the heat and leave to cool. Ⓐ
2. Grease a 23 × 33 cm (9 × 13 inch) Swiss roll tin. Put the wholewheat flour into a mixing bowl. Sift the white flour, baking powder and salt into the bowl. Dice the margarine and rub in until the mixture resembles fine breadcrumbs.
3. Stir in all the milk and mix to form a soft dough. Knead gently until free from cracks then roll out on a lightly floured surface to a 25 × 35 cm (10 × 14 inch) rectangle and use to line the base and sides of the prepared tin. Trim the edges.
4. Spoon the cooled tomato mixture evenly over the dough. Slice the mushrooms and scatter over. Cover with slices of cheese. Bake in a preheated oven for 20-25 minutes, then top with the salami and bake for a further 10 minutes Ⓕ
5. Leave the pizza to cool in the tin for 10 minutes, then cut into wedges and serve warm, with a green salad.

Ⓐ The topping mixture can be prepared up to 2 days in advance, covered tightly with cling film and kept chilled.
Ⓕ Freeze for up to 1 month. Thaw for 2 hours at room temperature, then cover with foil and reheat at 180°C, 350°F, Gas Mark 4 for 20 minutes until heated through.

Deluxe Cheeseburgers

450 g (1 lb) lean minced beef
1 small onion, peeled and finely chopped
½ teaspoon salt
freshly ground black pepper
2 tablespoons vegetable oil
4 slices of processed Cheddar cheese
8 crisp lettuce leaves
1 small onion, thinly sliced and separated into rings
4 sesame seed baps, split and warmed
1 large tomato, thinly sliced
2 tablespoons burger relish

PREPARATION TIME: *10 minutes*
COOKING TIME: *10-12 minutes*

1. Put the minced beef into a bowl. Add the chopped onion and salt and pepper to taste. Stir well to mix.
2. Divide the mixture into 4 equal portions and shape each into a 10 cm (4 inch) round burger, about 1 cm (½ inch) thick. Ⓐ
3. Heat the oil in a frying pan, add the burgers and fry over a moderate heat for 5-6 minutes on each side. Top each with a slice of cheese and remove from the heat
4. Place 2 lettuce leaves and some onion rings on each warmed bap base, then place a burger on each. Top with tomato slices and burger relish. Cover with the remaining bap halves and serve at once.

Ⓐ Can be prepared in the morning, covered with cling film and kept in the refrigerator.

VARIATION:
Add ¼ teaspoon dried mixed herbs to the minced beef mixture and serve the burgers with coleslaw instead of relish.

Top to bottom: Greek-Style Peppers; Deluxe Cheeseburgers; Wholewheat Pepperoni Pizza Tray.

Finnan Haddie Potato Nests

4 large old potatoes, scrubbed
225 g (8 oz) smoked haddock
25 g (1 oz) butter
salt
freshly ground black pepper
2 tablespoons single cream
50 g (2 oz) Edam cheese, grated

PREPARATION TIME: *10 minutes*
COOKING TIME: *1¼ hours*
OVEN: *200°C, 400°F, Gas Mark 6*

1. Prick the potatoes all over with a fork, then bake in a preheated oven for 1-1¼ hours until soft when squeezed gently.
2. Meanwhile, place the smoked haddock in a saucepan with water just to cover and cook over a gentle heat for 10 minutes until cooked through. Strain and leave to cool slightly, then flake the smoked haddock finely, discarding the skin and bones. Ⓐ
3. Cut the potatoes in half lengthways and scoop out the flesh, taking care not to pierce the skins. Mix the potato with the butter and season to taste with salt and pepper. Mix in the flaked smoked haddock and the cream and spoon the mixture back into the potato skins.
4. Sprinkle the stuffed potatoes with cheese and return to the oven for a further 15 minutes until the cheese has melted and the filling is heated through. Serve hot.

Ⓐ The smoked haddock can be cooked several hours in advance, covered with cling film and kept in the refrigerator.

Top to bottom: Crispy Cod Bites; Saucy Cabbage Parcels; Tartare Sauce; Finnan Haddie Potato Nests.

Saucy Cabbage Parcels

SERVES 6

2 tablespoons vegetable oil
350 g (12 oz) minced beef
2 medium onions, peeled and
    finely chopped
1 large carrot, scraped and
    finely chopped
50 g (2 oz) long-grain white
    rice
¼ teaspoon curry powder
    (optional)
300 ml (½ pint) beef stock
salt
freshly ground black pepper
75 g (3 oz) frozen sweetcorn,
    thawed
12 large cabbage leaves
1 × 400 g (14 oz) can tomatoes
1 teaspoon granulated sugar

PREPARATION TIME: *15 minutes*
COOKING TIME: *1¼ hours*
OVEN: *190°C, 375°F, Gas Mark 5*

Cabbage leaves, stuffed with a tasty savoury mince mixture and baked in a tangy tomato sauce make an unusual supper meal, served with crusty bread. For a more substantial meal, serve these delicious parcels with creamed or sauté potatoes.

1. Heat 1 tablespoon of the oil in a saucepan, add the minced beef, half the chopped onions and the carrot and fry over a moderate heat for 5 minutes, stirring frequently. Add the rice and curry powder, if using, stir well and cook for a further 2 minutes.
2. Stir in 150 ml (¼ pint) of the stock, season to taste with salt and pepper and bring to the boil. Cover and simmer gently for 15 minutes. Remove from the heat and stir in the sweetcorn. Ⓐ
3. Meanwhile, place the cabbage leaves in a saucepan, pour in boiling water to cover and boil gently for 5 minutes. Drain well, then plunge into cold water to prevent discoloration, and drain well again. Pat the leaves dry on absorbent paper and trim off about 1 cm (½ inch) of the thick centre stalks. Ⓐ
4. Make the sauce: heat the remaining oil in a saucepan, add the remaining chopped onion and fry over a gentle heat for 5 minutes, until soft and lightly coloured. Add the tomatoes with their juice and the remaining stock, with the sugar, to the pan. Bring to the boil, then lower the heat and simmer for 10 minutes. Remove from the heat and allow to cool slightly, then process in a blender for 30 seconds until smooth. Ⓐ
5. Divide the mince mixture into 12 equal portions and spread along the centre stalk of each cabbage leaf to within 2.5 cm (1 inch) of the edges. Fold in the stalk end and top edge, then fold the side edges over to form neat parcels.
6. Arrange the parcels, side by side and join sides down, close together in a greased shallow ovenproof dish. Pour over half the quantity of tomato sauce. Ⓐ Ⓕ
7. Cook in a preheated oven for 25-30 minutes, until cooked through. Serve hot with the remaining hot tomato sauce and crusty bread.

Ⓐ The mince mixture, cabbage leaves and tomato sauce can be prepared the previous day, stored separately and kept in the refrigerator. The Cabbage Parcels can be prepared the previous day, covered with cling film and kept in the refrigerator. Return to room temperature before cooking. Ⓕ Freeze for up to 2 months. Thaw overnight in the refrigerator then follow instructions given in step 7. Ⓜ Or microwave on Defrost for 25-30 minutes, then stand for 20 minutes before following step 7.

Tartare Sauce

MAKES just over 150 ml (¼ pint)

1 quantity prepared Mayonnaise
    (page 32), or use good-quality
    bought mayonnaise
1 tablespoon finely chopped
    capers
1 tablespoon finely chopped
    gherkins
2 teaspoons finely chopped
    onion
2 teaspoons finely chopped
    fresh parsley

PREPARATION TIME: *5 minutes,
plus making mayonnaise*

Place all the ingredients in a bowl and stir well to mix. Serve chilled. Ⓐ

Ⓐ Will keep for up to 3 days in the refrigerator.

Crispy Cod Bites

450 g (1 lb) cod fillets, skinned
    and boned
3 tablespoons plain flour
salt
freshly ground black pepper
150 g (5 oz) fresh white
    breadcrumbs
1½ tablespoons grated
    Parmesan cheese
2 tablespoons chopped fresh
    parsley
2 eggs, beaten
vegetable oil, for deep frying

TO GARNISH:
lemon wedges

PREPARATION TIME: *15 minutes*
COOKING TIME: *12-14 minutes*

Strips of cod, dipped in beaten egg, coated in a tasty breadcrumb mixture and deep-fried are easy to prepare and cook and are sure to be popular with the whole family. Serve piping hot with Tartare Sauce (opposite). They make an attractive dish to serve at a supper party too when served in a basket.

1. Cut the cod fillets diagonally into 5 cm × 5 mm (2 × ¼ inch) strips, 1 cm (½ inch) thick.
2. Season the flour with salt and pepper to taste and spread out on a plate. Mix together the breadcrumbs, Parmesan cheese and parsley and spread out on a separate plate.
3. Toss the cod strips in seasoned flour, dip in beaten egg and then coat in the breadcrumb mixture. Ⓐ
4. Heat oil in a deep-fryer to 180°-190°C/350°-375°F or until a cube of bread browns in 30 seconds. Fry half the breaded cod strips for 6-7 minutes until lightly golden brown and cooked through. Drain on absorbent paper and keep warm while cooking the remainder in the same way.
5. Garnish with lemon wedges and serve hot with Tartare Sauce (opposite), chips and peas.

Ⓐ The cod strips can be prepared 2 hours in advance, covered with cling film and kept chilled.

Chicken Schnitzels

4 boneless chicken breast
    fillets
1½ tablespoons plain flour
salt
freshly ground black pepper
1 egg, beaten
1 tablespoon milk
100 g (4 oz) fresh white
    breadcrumbs
25 g (1 oz) butter
1 tablespoon vegetable oil

TO GARNISH:
lemon wedges
watercress sprigs

PREPARATION TIME: *10 minutes*

COOKING TIME: *15-20 minutes*

The chicken breast fillets
need to be beaten out thinly
to ensure that they will be
cooked through in the time
stated in the recipe.

1. Place 1 chicken breast at a
time between 2 sheets of
greaseproof paper and beat
out with a rolling pin or meat
mallet to make a thin
escalope, no thicker than
5 mm (¼ inch).

2. Season the flour with salt
and pepper and spread out
on a plate. Beat together the
egg and milk in a shallow
dish.

3. Coat the escalopes in
seasoned flour, then dip into
the egg and milk and coat
with breadcrumbs, pressing
them on firmly with the
palms of the hands. Ⓐ

4. Heat 15 g (½ oz) of the
butter and ½ tablespoon of
the oil in a large frying pan.
Add 2 escalopes and fry over
a moderate heat for 4-5
minutes on each side or until
golden brown and cooked
through. Keep warm while
frying the remaining
escalopes in the same way.

5. Arrange the escalopes on
a warmed serving dish,
garnish with lemon wedges
and watercress. Serve at once
with a mixed salad and sauté
potatoes.

Ⓐ The escalopes can be
coated in the morning,
covered with cling film and
kept in the refrigerator.

Beany Pork Supper Soup

SERVES 6

---

2 tablespoons vegetable oil
450 g (1 lb) belly pork rashers,
    rinded, boned, trimmed and
    cut into 1 cm (½ inch)
    pieces
1 garlic clove, peeled and
    crushed
2 medium onions, peeled,
    quartered and thinly sliced
3 medium carrots, scraped and
    thinly sliced
1½ tablespoons plain flour
1 litre (1¾ pints) chicken
    stock
2 courgettes, trimmed and cut
    into 5 mm (¼ inch) thick
    slices
1 × 435 g (15 oz) can red kidney
    beans, drained
1½ tablespoons chopped fresh
    parsley
salt
freshly ground black pepper

PREPARATION TIME: *15 minutes*

COOKING TIME: *40 minutes*

Serve this hearty soup on its
own or with slices of crusty
bread or Hot Cheesy Garlic

Bread for a more substantial
meal.

1. Heat 1 tablespoon of the
oil in a flameproof casserole.
Add the belly pork and fry
over a moderate heat for 10
minutes, stirring frequently.
Remove the pork from the
casserole with a slotted
spoon and reserve.

2. Add the remaining oil to
the casserole. Add the garlic,
onions and carrots to the
casserole and fry over a
gentle heat for 3 minutes.

3. Sprinkle in the flour, stir
well and cook for 1 minute,
then stir in the stock and
bring to the boil. Return the
pork to the casserole, cover,
lower the heat and simmer
gently for 15 minutes.

4. Add the courgettes, beans
and parsley to casserole.
Return to the boil and
simmer gently for 10
minutes. Season to taste with
salt and pepper and serve hot
with crusty bread or with the
Hot Cheesy Garlic Bread
(page 29).

Broccoli Cheese Crisp

450 g (1 lb) fresh or frozen
    broccoli
100 g (4 oz) streaky bacon
    rashers, rinded, boned and
    cut into bite-sized pieces
40 g (1½ oz) butter or hard
    margarine
50 g (2 oz) plain flour
450 ml (¾ pint) milk
½ teaspoon made English
    mustard
100 g (4 oz) Cheddar cheese,
    grated
salt
freshly ground black pepper
5 tablespoons fresh white or
    brown breadcrumbs

PREPARATION TIME: *10 minutes*

COOKING TIME: *35-40 minutes*

OVEN: *190°C, 375°F, Gas Mark 5*

A tasty variation on the
cauliflower cheese theme.

1. Cook the broccoli in a
saucepan containing a little
boiling salted water until just
tender, for about 8-10
minutes if fresh, or
according to packet
instructions if frozen. Drain
the broccoli well and place
in a greased shallow
ovenproof dish. Ⓐ

2. Fry the bacon in its own
fat in a saucepan for 3-4
minutes, until crisp and
golden brown. Remove the
bacon with a slotted spoon
and scatter over the broccoli.

3. Heat 25 g (1 oz) of the
butter or margarine with the

fat in the pan, stir in the flour
and cook for 1 minute,
stirring. Gradually stir in the
milk and bring to the boil,
stirring all the time with a
wooden spoon. Lower the
heat and simmer for 2
minutes, stirring. Remove
from the heat.

4. Stir in the mustard, 75 g
(3 oz) of the cheese and salt
and pepper to taste. Pour the
sauce over the broccoli and
bacon in the dish.

5. Melt the remaining butter
or margarine in a frying pan,
add the breadcrumbs and fry
over a moderately high heat
for 1 minute, stirring all the
time. Remove from the heat,
mix the fried crumbs with

the remaining cheese and
sprinkle over the dish. Ⓐ

6. Place the dish on a baking
sheet and cook in a
preheated oven for 25-30
minutes until heated
through and golden brown.
Serve hot with toast.

Ⓐ The broccoli can be
prepared in the morning,
covered with cling film and
kept in a cool place.

The broccoli cheese can
be completed in the
morning, covered with cling
film and kept in a cool place.

Top to bottom: Beany Pork Supper
Soup; Broccoli Cheese Crisp; Chicken
Schnitzels.

Pancake Parade

Basic Pancakes

MAKES 8

100 g (4 oz) plain white flour
pinch of salt
1 egg
150 ml (¼ pint) milk
150 ml (¼ pint) cold water
1-2 tablespoons vegetable oil

TO FINISH:
caster sugar, to taste
lemon wedges

PREPARATION TIME: *5 minutes*

COOKING TIME: *2-3 minutes for each pancake*

To keep pancakes warm, stack them between 2 plates over a pan of gently simmering water. A batch of pancakes in the freezer is useful for making the quick savoury or sweet dishes described here. To prevent them sticking together when frozen, stack them up individually between pieces of cling film or greaseproof paper.

1. Sift the flour with the salt into a bowl and make a well in the centre. Add the egg and gradually stir in half of the milk and water.
2. Beat thoroughly with a wooden spoon, gradually drawing the flour into the liquid, to make a smooth batter. Stir in the remaining milk and water and beat until well mixed. Pour the mixture into a jug. Ⓐ

3. Heat a little of the oil in a 15-18 cm (6-7 inch) frying pan, swirling it over the base and sides, and pour off any excess into a heatproof jug or basin. Return the pan to the heat and pour in sufficient batter to coat the base of the pan thinly, tilting the pan quickly as you pour to spread the batter evenly.
4. Cook over a high heat, for 1½-2 minutes, until the underside is golden brown, then, using a palette knife, turn the pancake over and cook for another minute, until the other side is golden brown.
5. Remove the pancake and keep warm while frying the remaining batter in the same way, to make 8 pancakes in all, adding more oil to the pan as necessary. Ⓐ Ⓕ
6. Either roll the pancakes or fold them in half and then in half again to form triangles. Arrange the pancakes on a warmed serving dish and serve hot with caster sugar and lemon wedges.

Ⓐ The batter can be prepared several hours in advance, covered with cling film and kept in the refrigerator. Beat well with a wooden spoon before using. Pancakes can be prepared 2 days in advance, then stacked individually between pieces of cling film or greaseproof paper, placed in a polythene bag and kept chilled.
Ⓕ Freeze for up to 6 months. Reheat from frozen in stacks of 4, wrapped in foil, at 200°C, 400°F, Gas Mark 6 for 20 minutes, or heat individual pancakes in a lightly greased frying pan over a medium heat for 30 seconds on each side.
Ⓜ Or microwave in stacks of 4 on Defrost for 1½-2 minutes. Stand for 5 minutes, then roll or fold and heat on Maximum (Full) for 1-1½ minutes.

VARIATION:
Wholewheat Pancakes: replace the white flour with 100 g (4 oz) plain wholewheat flour.

Apple Spice Favourite

MAKES 8

1 quantity of Basic Pancakes (above)
750 g (1½ lb) cooking apples, peeled, cored and sliced
40 g (1½ oz) butter
1 tablespoon cold water
75 g (3 oz) soft light brown sugar
¼-½ teaspoon ground cinnamon
1 tablespoon icing sugar
1 tablespoon desiccated coconut

PREPARATION TIME: *7 minutes, plus making pancake batter*

COOKING TIME: *30-35 minutes, plus cooking pancakes*

OVEN: *190°C, 375°F, Gas Mark 5*

1. Make 8 pancakes following instructions given in Basic Pancakes recipe.
2. Put the apples, butter, water, sugar and cinnamon into a saucepan and cook over a moderate heat for 15-20 minutes until the apples are very tender. Beat the apple mixture thoroughly until smooth.
3. Place the pancakes flat on a board and spread each one with a portion of the apple mixture. Roll up the pancakes and arrange in a lightly greased shallow ovenproof dish. Mix together the icing sugar and desiccated coconut and sprinkle over the pancakes.
4. Cook in a preheated oven for 15 minutes until well heated through. Serve hot with whipped cream or ice cream, if liked.

Buttered Banana Ice Pancakes

MAKES 8

1 quantity of Basic Pancakes (above)
25 g (1 oz) butter
2 medium bananas, peeled and cut into 1 cm (½ inch) slices
a little icing sugar, sifted
4 scoops of vanilla or chocolate ice cream

PREPARATION TIME: *5 minutes, plus making pancake batter*

COOKING TIME: *3-4 minutes, plus cooking pancakes*

1. Make 8 pancakes following instructions given in Basic Pancakes recipe and keep warm while preparing the filling.
2. Melt the butter in a frying pan, add the banana slices and fry over a gentle heat, turning frequently, for 3-4 minutes.
3. Place 2 folded pancakes on each of 4 hot serving dishes and spoon over the hot banana slices. Dust with icing sugar and top each portion with a scoop of ice cream. Serve immediately.

Clockwise from the bottom: Bacon Bounty Pancakes; Orange Syrup Pancakes; Buttered Banana Ice Pancakes; Apple Spice Favourite; Basic Pancakes.

Bacon Bounty Pancakes

MAKES 8

1 quantity of Basic Pancakes
  (page 86)
40 g (1½ oz) butter or hard
  margarine
1 medium onion, peeled and
  finely chopped
225 g (8 oz) bacon steaks, cut
  into small dice
100 g (4 oz) button
  mushrooms, wiped and
  sliced
25 g (1 oz) plain flour
300 ml (½ pint) milk
salt
freshly ground black pepper
50 g (2 oz) Cheddar cheese,
  grated

PREPARATION TIME: *10 minutes,
plus making pancake batter*

COOKING TIME: *25-30 minutes,
plus cooking pancakes*

OVEN: *200°C, 400°F, Gas Mark 6*

1. Make 8 pancakes
following instructions given
in Basic Pancakes recipe.
2. Melt the fat in a saucepan.
Add the onion, bacon and
mushrooms and fry over a
moderate heat for 5 minutes,
until softened.
3. Stir in the flour and cook
for 1 minute, stirring.
Gradually stir in the milk and
bring to the boil, stirring all
the time. Lower the heat and
simmer for 2 minutes,
stirring. Season to taste with
salt and pepper.
4. Place the pancakes flat on
a board and spread a portion
of filling over half of each
one. Fold the pancakes in
half and then in half again to
form triangles. Arrange them
slightly overlapping, in a
greased shallow ovenproof
dish and sprinkle with the
cheese. Ⓐ Ⓕ
5. Cook in a preheated oven
for 15-20 minutes until the
pancakes are heated through
and the cheese has melted.
Serve hot with a mixed salad.

Ⓐ The pancakes can be
prepared the previous day,
covered with cling film and
kept in the refrigerator. Cook
for 10 minutes longer than
given in stage 5, covering
with foil after 20 minutes to
prevent over-browning.
Ⓕ Freeze for up to 1 month.
Thaw for 3 hours at room
temperature then follow
instructions given in step 5.
Ⓜ Or microwave on Defrost
for 8-12 minutes, then stand
for 5 minutes before
following instructions from
step 5.

Orange Syrup Pancakes

MAKES 8

1 quantity of Basic Pancakes
  (page 86)
3 medium oranges, peeled, all
  pith removed and cut into
  segments
4 tablespoons golden syrup or
  clear honey

PREPARATION TIME: *5 minutes,
plus making pancake batter*

COOKING TIME: *3 minutes, plus
cooking pancakes*

1. Make 8 pancakes
following instructions given
in Basic Pancakes recipe and
keep warm while preparing
the orange sauce.
2. Place the orange
segments in a saucepan, add
the golden syrup or honey
and heat through over a
gentle heat until the syrup or
honey is melted.
3. Roll the pancakes up and
arrange on a warmed serving
dish. Spoon over the hot
sauce and serve at once.

Gruyère Tomato Tart

SERVES 6

225 g (8 oz) plain white flour
a pinch of salt
a good pinch of cayenne pepper
  (optional)
50 g (2 oz) wholewheat flour
75 g (3 oz) hard margarine,
  diced
50 g (2 oz) lard, diced
3 tablespoons cold water
15 g (½ oz) butter
1 small onion, peeled and thinly
  sliced
2 eggs, beaten
100 g (4 oz) Gruyère cheese,
  finely chopped
freshly ground black pepper
2 medium tomatoes, thinly
  sliced

TO GLAZE:
beaten egg or milk

PREPARATION TIME: *15 minutes*
COOKING TIME: *40-45 minutes*
OVEN: *190°C, 375°F, Gas Mark 5*

1. Sift the white flour, with
the salt and cayenne pepper,
if using, into a mixing bowl.
Mix in the wholewheat flour,
add the margarine and lard
and rub in until the mixture
resembles fine
breadcrumbs.
2. Add the water and mix to
form a fairly firm dough.
Knead lightly until free from
cracks. A
3. Roll out two-thirds of the
pastry on a lightly floured
board or work surface to a
28 cm (11 inch) round and
use a line a 23 cm (9 inch) pie
plate.
4. Melt the butter in a
saucepan, add the onion and
cook over a gentle heat for 3
minutes. Meanwhile, mix
together the beaten eggs and
cheese and season to taste
with salt and pepper. Spoon
on to the pastry and cover
with onions. Top with the
tomato slices and season
lightly with salt and pepper.
5. Roll out the remaining

pastry to a 25 cm (10 inch)
round. Dampen the pastry
edges and use to cover the
pie. Seal the edges together
firmly and trim. Make a small
hole in the centre of the pie.
6. Re-knead and re-roll the
pastry trimmings and cut out
leaves. Brush the pie with
beaten egg or milk. Decorate
with leaves and brush with
beaten egg or milk.
7. Place on a preheated
baking sheet and bake in a
preheated oven for 40-45
minutes until cooked
through and golden brown.
Serve hot or cold.

A The pastry dough can be
prepared the previous day,
wrapped in cling film and
kept in the refrigerator.

Piquant Bacon Puffs

MAKES 8

2 bacon steaks, weighing about
  225 g (8 oz), chopped
3 tablespoons mango chutney,
  large pieces of mango
  chopped
100 g (4 oz) Cheddar cheese,
  grated
1 medium onion, peeled and
  finely chopped
1 × 370 g (14 oz) packet frozen
  puff pastry, thawed

TO GLAZE:
a little beaten egg

PREPARATION TIME: *15 minutes*
COOKING TIME: *30 minutes*
OVEN: *200°C, 400°F, Gas Mark 6*

1. Put the bacon, mango
chutney, cheese and onion
into a bowl and stir until well
mixed.
2. Roll out the pastry on a
lightly floured board or work
surface to a 40×30 cm
(16×12 inch) rectangle. Cut
in half lengthways, then cut
each half into 4 squares.
3. Divide the filling into 8
equal portions and place in
the centre of each pastry
square. Dampen the pastry
edges and bring together
over the top of the filling.
Seal the edges together
firmly to enclose the filling
completely and form neat
oblongs.
4. Place the puffs join sides
down on a lightly greased
baking sheet. A Brush the
tops and sides with beaten
egg and cut 3 slashes across

the top of each one, using a sharp knife.

5. Bake in a preheated oven for 30 minutes or until the pastry is golden brown, well risen, and cooked through. Ⓕ Serve hot or cold.

Ⓐ The puffs can be prepared 3-4 hours in advance, covered with cling film and kept in the refrigerator.
Ⓕ Freeze for up to 1 month. Thaw for 3 hours at room temperature than place on a baking sheet and refresh at 180°C, 350°F, Gas Mark 4 for 15-20 minutes.
Ⓜ Or microwave on Defrost for 10-12 minutes, then stand for 10 minutes before refreshing in conventional oven as above.

French Onion Flan

SERVES 6-8

90 g (3½ oz) butter
450 g (1 lb) onions, peeled and thinly sliced
salt
freshly ground black pepper
2 teaspoons tomato purée
225 g (8 oz) plain flour
pinch of salt
50 g (2 oz) lard
3 tablespoons cold water
3 eggs
150 ml (¼ pint) milk

| PREPARATION TIME: *15 minutes* |
| COOKING TIME: *1¼ hours* |
| OVEN: *200°C, 400°F, Gas Mark 6* |

1. Melt 40 g (1½ oz) of the butter in a frying pan. Add the onions with the tomato purée, season lightly, stir well and cook over a gentle heat, stirring occasionally, for 15 minutes. Remove from the heat and leave to cool.
2. Meanwhile sift the flour with the salt into a mixing bowl and rub in the remaining 50 g (2 oz) butter and the lard with the fingertips, until the mixture resembles fine breadcrumbs. Stir in the water and mix to form a fairly firm dough. Knead lightly until free from cracks.
3. Roll out the pastry on a lightly floured board or work surface to a 30 cm (12 inch) round and use to line a 25 cm (10 inch) loose-bottomed fluted flan tin set on a baking sheet.
4. Fold the excess pastry over the edge of the tin and run a rolling pin firmly over the top to cut through the pastry and give a neat edge. Prick the base all over with a fork.
5. Line the pastry-lined tin with a round of greaseproof paper or foil and fill with baking beans. Bake in a preheated oven for 15 minutes. Remove the paper and beans and return to the oven for a further 5-10 minutes until the pastry is dry and cooked through. Remove from the oven. Ⓐ Ⓕ
6. Arrange the onions in the flan case. Beat the eggs with the milk and salt and pepper to taste and strain into the flan case. Bake in a preheated oven for 30-35 minutes until the filling is set and lightly golden. Ⓕ Serve hot or cold.

Ⓐ The flan case can be baked a week in advance, then stored in an airtight tin.
Ⓕ Freeze for up to 3 months. Thaw at room temperature for 1 hour before adding the filling and cooking following the instructions given in step 6. The cooked, filled flan case can be frozen for up to 2 months. Thaw for 1½-2 hours at room temperature, then reheat on a baking sheet at 180°C, 350°F, Gas Mark 4 for 20 minutes, covering with foil if necessary during cooking to prevent over-browning.
Ⓜ Or microwave flan case on Defrost for 2-3 minutes, then stand for 5 minutes before proceeding from step 6. Microwave filled flan case for 10-12 minutes on Defrost, then stand for 15 minutes before heating in a conventional oven as above.

Left to right: Piquant Bacon Puffs; French Onion Flan; Gruyère Tomato Tart.

Hungarian Meatballs

4 tablespoons vegetable oil
2 medium onions, peeled and
  finely chopped
2 celery sticks, trimmed and
  thinly sliced
1 green pepper, cored, seeded
  and diced
75 g (3 oz) button mushrooms,
  wiped and quartered
2 teaspoons paprika pepper
2 tablespoons plain flour
150 ml (¼ pint) beef stock
1 × 400 g (14 oz) can tomatoes
salt
freshly ground black pepper
450 g (1 lb) lean minced beef
1 egg, beaten
150 ml (¼ pint) soured cream
  or plain unsweetened yogurt

PREPARATION TIME: *15 minutes*
COOKING TIME: *45 minutes*

Mild, sweet-flavoured
paprika pepper (not to be
confused with hot cayenne
pepper) is a most useful
ingredient to have to add
flavour and colour to many
dishes. Sprinkle a little on to
chicken or egg salads, or add
a little to taste to the dressing,
whether vinaigrette or
mayonnaise. Add a teaspoon
to stews, casseroles and
gravies.

1. Heat half the oil in a
saucepan. Add all but 2
tablespoons of the onions to
the pan with the celery,
green pepper and
mushrooms and fry over a
gentle heat for 3 minutes.
2. Stir in the paprika pepper
and 1 tablespoon of the flour
and cook for 1 minute. Add
the stock and the tomatoes
with their juice, breaking up
the tomatoes roughly with a
wooden spoon. Season to
taste with salt and pepper.
Bring to the boil, then lower
the heat, cover and simmer
for 20 minutes. Ⓐ
3. Meanwhile, place the
minced beef, reserved
chopped onion, egg and ½
teaspoon of salt in a bowl and
stir well to mix. Divide the
mixture into 20 portions,
shape into balls and roll in
the remaining flour. Ⓐ
4. Heat the remaining oil in
a frying pan, add the
meatballs and fry over a
moderate heat for 10
minutes, turning frequently
until browned all over. Drain
on absorbent paper.
5. Add the meatballs to the
tomato sauce and cook
gently for a further 10
minutes. Remove from the
heat Ⓕ and stir the soured
cream or yogurt into the
sauce. Reheat gently without
boiling and serve with
noodles or boiled rice.

Ⓐ The sauce and meatballs
can be prepared several
hours in advance and kept in
the refrigerator. Reheat the
sauce gently before
proceeding with step 4.
Ⓕ Freeze for up to 3 months.
Thaw overnight in the
refrigerator, then reheat in a
covered pan for 25 minutes
before stirring in the soured
cream.
Ⓜ Or microwave on Defrost
for 25-30 minutes, breaking
up gently as soon as possible,
before reheating as above.

Hawaiian Fritters

1 × 225 g (8 oz) can pineapple
  slices, drained, with juice
  reserved
2 tablespoon golden syrup
vegetable oil, for deep frying
75 g (3 oz) plain flour
3 teaspoons vegetable oil
120 ml (4 fl oz) cold water
2 tablespoons desiccated
  coconut
1 egg white
2 medium bananas, peeled and
  cut into chunks

PREPARATION TIME: *15 minutes*
COOKING TIME: *10 minutes*

1. Pat the pineapple dry on
absorbent paper. Place the
pineapple juice and golden
syrup in a saucepan, bring to
the boil and boil gently for 10
minutes.
2. Meanwhile heat the oil
for deep frying to 180°-
190°C/350°-375°F or until a
cube of bread browns in 30
seconds.
3. Sift the flour into a bowl.
Mix together the 3 teaspoons
oil and the water and add to
the flour; mix well to form a
smooth batter. Stir in the
coconut.
4. Whisk the egg white until
stiff and gently fold into the
batter, using a large metal
spoon. Dip the pineapple
slices and banana chunks in
the batter and fry in the hot
oil for about 6 minutes or
until golden brown and
heated through. Drain on
absorbent paper.
5. Arrange the fritters on a
warmed serving plate and
spoon over the hot syrup.
Serve hot with ice cream.

Hungarian Meatballs; Hawaiian Fritters.

Rösti

SERVES 6

1 kg (2 lb) even-sized potatoes, scrubbed but not peeled
1 small onion, peeled and finely chopped
salt
freshly ground black pepper
50 g (2 oz) butter

PREPARATION TIME: *10 minutes, plus cooling*

COOKING TIME: *30 minutes*

This Swiss potato dish is delicious served on its own as a snack or supper dish and also makes an excellent accompaniment to grilled or roast meat, sausages, or bacon and eggs.

1. Cook the potatoes in a saucepan of boiling salted water for 8 minutes (do not over-cook). Drain well and return to the pan. Place over a moderate heat for a few seconds, shaking the pan frequently, to dry off.

Remove from the heat and leave to cool completely for several hours. Ⓐ
2. Skin the potatoes and grate them coarsely into a bowl. Add the onion and season to taste with salt and pepper. Stir well to mix.
3. Melt the butter in a heavy-based frying pan, add the potato mixture and fry over a moderate heat for about 8 minutes, turning the mixture occasionally until lightly golden on the underside.
4. Turn the mixture over and, using a fish slice, pat down gently to form a neat cake covering the base of the pan. Cook for a further 15 minutes until golden brown on the underside.
5. Loosen with a palette knife and invert on to a hot serving plate. Cut into wedges and serve at once.

Ⓐ The potatoes can be cooked the previous day, then kept in a cool place.

Golden Chicory and Ham Mornay

4 chicory heads, trimmed but left whole
1 tablespoon lemon juice
4 thin slices of cooked ham
a little mild burger mustard (optional)
50 g (2 oz) butter or hard margarine
50 g (2 oz) plain flour
150 ml (¼ pint) chicken stock
325 ml (11 fl oz) milk
2 tablespoons chopped fresh parsley
75 g (3 oz) Lancashire cheese, grated or finely crumbled
2 hard-boiled eggs, shelled and coarsely chopped
salt
freshly ground black pepper

PREPARATION TIME: *10 minutes*

COOKING TIME: *1 hour 5 minutes*

OVEN: *200°C, 400°F, Gas Mark 6*

1. Put the chicory into a saucepan with the lemon juice and add enough water to cover. Bring to the boil, then lower the heat and cook for 15 minutes. Drain well and dry on absorbent paper.
2. Spread the ham slices with mustard, if using, and wrap a slice round each chicory head. Place the ham-wrapped chicory join side down, in a greased shallow ovenproof dish (or use individual dishes if preferred).
3. Melt the butter or margarine in a saucepan, add the flour and cook for 1 minute, stirring. Stir in the stock and milk and bring to the boil, stirring. Lower the heat and simmer for 2 minutes, stirring all the time.

4. Remove from the heat and stir in the parsley, 40 g (1½ oz) of the cheese and the hard-boiled eggs. Season to taste with salt and pepper. Pour the sauce over the chicory and sprinkle with the remaining cheese. Ⓐ
5. Cook in a preheated oven for 30-35 minutes until heated through and light golden. Serve hot with crusty bread or buttered toast.

Ⓐ Can be prepared 3-4 hours in advance, covered with cling film and kept in a cool place.

VARIATION:
Replace the chicory with medium leeks, trimmed and washed thoroughly. Cook the leeks in a lightly

buttered, covered saucepan for 10 minutes before wrapping in the ham slices. Follow instructions given from step 3.

Top to bottom: Rösti; Golden Chicory and Ham Mornay.

Dreamy Baked Alaska

SERVES 6

SPONGE:
2 eggs
50 g (2 oz) caster sugar
50 g (2 oz) plain flour

FILLING AND TOPPING:
3 tablespoons raspberry jam
1 × 400 g (14 oz) can raspberries, drained, with juice reserved
3 egg whites
175 g (6 oz) caster sugar
15 g (½ oz) toasted flaked almonds, chopped (optional)
1 × 483 ml (17 fl oz) packet vanilla or Neapolitan ice cream

PREPARATION TIME: *10 minutes*
COOKING TIME: *18-20 minutes*
OVEN: *190°C, 375°F, Gas Mark 5;*
THEN: *220°C, 425°F, Gas Mark 7*

This popular dessert always looks impressive and is so easy to make. To be certain of success every time, pile the meringue topping over the filling to enclose it completely, making sure there are no gaps.

1. Grease an 18 cm (7 inch) round sandwich cake tin and line the base with greased greaseproof paper.
2. Make the sponge: place the eggs and sugar in a large heatproof bowl set over a saucepan of gently simmering water. Whisk the mixture with an electric hand whisk for about 3 minutes until light, creamy and thick and the whisk leaves a trail when lifted for a few seconds.
3. Remove the bowl from the heat and whisk until the mixture is cold.
4. Sift the flour over the mixture and fold in very gently, using a large metal spoon.
5. Pour the mixture into the prepared tin and level the surface. Bake in a preheated oven for 15 minutes, until the sponge is well risen and cooked through. Turn out on to a wire rack, remove the lining paper and leave to cool completely. Ⓐ Ⓕ
6. Split the cake into 2 thin layers. Spread the bottom layer with jam and cover with the top layer. Place the cake on an ovenproof serving plate. Spoon 3 tablespoons of the reserved raspberry juice over the cake.
7. Whisk the egg whites until stiff. Whisk in 75 g (3 oz) of the sugar until the mixture is stiff and glossy. Gently fold in the remaining sugar and almonds, if using, using a large metal spoon.
8. Place the ice cream block on the centre of the cake and spoon over the raspberries. Pile the meringue mixture on top, spreading it out to cover the cake, ice cream and fruit completely, making sure there are no gaps.
9. Increase the oven temperature and bake the alaska in a preheated oven for 3-5 minutes, until the meringue is light golden. Serve at once.

Ⓐ The sponge cake can be prepared 2 days in advance, then stored in an airtight tin.
Ⓕ Freeze for up to 4 months. Thaw for 2 hours at room temperature, then follow instructions from step 5.
Ⓜ Or microwave on Defrost for 2-4 minutes, then stand for 5 minutes before following instructions from step 5.

Sticky Glazed Apples; Dreamy Baked Alaska.

Sticky Glazed Apples

4 medium cooking apples, cored
50 g (2 oz) sultanas
50 g (2 oz) soft light brown sugar
25 g (1 oz) butter, cut into 4 pieces
6 tablespoons fresh or unsweetened orange juice
100 g (4 oz) golden syrup

PREPARATION TIME: *10 minutes*
COOKING TIME: *50 minutes*
OVEN: *190°C, 375°F, Gas Mark 5*

1. Using a sharp knife, cut through the skins of the apples, around the circumference of each one, to prevent the skins from bursting.
2. Arrange the apples in a buttered shallow ovenproof dish. Mix together the sultanas and sugar and spoon into the cavities in the apples. Top each with a piece of butter.
3. Heat the orange juice and golden syrup in a pan until the syrup is melted, then spoon over the apples in the dish. Ⓐ
4. Cook in a preheated oven, basting with the orange mixture occasionally, for 50 minutes or until the apples are tender. Serve hot with custard, cream or ice cream.

Ⓐ Can be prepared in the morning, covered with cling film and kept at room temperature.

VARIATION:
Replace the orange juice with unsweetened pineapple or apple juice. Fill the apples with chopped marzipan and mixed nuts.

Bonfire and Other Late Night Treats

Piquant Cheesy Potatoes

4 large old potatoes, scrubbed
25 g (1 oz) butter
100 g (4 oz) Cheddar cheese, grated
100 g (4 oz) sliced cooked ham, chopped
2 tablespoons sweetcorn or tomato relish
salt
freshly ground black pepper

PREPARATION TIME: *10 minutes*
COOKING TIME: *1¼-1½ hours*
OVEN: *200°C, 400°F, Gas Mark 6*

1. Prick the potatoes all over with a fork and wrap in foil to enclose completely. Bake in a preheated oven for 1-1¼ hours, until soft when squeezed gently.
2. Cut a large cross in each potato, cutting through the foil. Very carefully squeeze each potato and scoop out the potato flesh taking care not to pierce the potato skins or foil.
3. Put the potato into a bowl, add the butter and mash well until smooth. Stir in the cheese, ham, sweetcorn or relish and salt and pepper to taste, and mix well.
4. Spoon the mixture back into the potato skins, return to the oven and cook for a further 15 minutes until the filling is well heated through. Serve hot.

VARIATION:
Add 100 g (4 oz) smoked mackerel, 100 g (4 oz) curd cheese, a squeeze of lemon juice and a little horseradish sauce (if liked) to the potato and butter at step 3, in place of the cheese mixture.

Bacon-Wrapped Corn Cobs

4 medium corn-on-the-cobs, trimmed and husks removed
8-12 streaky bacon rashers, rinded
50 g (2 oz) butter, melted
salt
freshly ground black pepper

PREPARATION TIME: *10 minutes*
COOKING TIME: *13 minutes*

1. Cook the corn-on-the-cobs in a saucepan of boiling water for 8 minutes. Drain well and pay dry on absorbent paper.
2. Place the bacon rashers on a board and, using the flat side of a knife, stretch each rasher to double its length.
3. Wrap 2-3 bacon rashers around each corn cob. Secure with small pieces of wooden cocktail sticks.
4. Arrange the corn-on-the-cobs in a grill pan, brush all over with melted butter and cook under a preheated hot grill for about 5-10 minutes, turning frequently and brushing with the butter, until the bacon is golden brown and the corn is cooked through. Remove the cocktail sticks.
5. Arrange the corn-on-the-cobs on a warmed serving dish. Pour over the melted butter from the grill pan and season with salt and pepper. Serve hot with corn skewers.

Bacon-Wrapped Corn Cobs; Piquant Cheesy Potatoes.

Onion Tortilla

40 g (1½ oz) butter
1 large onion, peeled, halved and thinly sliced
100 g (4 oz) cabbage, finely shredded
3 eggs, beaten
1 tablespoon cold water
salt
freshly ground black pepper
100 g (4 oz) Cheddar or Edam cheese, finely grated

TO GARNISH:
tomato wedges

PREPARATION TIME: *10 minutes*

COOKING TIME: *about 10 minutes*

1. Melt 25 g (1 oz) of the butter in a saucepan, add the onion and cabbage and cook over a gentle heat for 3 minutes, stirring frequently.
2. Beat the eggs with water and salt and pepper to taste. Stir in half the cheese.
3. Melt the remaining butter in a 23 cm (9 inch) frying pan. Add the onion and cabbage mixture, pour over the egg and cheese mixture and cook over a moderately high heat for 3 minutes or until lightly golden on the underside.
4. Sprinkle the surface of the tortilla with the remaining cheese and place under a preheated medium hot grill for 2-3 minutes until the cheese is melted and the tortilla is set. Cut into wedges, garnish with tomatoes and serve hot with a green salad.

Barabrith

MAKES a 1 kg (2 lb) cake

300 ml (½ pint) cold tea, strained
100 g (4 oz) sultanas
100 g (4 oz) seedless raisins
225 g (8 oz) soft light brown sugar
2 tablespoons beaten egg
350 g (12 oz) self-raising flour, sifted
1 teaspoon ground mixed spice

PREPARATION TIME: *10 minutes, plus soaking overnight*

COOKING TIME: *2¼ hours*

OVEN: *160°C, 325°F, Gas Mark 3;*

THEN: *140°C, 275°F, Gas Mark 1*

This traditional Welsh teabread improves with keeping for a week before serving, thinly sliced and buttered. As long, slow cooking is involved it's well worth making two at the same time.

1. Put the tea, sultanas, raisins and sugar into a bowl.
Stir and leave to soak overnight.
2. Grease a 1 kg (2 lb) loaf tin and line the base and sides with greased greaseproof paper.
3. Add the egg to the tea mixture and fold in the flour and mixed spice. Turn the mixture into the prepared tin and smooth the surface.
4. Bake in a preheated oven for 1 hour. Cover with foil to prevent over-browning and lower the heat. Bake for a further 1¼ hours.
5. Turn out of the tin on to a wire rack, remove the lining paper and leave to cool completely. F Store in an airtight tin for 1 week before serving thinly sliced and buttered.

F Freeze for up to 6 months. Thaw for 3-4 hours at room temperature before serving. M Or microwave on Defrost for 5-8 minutes, then stand for 15 minutes before serving.

Tasty Beef Pittas

15 g (½ oz) butter
½ tablespoon vegetable oil
1 large onion, peeled and thinly sliced
350 g (12 oz) minute steak or quick-frying steak, cut into narrow 2.5-5 cm (1-2 inch) strips about 5 mm (¼ inch) thick
4 pitta breads, warmed
3 crisp lettuce leaves, finely shredded
2 medium tomatoes, chopped
7.5 cm (3 inch) piece cucumber, cut into thin strips
salt
freshly ground black pepper
2 tablespoons mayonnaise (optional)

PREPARATION TIME: *15 minutes*

COOKING TIME: *8-13 minutes*

Warmed pitta breads (white or wholemeal) make perfect 'pockets' for all kinds of delicious fillings, such as fried sliced sausages, baked beans, beefburgers, fish fingers, slices of ham, rashers of crisp fried bacon and scrambled egg – to name but a few! If eating out-of-doors, supply paper napkins to hold them in.

1. Heat the butter and oil in a frying pan. Add the onion and cook over a gentle heat for 3-5 minutes. Add the steak strips and fry over a moderately high heat for 5-8 minutes, stirring frequently, until cooked as liked.
2. Cut off a 1 cm (½ inch) slice from a long side of each warmed pitta bread and open out to form a pocket.
3. Fill the pitta bread two-thirds full with shredded lettuce, tomato and cucumber strips. Top with the fried steak and onions and season with salt and pepper. Add a spoonful of mayonnaise to each pitta, if using. Serve hot.

Sticky Nut Gingerbread

MAKES a 28×18 cm (11×7 inch) cake

225 g (8 oz) plain flour
½ teaspoon salt
½ teaspoon ground mixed spice
1½ teaspoons ground ginger
1 teaspoon bicarbonate of soda
40 g (1½ oz) crystallized or stem ginger, finely chopped (optional)
75 g (3 oz) golden syrup
75 g (3 oz) black treacle
75 g (3 oz) hard margarine
75 g (3 oz) soft dark brown sugar
2 eggs, beaten
200 ml (7 fl oz) milk
25 g (1 oz) flaked almonds

PREPARATION TIME: *10 minutes*
COOKING TIME: *45-50 minutes*
OVEN: *160°C, 325°F, Gas Mark 3*

If possible, store gingerbread for at least 3 days before serving, as it improves with keeping.

Gingerbread keeps well, for 1-2 weeks, stored in an airtight tin.

1. Grease a 28×18 cm (11×7 inch) shallow baking tin and line the base and sides with greased greaseproof paper, allowing paper to stand 2.5 cm (1 inch) above the sides of the tin.
2. Sift the flour with the salt, mixed spice, ground ginger and bicarbonate of soda into a mixing bowl. Add the chopped ginger, if using, and mix well.
3. Put the golden syrup, black treacle, margarine and sugar into a saucepan and heat gently until melted. Stir the warm mixture into the flour and add the eggs and milk; stir very thoroughly to mix.
4. Pour the mixture into the prepared tin and sprinkle the surface with almonds. Bake in a preheated oven for 45-50 minutes until well risen and firm to the touch.
5. Leave to cool in the tin, then turn out and carefully remove the lining paper. F Cut into squares when ready to serve.

F Freeze for up to 6 months. Thaw for several hours at room temperature before serving.
M Or microwave on Defrost for 7-10 minutes, then stand for 30 minutes before serving.

VARIATIONS:
Replace the crystallized or stem ginger with sultanas, chopped almonds or cut mixed peel.

This also makes a delicious hot pudding, served with custard or ice cream. When ready to serve, wrap pieces in foil and heat at 180°C, 350°F, Gas Mark 4 for 15-20 minutes.

Hot Frothy Chocolates

900 ml (1½ pints) milk
4 tablespoons drinking chocolate
16 marshmallows

PREPARATION TIME: *3 minutes*
COOKING TIME: *3 minutes*

1. Put the milk and drinking chocolate into a saucepan and bring to the boil, whisking continuously.
2. Pour the mixture into a warmed blender goblet, add 12 of the marshmallows and blend for 45 seconds until the marshmallows are melted.
3. Pour into 4 mugs and top each with a marshmallow. Serve at once.

Left to right: Tasty Beef Pittas; Onion Tortilla; Sticky Nut Gingerbread; Hot Frothy Chocolates; Barabrith.

Sonia Allison's

Halloween Supper

Witches, warlocks, wizards and hobgoblins add a note of devilment to Halloween night on 31 October, and a supper party for this spooky occasion is bound to delight and excite the children – and win approval from the grown-ups as well!

Witches' Cauldron Broth

SERVES 8

stock, cooked carrots and
  onions, chopped, left over
  from the Glazed Chicken
  Drumsticks (opposite)
600 ml (1 pint) hot water
2 large celery sticks, thinly
  sliced
1 small turnip, diced
1 parsnip, diced
2 large leeks, trimmed and
  thinly sliced
175 g (6 oz) white cabbage,
  finely shredded
175 g (6 oz) red cabbage, finely
  shredded
225 g (8 oz) fennel, coarsely
  grated
100 g (4 oz) mushrooms, sliced
2 teaspoons salt
100 g (4 oz) long-grain rice

TO GARNISH:
3 tablespoons chopped fresh
  parsley

PREPARATION TIME: *45 minutes by hand, 15-20 minutes using a food processor*

COOKING TIME: *40 minutes*

A heartening brew for a chilly night, coloured an attractive pink by the red cabbage. The portions are generous and any leftovers can be frozen.

1. Pour the stock into a large saucepan and add the pre-cooked carrots, onions and water.
2. Stir in all the remaining vegetables with the salt. Bring to the boil, stirring. Lower the heat, cover and simmer for 30 minutes.
3. Stir in the rice and cook for a further 20 minutes. Taste and adjust the seasoning. Ladle the soup into heated soup bowls and sprinkle each with parsley.

Witches' Cauldron Broth; Glazed Chicken Drumsticks.

Glazed Chicken Drumsticks

SERVES 8

16 chicken drumsticks, each
   75-100 g (3-4 oz)
1.2 litres (2 pints) boiling water
2 teaspoons salt
100 g (4 oz) onions, peeled
100 g (4 oz) carrots, scraped

TO GLAZE:
40 g (1½ oz) butter
1½ tablespoons clear honey
2 teaspoons Worcestershire
   sauce
1½ teaspoons soy sauce
1½ teaspoons malt vinegar
½ teaspoon salt
½ teaspoon garlic powder

PREPARATION TIME: *15 minutes*

COOKING TIME: *35-40 minutes*

1. Put the drumsticks into a large pan with the water, salt, whole onions and carrots. Bring to the boil and skim off the scum. Lower the heat, cover and simmer gently for 30 minutes.

2. Meanwhile, prepare the glaze. Place all the ingredients in a small pan and heat slowly until the butter is melted. Remove from the heat and set aside.

3. Transfer the drumsticks from the pan to a plate. Reserve the stock and vegetables for the Witches' Cauldron Broth (left).

4. Pat the drumsticks dry with absorbent kitchen paper ⒡, then arrange in a grill pan. Brush with the glaze and cook under a preheated hot grill for 4-5 minutes on each side until golden brown, brushing once or twice with the remaining glaze. Serve hot or cold.

⒡ Freeze unglazed for up to 2 months. Thaw overnight in the refrigerator or for 3-4 hours at room temperature. Glaze and grill as above.

Wizard's Scones

MAKES 10

225 g (8 oz) self-raising flour
½ teaspoon baking powder
½ teaspoon English mustard
  powder
½ teaspoon paprika
½ teaspoon milk curry powder
1 teaspoon salt
25 g (1 oz) hard margarine or
  white cooking fat, diced
150 ml (¼ pint) cold milk
1 tablespoon cold water
a little extra milk, to glaze

PREPARATION TIME: *7 minutes*
COOKING TIME: *10-12 minutes*
OVEN: *230°C, 450°F, Gas Mark 8*

1. Sift the flour with the baking powder, spices and salt into a mixing bowl. Add the margarine or cooking fat and rub in with the fingertips until the mixture resembles fine bread crumbs.
2. Add the milk and water all at once and stir with a fork to form a soft dough.
3. Turn on to a lightly floured board or work surface and knead quickly until smooth. Roll out to a 1 cm (½ inch) thickness and cut out 10 shapes with a 5 cm (2 inch) shaped biscuit cutter.
4. Place the dough rounds well apart on a greased baking sheet and brush the tops with milk. Bake for 10-12 minutes or until well-risen and golden brown. Transfer to a wire tray and leave to cool. F

F Freeze for up to 2 months. Thaw for 2-3 hours at room temperature. Reheat for 7 minutes at 180°C, 350°F, Gas Mark 4.

Left to right: Wizard's Scones; Pumpkin Pie; Spice Biscuits.

Pumpkin Pie

SERVES 8

225 g (8 oz) plain flour
pinch of salt
50 g (2 oz) lard
50 g (2 oz) butter or margarine, diced
2 tablespoons cold water

FILLING:
1 × 400 g (14 oz) can pumpkin purée
175 g (6 oz) caster sugar
1 tablespoon cornflour
1 tablespoon black treacle
2 teaspoons mixed spice
150 ml (¼ pint) single cream
3 eggs, size 3, well-beaten

PREPARATION TIME:	*20 minutes*
COOKING TIME:	*45 minutes, plus resting*
OVEN:	*200°C, 400°F, Gas Mark 6*

This pie is traditionally quite sweet, so serve in small portions.

1. Place the flour and salt in a bowl. Add the butter or margarine and rub in until the mixture resembles fine breadcrumbs. Add the water and mix to form a fairly firm dough. Knead lightly.
2. Roll out the pastry fairly thinly on a floured board or work surface and use to line the base and sides of a 23 cm (9 inch), lightly greased, fluted flan dish.
3. To make the filling, put all the ingredients into a mixing bowl and beat with a wooden spoon until thoroughly combined. Pour the mixture into the pastry case.
4. Bake in a preheated oven for 45 minutes, then open the oven door, switch off the heat and leave the pie in the oven for a further 15 minutes.
5. Serve the pie warm, cut into wedges, with whipped cream.

VARIATIONS:
For home-made pumpkin purée, place 750 g (1½ lb) pumpkin on a greased baking tray, cut side down. Cook for 1 hour in the oven preheated to 180°C, 350°F, Gas Mark 4. Scoop out the flesh and pass through a nylon mesh sieve. Drain off as much liquid as possible, pressing with the back of a wooden spoon, then measure out 400 g (14 oz) of the pulp.

Spice Biscuits

MAKES 20

100 g (4 oz) plain flour
1 teaspoon mixed spice
1 teaspoon ground cinnamon
100 g (4 oz) butter, softened
50 g (2 oz) caster sugar

PREPARATION TIME:	*12 minutes*
COOKING TIME:	*15-20 minutes*
OVEN:	*180°C, 350°F, Gas Mark 4*

1. Sift the flour with the spices into a mixing bowl.
2. In another bowl, cream the butter with the sugar until light and fluffy.
3. Fork the spiced flour into the creamed mixture, until thoroughly blended. Place teaspoonfuls of the mixture on a greased baking sheet, spacing them well apart.
4. Bake in a preheated oven for 15-20 minutes or until light golden-brown. Transfer to a wire rack and leave to cool completely. Store the biscuits in an airtight container.

FIVE

WEEKEND COOKING

Liver and Mushroom Pâté

SERVES 4-5

65 g (2½ oz) butter
1 garlic clove, peeled and chopped
1 medium onion, peeled and thinly sliced
4 rashers streaky bacon, rinded and diced
100 g (4 oz) button mushrooms, sliced
225 g (8 oz) chicken livers, trimmed
150 ml (¼ pint) chicken stock
2 hard-boiled eggs, shelled and chopped
1½ tablespoons single cream
salt
freshly ground black pepper

TO GARNISH:
4 bay leaves
black peppercorns

PREPARATION TIME: *15 minutes, plus chilling*

COOKING TIME: *20 minutes*

A smooth-textured pâté with a mild flavour, which is delicious served either as a starter with crisp biscuits, or as a snack with crusty bread and tomatoes.

1. Melt 40 g (1½ oz) of the butter in a frying pan. Add the garlic, onion and bacon and fry over a moderate heat for 5 minutes.
2. Stir in the mushrooms and chicken livers and fry for a further 5 minutes, stirring frequently.
3. Add the stock and bring to the boil. Cover with a lid or foil and cook over a gentle heat for 10 minutes.
4. Strain the mixture and process in a food processor or blender for about 30 seconds, until smooth. Add the hard-boiled eggs, cream and salt and pepper to taste and blend again until smooth

and thoroughly combined. Add a little stock to blend if necessary.
5. Turn the mixture into a 300 ml (½ pint) serving dish and smooth the surface. Ⓐ Ⓕ Melt the remaining butter and pour over the top of the pâté. Garnish with the bay leaves and peppercorns, then chill in the refrigerator for at least 4 hours before serving.

Ⓐ Can be prepared 2 days in advance, covered with cling film and kept chilled.
Ⓕ Freeze for up to 1 month. Thaw overnight in the refrigerator before covering with melted butter and garnishing with bay leaves and peppercorns.
Ⓜ Or microwave on Defrost for 4-6 minutes, then stand for 1 hour before covering with melted butter.

Farmhouse Terrine

SERVES 8-10

10 rashers streaky bacon, rinded and boned
450 g (1 lb) pig's liver, coarsely minced
450 g (1 lb) lean pork, coarsely minced
1 medium onion, peeled and finely chopped
2 garlic cloves, peeled and crushed
½ teaspoon dried thyme or mixed herbs
1 tablespoon dry sherry
50 g (2 oz) fresh wholemeal breadcrumbs
½ teaspoon salt
freshly ground black pepper

PREPARATION TIME: *20 minutes, plus setting and chilling overnight*

COOKING TIME: *2½ hours*

OVEN: *160°C, 325°F, Gas Mark 3*

An attractive, chunky pâté which is bacon-lined and

made with a tasty mixture of lean pork and pig's liver, flavoured with onion, garlic, herbs and sherry. Serve cut into thick slices, with French or Granary bread and a green salad.

1. Place the bacon rashers on a board and flatten them with the flat side of a knife until double their original length.
2. Line a 1 kg (2 lb) loaf tin with bacon rashers, arranging them crossways and slightly overlapping along the length of the tin, allowing the ends to overlap the rim of the tin on each of the longer sides.
3. Place the liver, pork, onion, garlic, herbs, sherry, breadcrumbs and salt and pepper to taste in a bowl and stir well to mix.
4. Turn the mixture into the bacon-lined tin and smooth

the surface. Fold the overlapping ends of the bacon rashers over the mixture.
5. Cover the tin tightly with foil and place in a roasting tin. Pour in cold water to come halfway up the sides of the loaf tin. Cook in a preheated oven for 2½ hours.
6. Remove the foil and cover with fresh foil, weight down and leave to cool for 3 hours. Then chill overnight, in the refrigerator, still weighted down. Ⓕ
7. Run a knife around the edge of the terrine and turn on to a serving plate. Serve cut into chunky slices.

Ⓕ Freeze for up to 1 month. Thaw overnight in the refrigerator.
Ⓜ Or microwave on Defrost for 12-15 minutes, then stand for 2-3 hours.

Creamed Smoked Mackerel Pots

1 medium smoked mackerel, about 225 g (8 oz), skinned, boned and finely flaked
65 g (2½ oz) butter, melted
50 g (2 oz) full fat soft cheese
1 teaspoon lemon juice
1 tablespoon chopped fresh parsley
½-1 teaspoon creamed horseradish (optional)
freshly ground black pepper

TO GARNISH:
lemon slices
parsley sprigs

PREPARATION TIME: *10 minutes*

This unusual pâté – a combination of succulent smoked mackerel and full fat soft cheese, flavoured with parsley and creamed horseradish – is quick and easy to make and delicious served with bread or wholewheat crackers.

1. Place the mackerel in a bowl. Add 25 g (1 oz) of the melted butter with the cheese and stir well to mix.
2. Stir in the lemon juice, parsley, creamed horseradish, if using, and pepper to taste. Mix thoroughly until well combined.
3. Divide the mixture evenly between 4 small individual ramekins or serving pots and smooth the surfaces.
4. Pour the remaining melted butter over each ramekin and chill in the refrigerator for at least 2 hours before serving, garnished with lemon slices and parsley sprigs.

Clockwise from the left: Liver and Mushroom Pâté; Farmhouse Terrine; Creamed Smoked Mackerel Pots.

Country Casserole with Herb Dumplings

40 g (1½ oz) beef dripping

750 g (1½ lb) leg of beef, trimmed and cut into bite-sized pieces

1 medium onion, peeled and sliced

2 large leeks, trimmed and thickly sliced

1 medium turnip, peeled and cut into 1 cm (½ inch) dice

1 medium parsnip, peeled and thinly sliced

6 medium carrots, scraped and sliced

2 celery sticks, trimmed and cut into 1 cm (½ inch) slices

2 tablespoons plain flour

1.2 litres (2 pints) beef stock

salt

freshly ground black pepper

HERB DUMPLINGS:

100 g (4 oz) self-raising flour

pinch of salt

1 tablespoon chopped fresh parsley or chives

50 g (2 oz) shredded suet

about 4 tablespoons cold water

TO GARNISH:

chopped fresh parsley

PREPARATION TIME: *15 minutes*	
COOKING TIME: *about 2½ hours*	
OVEN: *180°C, 350°F, Gas Mark 4*	

The secret of successful dumplings is to add the water to the dough mixture when ready to cook dumplings and, once they have been added to the simmering stew or casserole, to ensure that the stew remains at simmering point throughout the dumplings' cooking time.

1. Melt the dripping in a flameproof casserole. Add the beef and vegetables and fry over a moderate heat for 5 minutes, stirring frequently.

2. Stir in the flour and cook for 1 minute, then gradually stir in the stock with salt and pepper to taste. Bring to the boil. Remove from the heat, cover and cook in a preheated oven for 2 hours or until the beef is tender. A F

3. Make the dumplings: sift the flour with the salt into a mixing bowl, and stir in the parsley or chives and suet. Stir in the water all at once and mix quickly to form a soft dough. Divide the dough into 8 equal pieces and shape into neat balls.

4. Remove the casserole from the oven, stir well and arrange the dumplings on top. Cover again, return to the oven and cook for a further 15-20 minutes until the dumplings are well-risen and light and fluffy.

5. Sprinkle the dumplings with chopped parsley and serve at once.

A Can be prepared the previous day and kept chilled. Reheat gently until simmering before adding dumplings and covering and cooking on the hob for 15-20 minutes.

F Freeze for up to 3 months. Reheat gently from frozen until piping hot then follow instructions given from step 3.

M Or microwave on Defrost for 25-30 minutes, breaking down with a spoon every few minutes. Stand for 20 minutes before following instructions from step 3.

Clockwise from the bottom:
Skewered Lamb Korma; Guard of Honour; Country Casserole with Herb Dumplings.

Guard of Honour

SERVES 6

2 pieces of best end of neck of lamb, each piece with 6 cutlets
40 g (1½ oz) butter
50 g (2 oz) button mushrooms, finely chopped
1 medium onion, peeled and finely chopped
4 rashers streaky bacon, rinded, boned and finely chopped
100 g (4 oz) fresh white breadcrumbs
1 egg, beaten
salt
freshly ground black pepper
1 tablespoon vegetable oil

TO GARNISH:
cutlet frills
watercress sprigs

PREPARATION TIME: *15 minutes*
COOKING TIME: *1 hour 35 minutes*
OVEN: *180°C, 350°F, Gas Mark 4*

When buying the meat, ask the butcher to prepare the best ends of lamb by chining them and trimming away 1 cm (½ inch) of meat and fat from the top of each cutlet bone.

1. Using a sharp knife, score the fatty sides of each best end in a diamond pattern. Place the 2 best ends together, fatty sides outwards, and interlace the cutlet bones at the top to form a Guard of Honour. Tie together with string between every 2 cutlets. A
2. Make the stuffing: melt the butter in a saucepan, add the mushrooms, onion and bacon and fry over a gentle heat for 5 minutes. Stir in the breadcrumbs and egg, with salt and pepper to taste, and stir well to mix. A
3. Spoon the stuffing inside the Guard of Honour. Cover the exposed bone ends of each trimmed cutlet bone with pieces of foil to prevent burning during cooking.
4. Stand the joint upright in a roasting tin, pour over the oil and season with salt and pepper.
5. Roast in a preheated oven for 1½ hours or until the lamb is cooked through and tender. Remove the string and foil and transfer the joint to a heated serving dish. Garnish each cutlet bone with a cutlet frill and arrange watercress sprigs around the base of the joint. Serve hot with a selection of vegetables and gravy.

A Meat and stuffing can be prepared the previous day, stored separately covered with cling film, and kept chilled.

Skewered Lamb Korma

150 ml (¼ pint) plain unsweetened yogurt
3 tablespoons vegetable oil
1 medium onion, peeled and finely chopped
2 cloves garlic, peeled and crushed
1 cm (½ inch) piece fresh root ginger, peeled and grated (optional)
¼ teaspoon chilli powder
½ teaspoon garam masala
1 teaspoon lemon juice
salt
freshly ground black pepper
750 g-1 kg (1½-2 lb) lean boneless lamb, trimmed and cut into 2.5 cm (1 inch) pieces
1 medium onion, peeled, quartered and separated into layers

PREPARATION TIME: *15 minutes, plus marinating*
COOKING TIME: *25-30 minutes*

1. Place the yogurt, 2 tablespoons of the oil and chopped onion in a large bowl. Stir in the garlic and ginger, if using, then stir in the chilli powder, garam masala, lemon juice and salt and pepper to taste.
2. Add the lamb and stir well, then cover and leave to marinate for 3-4 hours in the refrigerator, stirring occasionally. A
3. Lift the pieces of lamb from the marinade and thread fairly loosely on to 4 skewers, alternating with the onion layers.
4. Place the lamb skewers in a grill pan, spoon over the reserved marinade and drizzle over the remaining oil. Cook under a moderately hot grill for 25-30 minutes, turning and brushing often with the marinade.
5. Serve hot on a bed of boiled rice with side dishes of chopped tomatoes mixed with finely chopped fresh mint, and mango chutney.

A Can be prepared and left to marinate overnight, covered with cling film and kept chilled.

Minted Roast Lamb with Watercress Stuffing

SERVES 6-8

50 g (2 oz) butter
1 medium onion, peeled and finely chopped
2 sticks celery, trimmed and finely chopped
1 bunch watercress, stalks trimmed and finely chopped
1½ tablespoons mint jelly
100 g (4 oz) fresh white breadcrumbs
1 egg, beaten
salt
freshly ground black pepper
1½ kg (3-3½ lb) shoulder of lamb, boned
1 tablespoon vegetable oil

TO GARNISH:
mint sprigs

PREPARATION TIME: *10-15 minutes*
COOKING TIME: *about 1½ hours*
OVEN: *190°C, 375°F, Gas Mark 5*

Try this unusual way of stuffing a lamb shoulder. It is beautifully easy to carve. Ask the butcher to bone the shoulder for you.

1. Melt half the butter in a saucepan, add the onion and celery and cook over a gentle heat for 3 minutes. Add the watercress to the pan and cook for a further 3 minutes.
2. Add the remaining butter and heat until melted. Remove the pan from the heat, then stir in ½ tablespoon of the mint jelly with the breadcrumbs, egg and salt and pepper to taste. Leave to cool. Ⓐ
3. Use the mixture to stuff the cavity in the lamb. Shape the lamb into a neat round and tie securely with string.
4. Weigh the stuffed joint and calculate the cooking time at 20 minutes per 450 g

(1 lb), plus 30 minutes.
5. Heat the oil in a roasting tin, add the joint and season with salt and pepper. Roast in a preheated oven for all but 15 minutes of the calculated cooking time. Remove from the oven, cut away the string and brush with the remaining mint jelly. Return to the oven and cook for a further 15 minutes. Ⓕ
6. Garnish with mint and serve hot or cold.

Ⓐ The stuffing can be prepared the previous day, covered with cling film and kept chilled.
Ⓕ Freeze for up to 3 months. Thaw overnight in refrigerator. Serve cold.
Ⓜ Or microwave on Defrost for 8-10 minutes per 450g/1 lb, turning over every 10 minutes. Stand for 1 hour before serving.

Beef Pepperpot

2 tablespoons plain flour
1 teaspoon paprika pepper
salt
freshly ground black pepper
750 g (1½ lb) braising steak, trimmed and cut into 2.5 cm (1 inch) cubes
2 tablespoons vegetable oil
12 small onions or shallots, peeled
100 g (4 oz) button mushrooms, quartered
1 garlic clove, peeled and crushed (optional)
1 × 225 g (8 oz) can tomatoes
450 ml (¾ pint) beef stock
1 medium red pepper, cored, seeded and cut into 1 cm (1 inch) strips
1 medium green pepper, cored, seeded and cut into 1 cm (½ inch) strips

PREPARATION TIME: *25 minutes*
COOKING TIME: *2¼ hours*
OVEN: *160°C, 325°F, Gas Mark 3*

Bacon and Onion Pudding

SERVES 4-6

50 g (2 oz) butter
500 g (1¼ lb) lean boned collar of bacon, soaked overnight in cold water, then drained, trimmed of excess fat and cut into 2.5 cm (1 inch) pieces
2 medium onions, peeled and coarsely chopped
2 medium carrots, scraped and thinly sliced
50 g (2 oz) plain flour
300 ml (½ pint) chicken stock
freshly ground black pepper
1½-2 tablespoons chopped fresh parsley

SUET PASTRY:
225 g (8 oz) self-raising flour
a pinch of salt
100 g (4 oz) shredded suet
150 ml (¼ pint) cold water

PREPARATION TIME: *35 minutes, plus soaking*
COOKING TIME: *2½-3 hours*

This filling and tasty suet crust pudding is a perfect dish to serve the family on a cold winter day.

1. Melt the butter in a saucepan, add the bacon, onions and carrots and cook over a gentle heat for 10 minutes.
2. Stir in the flour and cook for 1 minute, then gradually pour in the stock and bring to the boil, stirring. Lower the heat and simmer for 2 minutes. Add pepper to taste and stir in the parsley. Remove from the heat and leave to cool. Ⓐ
3. Make the suet pastry: sift the flour with the salt into a mixing bowl. Stir in the suet, then add the water and mix to form a soft dough. Knead gently on a lightly floured board or work surface.
4. Cut off ¼ of the dough

and reserve for the lid. Roll out the remaining pastry to a round 10 cm (4 inches) larger than the top of a 1.2 litre (2 pint) pudding basin.
5. Grease the basin liberally with butter. Lightly dust the rolled out pastry with flour, then fold loosely in half and then into quarters. Lift the pastry into the basin, pointed end down, unfold and press neatly around the base and sides.
6. Spoon the cooled bacon mixture into the pastry-lined basin. Dampen the pastry edge. Roll out the reserved pastry to a round large enough to cover the top of the pudding. Place on top and seal the edges together firmly.
7. Cover with pleated greased greaseproof paper and pleated foil and tie securely with string. Place

the pudding in a large saucepan and pour in boiling water to come half-way up the sides of the basin.
8. Boil the pudding for 2½-3 hours until cooked through, topping up with more boiling water as required. Serve hot with boiled potatoes and peas or cabbage.

Ⓐ Can be prepared 3-4 hours in advance, covered with cling film and kept chilled.

Clockwise from the left:
Honey Roast Bacon with Peaches; Bacon and Onion Pudding; Beef Pepperpot; Minted Roast Lamb with Watercress Stuffing.

1. Spread the flour out on a plate, season with the paprika pepper, salt and pepper and use to coat the beef cubes, reserving any excess seasoned flour.
2. Heat the oil in a flameproof casserole, add the onions or shallots, mushrooms and garlic, if using, and fry over a moderate heat for 5 minutes, stirring frequently. Remove from the casserole with a slotted spoon and set aside on a plate.
3. Add the beef to the casserole and fry over a moderately high heat to seal and brown on all sides.
4. Return the onions, garlic and mushrooms to the casserole, stir in the reserved flour and cook for 1 minute. Stir in the tomatoes with their juice, breaking them up

with a wooden spoon. Stir in the stock and bring to the boil.
5. Cover the casserole and cook in a preheated oven for 1½ hours. F Stir in the red and green pepper strips, cover again and cook for a further 30 minutes. Serve hot with plain boiled rice.

F Freeze for up to 2 months. Thaw overnight in the refrigerator, then stir in the red and green pepper strips and reheat at 180°C, 350°F, Gas Mark 4 for 35-40 minutes.
M Or microwave on Defrost for 25-30 minutes. Stand for 20 minutes before heating through as in freezer instructions.

Honey Roast Bacon with Peaches

SERVES 6

1 × 1½-1¾ kg (3½-4 lb) boned collar of bacon, soaked overnight in cold water
1 bay leaf
1 small onion, peeled and quartered
1 × 425 g (15 oz) can peach halves, drained, with syrup reserved
2 tablespoons clear honey
about 40 whole cloves (optional)
1 tablespoon demerara sugar
2 good pinches of ground cinnamon

TO GARNISH:
watercress sprigs

PREPARATION TIME: *15 minutes, plus soaking overnight*
COOKING TIME: *2 hours*
OVEN: *190°C, 375°F, Gas Mark 5*

1. Drain the bacon and place rind side down in a large saucepan. Add the bay leaf and onion and pour in cold water to cover. Cover and bring to the boil, then lower the heat and simmer gently for 1½ hours.
2. Remove the bacon from the pan and allow to cool slightly. Strip off the skin, leaving the layer of fat on the bacon, and place the joint fat side up in a roasting tin. Using a sharp knife, score the fat into a diamond pattern.
3. Mix 2 tablespoons of the reserved peach syrup with the honey and brush the mixture over the scored bacon fat. Stud each diamond with cloves, if using.
4. Roast the bacon in a preheated oven for 25 minutes, until the topping is golden brown. F
5. Meanwhile place the remaining peach syrup with the peach halves in a saucepan, stir in the sugar and cinnamon and simmer gently for 10 minutes. F
6. Place the bacon joint on a heated serving dish. Remove the peach halves from the sauce, arrange them around the base of the joint and garnish with watercress sprigs. Pour the peach sauce into a warmed sauce boat and serve separately.

F Freeze the bacon joint and peaches in syrup separately for up to 1 month. Thaw bacon overnight in refrigerator; thaw peaches in syrup for 3 hours at room temperature. Serve cold.
M Or microwave bacon on Defrost for 8-10 minutes to the 450 g/1 lb, turning over every 10 minutes, then stand for 1 hour before serving. Microwave peaches on Defrost for 10-12 minutes, then stand for 10 minutes.

Cheesy-Crust Fish Pie

750 g (1½ lb) cod fillets, skinned and cut into bite-sized pieces
15 g (½ oz) butter
1 medium onion, peeled and finely chopped
1 clove garlic, crushed (optional)
1 × 225 g (8 oz) can tomatoes, chopped
100 g (4 oz) frozen peas, thawed
salt
freshly ground black pepper

TOPPING:
225 g (8 oz) self-raising flour
pinch of salt
50 g (2 oz) butter or hard margarine, diced
½ teaspoon dried mixed herbs
75 g (3 oz) Cheddar cheese, grated
120 ml (4 fl oz) milk

TO GLAZE:
a little milk

PREPARATION TIME: *25 minutes*
COOKING TIME: *about 45 minutes*
OVEN: *190°C, 375°F, Gas Mark 5*
THEN: *200°C, 400°F, Gas Mark 6*

Golden-brown cheese scones form the tempting topping on this simple-to-make fish pie.

1. Place the cod in an ovenproof dish. Melt the butter in a saucepan, add the onion and garlic, if using, and fry over a gentle heat for 5 minutes then sprinkle over the fish. Pour the tomatoes with their juice over the fish. Stir in the peas and season well with salt and pepper.
2. Cook in a preheated oven for 20 minutes.
3. Meanwhile, make the topping: sift the flour with the salt into a mixing bowl. Add the butter or margarine and rub in with the fingertips until the mixture resembles fine breadcrumbs. Stir in the herbs with 50 g (2 oz) of the cheese. Stir in the milk and mix to form a soft dough. Knead lightly until free from cracks.
4. Roll out on a lightly floured work surface to 1 cm (½ inch) thickness and, using a 5 cm (2 inch) round cutter, cut out 12 rounds. Re-knead and re-roll the trimmings and cut out 8 further rounds.
5. Arrange the scone rounds over the hot fish in the dish, brush with milk and sprinkle with the remaining grated cheese. Increase the oven temperature and cook, uncovered, for 15-20 minutes or until the scone topping is well risen, golden brown and cooked through. Serve hot.

VARIATIONS:
Replace the cod with smoked haddock. Add frozen (thawed) sweetcorn instead of the peas.

Cape Cod Pie

450 g (1 lb) cod fillets
250 ml (8 fl oz) milk
50 g (2 oz) butter or hard
   margarine
75 g (3 oz) button mushrooms,
   sliced
40 g (1½ oz) plain flour
75 g (3 oz) peeled prawns,
   coarsely chopped
salt
freshly ground black pepper
1 × 400 g (14 oz) packet frozen
   puff pastry, thawed

TO GLAZE:
a little beaten egg

PREPARATION TIME: *15-20
minutes*
COOKING TIME: *45 minutes*
OVEN: *200°C, 400°F, Gas Mark 6*

1. Place the cod in a
saucepan, add the milk and
cook over a gentle heat for 10
minutes, until tender. Drain,
reserving the cooking liquid,
and make up to 250 ml
(8 fl oz) with water.
2. Flake the cod finely,
discarding the skin and
bones.
3. Melt the butter or
margarine in a saucepan, add
the mushrooms and fry over
a gentle heat for 3 minutes.
Stir in the flour and cook for
1 minute. Gradually stir in
the reserved cooking liquid
and bring to the boil, stirring.
Lower the heat and simmer
for 2-3 minutes. Remove
from the heat and stir in the
flaked fish with the prawns
and salt and pepper to taste.
Leave to cool. Ⓐ
4. Roll out the pastry on a
lightly floured board or work
surface and trim to a
40 × 25 cm (16 × 10 inch)

rectangle, reserving the
trimmings. Cut the pastry
rectangle in half to give two
20 × 25 cm (8 × 10 inch)
pieces.
5. Place one piece of pastry
on a dampened baking sheet.
Spoon the cold fish mixture
on to the pastry and spread
out evenly to within 2 cm
(¾ inch) of the edges. Roll
out the remaining piece of
pastry to a 23 × 28 cm (9 × 11
inch) rectangle.
6. Dampen the edges of the
pastry on the baking sheet
and cover with the larger
piece of pastry. Press the
edges firmly together to seal.
Knock up and flute the edges
neatly. Make a small hole in
the centre of the pie.
7. Brush the pie with beaten
egg. Re-roll the pastry
trimmings and cut out pastry
leaves. Use to decorate the
pie and brush with more
beaten egg. Cook in a
preheated oven for 30-35
minutes until golden brown
and cooked through. Serve
hot with creamed potatoes
and peas.

Ⓐ Can be prepared 3-4 hours
in advance, covered with
cling film and kept chilled.

VARIATIONS:
Substitute cod with haddock,
coley or rock salmon.
   Flavour with 1 tablespoon
of chopped fresh parsley if
liked.
   Replace the mushrooms
with 2 hard-boiled eggs,
coarsely chopped.
   Omit the prawns and
increase the quantity of
mushrooms to 175 g (6 oz).

Celebration-Stuffed Plaice

750 g (1¾ lb) potatoes, peeled
   and cut into even-sized
   pieces
salt
freshly ground black pepper
75 g (3 oz) butter
1 tablespoons milk
8 plaice fillets, skinned and
   boned
100 g (4 oz) peeled prawns
1 small onion or shallot, peeled
   and finely chopped
1 tablespoon lemon juice
3 tablespoons dry white wine
1½ tablespoons plain flour
150 ml (¼ pint) chicken stock
50 g (2 oz) Cheddar cheese,
   grated
4 tablespoons single cream

TO GARNISH:
lemon butterflies
parsley sprigs

PREPARATION TIME: *15 minutes*
COOKING TIME: *45 minutes*
OVEN: *190°C, 375°F, Gas Mark 5*

1. Cook the potatoes in a
saucepan of boiling, salted
water for 15-20 minutes until
tender. Drain well and
return to the pan. Place over
a moderate heat for 1-2
minutes, shaking the pan
frequently to dry off.
2. Mash the potatoes well
and season with salt and
pepper to taste. Add 25 g
(1 oz) of the butter with the
milk. Stir well to mix and
beat thoroughly until
smooth.
3. Place the potato in a
piping bag fitted with a large
star nozzle and pipe a
decorative border around
the edge of a shallow
ovenproof dish. Ⓐ
4. Place the plaice fillets on a
board and cover half of each
one with the prawns and
onion or shallot. Season with
salt and pepper and fold over
the uncovered half of each
fillet.
5. Melt half the remaining
butter in a large frying pan.

Remove from heat, add the
folded plaice fillets and pour
over the lemon juice and
white wine.
6. Cover with a lid or foil
and poach gently for about 7
minutes, until the plaice is
just tender. Using a fish slice,
carefully lift the fillets from
the pan and arrange on the
potato-lined dish. Reserve
the cooking liquid.
7. Melt the remaining butter
in a saucepan, stir in the flour
and cook for 1 minute. Stir in
the reserved cooking liquid
with the stock. Bring to the
boil, stirring all the time.
Lower the heat and simmer
for 2 minutes, stirring.
8. Remove from the heat,
stir in the cheese and cream
and taste and adjust the
seasoning if necessary. Pour
the sauce over the plaice
fillets Ⓐ and cook in a
preheated oven for 15-20
minutes until piping hot and
lightly browned. Serve at
once, garnished with lemon
butterflies and parsley
sprigs.

Ⓐ The potato border can be
prepared the previous day,
covered with cling film and
kept chilled. The fish dish
can be prepared to this stage
3-4 hours in advance,
covered lightly and kept in a
cool place. Cook at 190°C,
375°F, Gas Mark 5 for 40-45
minutes until lightly golden.

VARIATION:
Replace the white wine with
vegetable or chicken stock if
preferred. Use white crab
meat, flaked, instead of
prawns.

Clockwise from the top: Cheesy-
Crust Fish Pie; Celebration-Stuffed
Plaice; Cape Cod Pie.

Oriental Duckling

1 × 1¾ kg (4 lb) oven-ready duckling
salt
5 tablespoons vegetable oil
1 large onion, peeled, quartered and thinly sliced
100 g (4 oz) button mushrooms, thickly sliced
1 garlic clove, peeled and crushed
1 small red pepper, cored, seeded and cut into thin strips
1 small green pepper, cored, seeded and cut into thin strips
225 g (8 oz) fresh beansprouts
1 tablespoon soy sauce
1 tablespoon cornflour
2-3 teaspoons dry sherry
300 ml (½ pint) chicken stock
100 g (4 oz) toasted blanched almonds
freshly ground black pepper

PREPARATION TIME: *20 minutes, plus cooling*
COOKING TIME: *about 2 hours 10 minutes*
OVEN: *180°C, 350°F, Gas Mark 4*

This Chinese-style dish is quick to prepare, provided the duckling is roasted several hours before needed as it has to have time to cool. If fresh bean sprouts are unavailable try using finely shredded Chinese leaves instead.

1. Weigh the duckling and calculate the cooking time at 30 minutes per 450 g (1 lb). Prick the duckling all over with a fork and place in a roasting tin. Sprinkle with salt and roast in a preheated oven for the calculated cooking time, until golden brown and cooked through. Leave to cool.
2. Strip the flesh and skin from the carcass and cut into thin strips.
3. Heat 2 tablespoons of the oil in a large frying pan. Add the onion, mushrooms, garlic, red and green pepper and fry for 4 minutes. Remove from the pan with a slotted spoon, transfer to a plate and keep warm. Heat the remaining oil in the pan, add the duck meat and skin and beansprouts and stir-fry for 3 minutes. Remove from the pan and keep warm.
4. Blend the soy sauce with the cornflour and sherry and stir into the chicken stock. Stir the mixture into the pan, bring to the boil, and then simmer for 2 minutes. Stir in the almonds and return all the ingredients to the pan. Taste and adjust the seasoning and heat through for 3 minutes.
5. Serve at once with boiled rice and crisp fried noodles.

Pork and Mushroom Carbonnade

3 tablespoons vegetable oil
2 large onions, peeled and sliced
175 g (6 oz) button mushrooms, quartered
750 g (1½ lb) boned spare rib of pork, trimmed and cut into bite-sized pieces
1½ tablespoons plain flour
300 ml (½ pint) light ale
300 ml (½ pint) chicken stock
2 teaspoons soft light brown sugar
salt
freshly ground black pepper
50 g (2 oz) butter, softened
1½ teaspoons French mustard
40 g (1½ oz) Cheddar cheese, grated
1 tablespoon chopped fresh parsley
8 × 2.5 cm (1 inch) thick slices of French bread

PREPARATION TIME: *20 minutes*
COOKING TIME: *2 hours 15 minutes*
OVEN: *180°C, 350°F, Gas Mark 4*

1. Heat 2 tablespoons of the oil in a flameproof casserole. Add the onions and mushrooms and fry over a gentle heat for 5 minutes. Remove from the casserole with a slotted spoon and set aside on a plate.
2. Heat the remaining oil in the casserole, add the pork and fry over a moderately high heat, stirring, until the meat is sealed and browned on all sides.
3. Stir in the flour and cook for 1 minute. Stir in the ale and stock and bring to the boil. Remove from the heat and return the onions and mushrooms to the casserole. Stir in the sugar with salt and pepper to taste. Cover and cook in a preheated oven for 1¾ hours. Remove the casserole from the oven. F
4. Mix together the butter, mustard, cheese and parsley and spread over the slices of French bread. Arrange the bread slices, cheese side up, on top of the casserole. Press the slices down into the gravy (they will rise again during cooking).
5. Return the casserole to the oven and cook, uncovered, for a further 30 minutes, until the bread topping is melted and golden. Serve hot with French beans or seasonal greens.

F Freeze for up to 1 month. Thaw overnight in the refrigerator, then finish as for steps 4 and 5.
M Or microwave on Defrost for 25-30 minutes. Stand for 20 minutes before finishing as for steps 4 and 5.

French Roast Chicken with Cream Sauce

75 g (3 oz) butter
1 teaspoon chopped fresh tarragon or parsley
salt
freshly ground black pepper
1 × 1½ kg (3-3½ lb) oven-ready roasting chicken
450 ml (¾ pint) chicken stock
1 tablespoon plain flour
3 tablespoons single cream

PREPARATION TIME: *10 minutes*
COOKING TIME: *1½ hours*
OVEN: *190°C, 375°F, Gas Mark 5*

1. Mix together 25 g (1 oz) of the butter with the tarragon or parsley and salt and pepper to taste. Place the mixture inside the chicken cavity.
2. Place the chicken in a roasting tin. Melt the remaining butter and pour over the chicken. Season with salt and pepper and pour 150 ml (¼ pint) of the chicken stock into the roasting tin.
3. Roast in a preheated oven for 1½ hours or until the chicken is cooked through and the juices run clear when the thickest part of the thigh is pierced with a fine skewer.
4. Transfer the chicken to a heated serving plate. Keep warm while making the sauce.
5. Pour off all but 2 tablespoons of the juices from the tin. Stir in the flour and cook for 1 minute. Stir in the remaining chicken stock and bring to the boil, stirring all the time. Stir in the cream, taste and adjust the seasoning if necessary and simmer gently for 3 minutes.
6. Pour the sauce into a warmed sauce boat and serve hot with the chicken.

Clockwise from the bottom: Oriental Duckling; French Roast Chicken with Cream Sauce; Pork and Mushroom Carbonnade.

Tropical Fruit Bowl

SERVES 3-4

1 tablespoon fresh lime juice
20-25 g (¾-1 oz) caster sugar
100 ml (3½ fl oz) water
1 passion fruit, halved and pulp
   and seeds scooped out
½ melon, seeded, peeled and
   cut into neat cubes
1-2 kiwi fruit, peeled, halved
   and sliced
100 g (4 oz) strawberries,
   hulled and halved
4 fresh lychees, peeled, stoned
   and halved, or use canned
   lychees
1 medium banana, peeled and
   sliced

TO DECORATE:
1 heaped tablespoon shredded
   coconut, toasted if liked

PREPARATION TIME: *25-30
minutes, plus chilling*
COOKING TIME: *3 minutes*

This lovely tropical salad is a
special occasion dessert but
the fruit can be varied
according to seasonal
availability, to make it less
expensive.

1. Place the lime juice, sugar
and water in a saucepan and
bring to the boil. Boil for 3
minutes, then remove from
the heat and leave to cool.
Stir in the passion fruit pulp
and seeds. Ⓐ
2. Place all the prepared
fruit in a serving bowl. Pour
over the cooled syrup and
stir well.
3. Chill for at least 2 hours
before serving, scattered
with shredded coconut.

Ⓐ Can be prepared the
previous day, covered tightly
with cling film and kept
chilled.

Top to bottom: Tropical Fruit Bowl;
Grapefruit Ratafia Soufflé; French
Raspberry Lattice Flan.

French Raspberry Lattice Flan

SERVES 8

225 g (8 oz) plain flour
pinch of salt
185 g (6½ oz) butter, diced
225 g (8 oz) caster sugar
1 egg yolk
1 tablespoon cold water
350 g (12 oz) fresh or frozen
   (thawed) raspberries
1 large cooking apple, peeled,
   cored and thinly sliced

TO GLAZE:
6 tablespoons seedless
   raspberry jam
2 teaspoons lemon juice

PREPARATION TIME: *30 minutes*
COOKING TIME: *45 minutes*
OVEN: *180°C, 350°F, Gas Mark 4*

Delicious served as a dessert
or at teatime.

1. Sift the flour with the salt into a bowl. Add 175 g (6 oz) of the butter and rub in with the fingertips until the mixture resembles fine breadcrumbs. Stir in 50 g (2 oz) of the sugar with the egg yolk and water and mix to form a fairly firm dough. Knead lightly until free from cracks. Ⓐ Chill in the refrigerator while preparing the filling.
2. Place raspberries and apple with the remaining sugar and butter in a saucepan and bring slowly to the boil, stirring until the sugar is dissolved. Boil gently, uncovered, for about 15 minutes or until most of the liquid has reduced and the mixture is quite thick. Remove from the heat and leave to cool. Ⓐ
3. Cut off one-third of the pastry and reserve. Roll out the remaining pastry on a lightly floured board or work surface to a 28 cm (11 inch) round.
4. Ease the pastry into a 23 cm (9 inch) loose-bottomed fluted flan tin, pressing pastry on to the base and up the sides of the tin. Press firmly into the flutes and fold the excess pastry over the rim of the flan tin. Run a rolling pin firmly across the top of the flan tin to trim and give a neat edge. Add the pastry trimmings to the reserved pastry and knead together lightly.
5. Spoon the cooled raspberry mixture into the pastry-lined tin. Roll out the remaining pastry and cut into ten 25 × 1 cm (10 × ½ inch) strips. Arrange half the strips one way over the filling and the remaining half the other way to form an attractive lattice design, trimming and dampening the ends, and sealing them well to the pastry flan edge.
6. Place the flan tin on a preheated baking sheet and bake in a preheated oven for 30-35 minutes until the pastry is golden brown and cooked through.
7. Remove the flan tin edge and place the flan, still on the tin base, on a serving plate.
8. Heat the raspberry jam and lemon juice in a saucepan until the jam is melted and the mixture is smooth. Spoon over the warm pastry lattice and sides of the flan to give a shiny finish. Leave to set for 5 minutes.
9. Serve warm or cold, with whipped or single cream.

Ⓐ The pastry and the filling can both be prepared the previous day, covered with cling film and kept chilled in the refrigerator.

Grapefruit Ratafia Soufflé

SERVES 8

15 g (½ oz) powdered gelatine
150 ml (¼ pint) freshly
   squeezed pink grapefruit
   juice, strained
2 tablespoons lemon juice
4 eggs, separated
175 g (6 oz) caster sugar
¼ teaspoon finely grated pink
   grapefruit rind
300 ml (½ pint) whipping
   cream
50 g (2 oz) ratafias, crushed
   finely

TO DECORATE:
150 ml (¼ pint) whipping
   cream, whipped
8 ratafias

PREPARATION TIME: *15 minutes,*
plus setting
COOKING TIME: *3 minutes*

This light, fluffy, cold soufflé has a refreshingly tangy flavour and makes a perfect ending to any meal. When pink grapefruit are unavailable use ordinary yellow grapefruit instead.

1. Prepare the soufflé dish: tie a band of double thickness greaseproof paper or foil around the outside of a 15 cm (6 inch) diameter, 1.2 litres (2 pint) capacity soufflé dish, to stand at least 5 cm (2 inches) above the rim of the dish.
2. Sprinkle the gelatine over the grapefruit juice in a small heatproof bowl and leave to soften for 10 minutes, until spongy. Stand the bowl in a saucepan of simmering water and stir until the gelatine is dissolved. Add the lemon juice and leave to cool for about 7 minutes, but do not allow it to set.
3. Place the egg yolks with the sugar and grapefruit rind in a heatproof bowl set over a saucepan of very hot water, off the heat. Whisk for about 3 minutes with an electric hand-held whisk until creamy, thick and pale. Remove from the heat and whisk constantly until the mixture is cold.
4. Whisk in the cooled gelatine mixture and leave in the refrigerator for about 7-10 minutes until just beginning to set around the edges.
5. Whisk the egg whites stiffly; whisk the cream until soft peaks form. Gently fold the egg whites and cream into the grapefruit mixture, using a large metal spoon.
6. Turn half the grapefruit mixture into the prepared soufflé dish. Cover with half the crushed ratafias and quickly top with the remaining grapefruit mixture. Smooth the surface and leave to set in a cool place (preferably not the refrigerator) for at least 3 hours, or overnight.
7. Carefully peel away the greaseproof paper or foil, using a knife to help. Coat the exposed sides of the soufflé with the remaining crushed ratafias. Decorate the top with 8 swirls of whipped cream and place a ratafia on each one.

VARIATION:
Omit the layer of ratafias in the centre of the soufflé if liked and coat the exposed sides of the soufflé with finely chopped walnuts.

Vanilla and Blackcurrant Ripple Ice

SERVES 4-5

150 ml (¼ pint) single cream
3 egg yolks
40-50 g (1½-2 oz) caster sugar
1 teaspoon vanilla essence
300 ml (½ pint) whipping
  cream
2 tablespoons blackcurrant
  jelly preserve

PREPARATION TIME: *15 minutes,
plus freezing*
COOKING TIME: *2-3 minutes*

1. Heat the single cream until hot but not boiling. Place the egg yolks in a heatproof bowl and mix with a fork.
2. Pour the hot cream on to the egg yolks, stirring all the time. Stir in the sugar and vanilla essence. Place the bowl over a saucepan of gently simmering water and stir for about 8-10 minutes with a wooden spoon until the mixture thickens and coats the back of the spoon. Strain into a bowl and leave to cool.
3. Whip the whipping cream until soft peaks form and lightly fold into the custard, using a large metal spoon.
4. Turn the mixture into a 1 kg (2 lb) loaf tin, cover and freeze for 1½ hours or until partly frozen.
5. Warm the blackcurrant jelly in a saucepan until smooth and melted. Leave to cool but do not allow to set. Meanwhile, turn the ice cream into a bowl, break up with a fork and whisk until smooth.
6. Return the mixture to the loaf tin. Make 3 holes along the centre of the ice cream and pour in the melted blackcurrant jelly. Run a knife through the jelly and ice cream to give a marble effect.
7. Freeze for at least a further 4 hours until completely frozen. F
8. Transfer the ice cream to the main compartment of the refrigerator for 30 minutes before required for serving, to soften slightly. Serve with fan wafers.

F Freeze for up to 3 months.

VARIATION:
Replace the blackcurrant jelly with the same quantity of seedless raspberry jam.

Coffee Parfait

3 teaspoons instant coffee
  powder
1 teaspoon drinking chocolate
2 teaspoons boiling water
¼ teaspoon vanilla essence
300 ml (½ pint) whipping
  cream
2 egg whites
50 g (2 oz) caster sugar
40 g (1½ oz) plain chocolate,
  grated

PREPARATION TIME: *15 minutes,
plus chilling*

1. Dissolve the coffee and drinking chocolate in the boiling water, then leave to cool. Add the vanilla essence.
2. Whisk the cream until stiff and fold in the coffee and chocolate mixture, using a metal spoon.
3. Whisk the egg whites stiffly, then gradually add the sugar, whisking well after each addition until very stiff and glossy.
4. Lightly fold the egg whites and 25 g (1 oz) of the grated chocolate into the cream mixture, using a metal spoon.
5. Spoon the mixture into 6 individual serving dishes, sprinkle with the remaining grated chocolate and serve chilled, with fan wafers.

Top to bottom: Strawberry Ice Cream; Coffee Parfait; Vanilla and Blackcurrant Ripple Ice.

Strawberry Ice Cream

SERVES 6

450 g (1 lb) fresh strawberries,
  hulled
4 tablespoons fresh orange
  juice
175 g (6 oz) caster sugar
450 ml (¾ pint) whipping
  cream

PREPARATION TIME: *15 minutes,
plus freezing*

1. Mash the strawberries finely and mix with the orange juice to form a smooth purée. Stir in the sugar.
2. Whip the cream until soft peaks form and fold into the strawberry purée.
3. Pour the mixture into a 1 kg (2 lb) loaf tin. Cover and freeze for 1½ hours or until partly frozen.
4. Turn the mixture into a bowl, break it up with a fork and whisk until smooth. Return the mixture to the loaf tin and freeze for at least a further 5 hours until completely frozen. F
5. Transfer the ice cream to the main compartment of the refrigerator for 25-30 minutes before required for serving, to soften slightly. Serve with fan wafers.

F Freeze for up to 3 months.

VARIATION:
Raspberry Ice Cream: Replace the strawberries with the same quantity of raspberries, or use a mixture of half strawberries and half raspberries.

Black Cherry Gâteau

MAKES a 23 cm (9 inch) round cake

225 g (8 oz) butter or hard margarine
225 g (8 oz) caster sugar
4 eggs
225 g (8 oz) self-raising flour, sifted
pinch of salt
2 tablespoons hot water

FILLING:
50 g (2 oz) soft margarine
100 g (4 oz) icing sugar
½ tablespoon cocoa powder
½ tablespoon hot water

TOPPING:
1 × 450 g (16 oz) can pitted black cherries, drained
450 ml (¾ pint) whipping cream
40 g (1½ oz) plain chocolate, grated

PREPARATION TIME: *20-25 minutes, plus cooling*
COOKING TIME: *20-25 minutes*
OVEN: *190°C, 375°F, Gas Mark 5*

1. Grease two 23 cm (9 inch) round sandwich cake tins and line the bases with greased greaseproof paper.
2. In a bowl, beat together the butter or margarine and sugar until light and fluffy. Add the eggs one at a time, beating well after each addition.
3. Add the flour with the salt and gently fold into the mixture, using a large metal spoon. Fold in the hot water, to give a fairly soft dropping consistency.
4. Divide the mixture evenly between the tins and smooth the surfaces. Bake in a preheated oven for 20-25 minutes until golden brown, cooked through and springy to the touch.
5. Turn the cakes on to a wire rack, carefully remove the lining papers and leave to cool completely. Ⓐ Ⓕ

6. Meanwhile to make the filling, beat together the margarine and icing sugar until smooth. Blend the cocoa powder with the hot water and add to the mixture. Beat thoroughly until the mixture is smooth and evenly blended. Ⓐ
7. Reserve 40 cherries for the topping and roughly chop the remainder. Add the chopped cherries to the buttercream and mix well.
8. Spread the top of one of the cooled cakes with the buttercream mixture. Place the remaining cake on top.
9. Whip the cream stiffly and use half of it to spread over the top and sides of the gâteau. Place the remaining cream in a piping bag fitted with a large star nozzle. Coat the sides of gâteau with the grated chocolate, reserving a little for decorating the finished gâteau.
10. Pipe a decorative border of cream around the top of the cake and arrange the reserved cherries inside the border. Pipe the remaining cream into swirls or rosettes in the centre of the gâteau and sprinkle with the remaining grated chocolate.

Ⓐ Sandwich cakes can be prepared the previous day and stored in an airtight tin.
Ⓕ Freeze for up to 3 months. Thaw for 3 hours at room temperature before following instructions given from step 6.
Ⓜ Or microwave on Defrost for 2-4 minutes, then stand for 5 minutes. Defrost the layers separately, before following instructions from step 6.

Black Cherry Gâteau.

Strawberry Chantilly Meringue

SERVES 6-8

3 egg whites
175 g (6 oz) caster sugar

FILLING:
300 ml (½ pint) whipping
   cream
a few drops of vanilla essence
1 tablespoon icing sugar
350 g (12 oz) strawberries,
   hulled and sliced
3 tablespoons raspberry jam,
   warmed and sieved
½ tablespoon lemon juice

PREPARATION TIME: *15 minutes,*
plus chilling

COOKING TIME: *4-5 hours*

OVEN: *110°C, 225°F, Gas Mark*
¼

Serve this luscious
meringue, cream and
strawberry layer gâteau
within 1 hour of assembling.

1. Line 2 baking sheets with
non-stick silicone paper or
lightly greased greaseproof
paper.
2. Whisk the egg whites
stiffly, fold in half the sugar
and whisk again until very
stiff and glossy.
3. Lightly fold in the
remaining sugar, using a
large metal spoon. Divide
the mixture into two and use
to form two 20 cm (8 inch)
rounds on the prepared
baking sheets.
4. Bake in a preheated oven
for 4-5 hours or until
completely dried out.
Carefully lift the meringue
rounds from the baking
sheets and remove the
paper. Leave to cool on a
wire rack. Ⓐ
5. Whisk together the
cream, vanilla essence and
icing sugar until soft peaks
form.
6. Place one meringue
round on a serving plate and
spread with half the cream.
Cover with half the sliced
strawberries and top with the
remaining meringue round.
7. Spread with the
remaining cream and cover
with the remaining sliced
strawberries.
8. Warm the jam with the
lemon juice until melted,
then bring to the boil.
Remove from the heat and
allow to cool, but do not
allow to set. Drizzle the
melted jam over the
strawberry topping, to give a
sticky glaze. Chill before
serving.

Ⓐ Can be prepared up to 3
weeks in advance, wrapped
in polythene bags and kept in
an airtight tin.

VARIATION:
Replace the strawberries
with raspberries, or a
mixture of black and
redcurrants.

Spicy Lemon Syrup Layer

SERVES 6-8

225 g (8 oz) self-raising flour
pinch of salt
¼ teaspoon ground cinnamon
100 g (4 oz) shredded suet
150 ml (¼ pint) cold water
75 g (3 oz) sultanas
1 tablespoon lemon juice
½ teaspoon finely grated lemon
   rind
200 g (7 oz) golden syrup

PREPARATION TIME: *15 minutes*

COOKING TIME: *2 hours*

1. Grease a 900 ml (1½ pint)
pudding basin.
2. Sift the flour with the salt
and cinnamon into a mixing
bowl. Stir in the suet, add the
water and mix to form a fairly
firm dough. Knead lightly
until free from cracks.
3. Divide the pastry in half,
cut one half into two equal
pieces and reserve. Mark the
remaining half into thirds:
cut off one-third and reserve.
4. Mix together the sultanas,
lemon juice and rind and
golden syrup.
5. Roll out the smallest
piece of pastry to a round
that fits the bottom of the
basin and place in position.
Cover with one-third of the
sultana mixture.
6. Roll out the two equal
pieces of pastry, one slightly
larger than the other, to fit
the basin. Place the smaller
one in position and cover
with half the remaining
sultana mixture.
7. Place the slightly larger
round on top and cover with
the remaining sultana
mixture. Roll out the
remaining large piece of
pastry to fit the top of the
basin and place in position.
8. Cover with pleated
greased greaseproof paper
and foil and tie securely with
string.
9. Place the pudding in a
large saucepan and pour in
boiling water to come half-
way up the sides of the basin.
Boil for 2 hours, topping up
with boiling water as
necessary. Turn the pudding
on to a heated serving dish
and serve with custard.

Cheesecake Tropica

SERVES 8

1 × 200 g (7 oz) packet Nice
  biscuits, finely crushed
90 g (3½ oz) butter, melted

FILLING:
15 g (½ oz) powdered gelatine
1 × 425 g (15 oz) can sliced
  mangoes, drained, with 3
  tablespoons of syrup
  reserved
175 g (6 oz) full fat soft cheese
50 g (2 oz) caster sugar
2 eggs, separated
¼ teaspoon finely grated
  orange rind
150 ml (¼ pint) plain
  unsweetened yogurt
150 ml (¼ pint) whipping
  cream

TO DECORATE:
150 ml (¼ pint) whipping
  cream, whipped
whole almonds

PREPARATION TIME: *25-30
minutes, plus chilling*
COOKING TIME: *2 minutes*

1. Mix the crushed biscuits
with the melted butter. Press
the mixture on to the base of
a 20 cm (8 inch) round,
loose-bottomed cake tin.
Chill for 30 minutes while
making the filling. **A**
2. Sprinkle the gelatine over
3 tablespoons of the
reserved mango juice in a
heatproof bowl and leave to
soften for 10 minutes, until
spongy. Stand the bowl in a
saucepan of simmering
water, stirring until the
gelatine dissolves. Leave to
cool for about 7 minutes, but
do not allow to set.
3. Place the cheese and
sugar in a bowl and beat well
until soft and creamy. Add
the egg yolks and orange
rind and beat thoroughly.
4. Reserve 3 mango slices
for decoration. Process the
remaining mangoes in a
blender, until smooth. Add
to the cheese mixture and
stir well to mix.
5. Whisk the cooled gelatine
liquid into the cheese
mixture and then whisk in
the yogurt. Whip the cream
until soft peaks form and fold
lightly into the mixture,
using a metal spoon.
6. Whisk the egg whites
stiffly and fold into the
mixture. Pour into the
prepared tin and leave to set
in a cool place for at least 3
hours. **F**
7. Carefully remove the side
of the tin and place the
cheesecake on a serving
plate, still on the tin base.
Decorate with whipped
cream, almonds and the
reserved mango slices, cut
into diamond shapes. Chill
for 2-3 hours before serving.

A Can be prepared the
previous day and kept
chilled.
F Freeze for up to 1 month.
Thaw overnight in the
refrigerator before following
instructions given in stage 7.

Top to bottom: Strawberry Chantilly
Meringue; Cheesecake Tropica; Spicy
Lemon Syrup Layer.

Delia Smith's
Christmas Fare

═══ MENU ═══

ROAST DUCK

MORELLO CHERRY SAUCE

SAUTÉED CAULIFLOWER WITH CORIANDER

RICH FRUIT CAKE

CHRISTMAS CAKE

Roast Duck

SERVES 4

1 duck, weighing about 2.75 kg (6 lb)
salt
freshly ground black pepper

TO GARNISH:
1 bunch of watercress

PREPARATION TIME: *20 minutes*

COOKING TIME: *about 3½ hours*

OVEN: *220°C, 425°F, Gas Mark 7*

1. The golden rule is never to put any sort of fat near a duck, because it has more than enough of its own. Just place the bird in a roasting tin, then prick the duck skin all over – going deep into the flesh – with a skewer (to leave little escape routes for the fat to run out). Season the duck quite liberally with salt and pepper, then place the tin on a highish shelf in the oven.

2. After 20 minutes turn the heat down to 180°C, 350°F, Gas Mark 4, then basically all you have to do is leave it alone for 3 hours – just once or twice pouring off the fat that has collected in the roasting tin. Pour the fat into a bowl – don't throw it away, it is lovely for roasting or sautéeing potatoes.

3. When the cooking time is up, remove the duck from the tin, first tipping it up to let excess fat drain out of the body cavity, and place it on a carving board. Leave it to "relax" for 5 minutes then either leave whole or divide it into portions: all you need do is cut the bird in half lengthways (i.e. along the length of the breast and through the backbone) with a sharp knife, then cut the halves into quarters – you may need the help of some kitchen scissors here. Leaving any escaped pieces of bone behind, sit the quarters up together on a warm serving dish and garnish with watercress.

NOTE:
It is best to place the duck on a rack in the roasting tin. If the rack from your grill pan will fit into the oven, use that.

Morello Cherry Sauce

175 g (6 oz) morello cherry jam
150 ml (¼ pint) red wine

PREPARATION TIME: *5 minutes*

COOKING TIME: *10 minutes*

I know this sauce sounds a bit unlikely, but it really is delicious and it takes no time at all to make. There's one vital point, though, and that's that the main ingredient must be *morello* cherry jam and no other kind (there are several brands on the market: one made by a Polish firm and another by an

Sautéed Cauliflower with Coriander

SERVES 2

1 smallish cauliflower
½ onion, finely chopped
1 level teaspoon whole
   coriander seeds
1 small clove of garlic
2 tablespoons olive oil
1 knob of butter
salt
freshly ground black pepper

PREPARATION TIME: *20 minutes*
COOKING TIME: *13-15 minutes*

Cauliflower florets, just tossed in oil and fried quickly, seem to retain their crunchiness and flavour – which they can so easily lose when cooked with water.

1. Separate the cauliflower into fairly small florets (about an inch long, including the stalk). Wipe them but don't wash them – they'll be cooked anyway at a fairly high temperature. Now heat the oil in your largest frying-pan and soften the onion in it for 5 minutes. Meanwhile chop the peeled clove of garlic finely and crush the coriander seeds with a pestle and mortar (or use the end of a rolling-pin and a small bowl).

2. When the onion is softened, turn the heat right up, and add the cauliflower. After a minute or two toss the pieces over by shaking the pan, then add the coriander seeds and continue to cook the cauliflower for about 5 minutes, seasoning it with a sprinkling of salt and pepper. Finally add the butter and garlic to the pan and cook for a further minute, until the cauliflower is an attractive nutty-golden colour, but still retains some bite. Serve straight away.

English firm well-known for high quality jams and preserves). The reason it's so good is that morello cherries are bitter, and any sharp fruit can better hold its own when combined with the large amount of sugar needed to make a preserve.

1. Simply combine the jam and the wine in a saucepan, and simmer without a lid for 10 minutes. Ⓐ This is enough for 4 people.

Ⓐ The sauce can be made well in advance and re-heated just before serving.

Left to right: Sautéed Cauliflower with Coriander; Roast Duck; Morello Cherry Sauce.

Rich Fruit Cake

450 g (1 lb) currants
175 g (6 oz) sultanas
175 g (6 oz) raisins
50 g (2 oz) glacé cherries,
    rinsed and finely chopped
50 g (2 oz) mixed peel, finely
    chopped
3 tablespoons brandy
225 g (8 oz) plain flour
½ teaspoon salt
¼ teaspoon freshly grated
    nutmeg
½ teaspoon mixed spice
50 g (2 oz) almonds, chopped –
    the skins can be left on
225 g (8 oz) soft brown sugar
1 dessertspoon black treacle
225 g (8 oz) unsalted butter
4 eggs
the grated rind of 1 lemon
the grated rind of 1 orange

PREPARATION TIME: *45 minutes,
plus soaking*

COOKING TIME: *4½-4¾ hours*

OVEN: *140°C, 275°F, Gas Mark 1*

1. Grease and line with greaseproof paper a 20 cm (8 inch) round cake tin, or an 18 cm (7 inch) square tin.
2. The night before you make the cake, place all the dried fruit and peel in a bowl and mix in the brandy. Cover the bowl with a cloth and leave to soak for at least 12 hours.
3. It is quite a good idea before you measure the treacle to place the tin in the warming drawer of the oven, so that it melts a little.
4. Sieve the flour, salt and spices into a large mixing bowl, and in a separate bowl cream the butter and sugar together until the mixture's light and fluffy (this in fact is the most important part of the cake, so don't cut any corners). Next beat up the eggs and – a tablespoonful at a time – add them to the creamed mixture, beating thoroughly after each addition. If it looks as if it might start to curdle, you can

prevent this happening by adding a little of the flour.
5. When all the egg has been added, fold in the flour and spices (fold, don't beat). Now stir in the fruit and peel that has been soaking, the nuts, the treacle and the grated lemon and orange rinds.
6. Spoon the mixture into the prepared cake tin, and spread it out evenly with the back of a spoon. (If you are not going to ice the cake, at this stage you can arrange some whole blanched almonds over the surface – but do it lightly, or else they disappear for ever into the cake!)
7. Tie a band of brown paper around the outside of the tin, and cover the top of the cake with a double square of greaseproof paper (with a hole in the middle approximately the size of a 50p). Bake the cake on the lower shelf of the oven for 4½-4¾ hours, and don't open the door to peek at it until at least 4 hours have passed. When the cake is cold, wrap it well in double greaseproof paper and store in an airtight tin. I like to "feed" it at odd intervals with brandy during the storage time. To do this, strip off the lining papers, make a few extra holes in the top with a thin darning needle and pour a few teaspoonfuls of brandy in to soak into the cake. Repeat this at intervals of a week or two.

Christmas Cake

A 20 cm (8 inch) round cake or
    an 18 cm (7 inch) square
    cake, made from the Rich
    Fruit Cake recipe (left)

FOR THE ALMOND PASTE*:
450 g (1 lb) ground almonds
225 g (8 oz) caster sugar
225 g (8 oz) icing sugar
2 eggs
2 egg yolks – reserve the whites
    for the royal icing (see
    below)
½ teaspoon almond essence
1 teaspoon brandy
1 teaspoon lemon juice
red, green and yellow food
    colouring
*Part of this is used to ice the
    cake, the rest is used to
    model the flower
    decorations

FOR THE ROYAL ICING:
4 egg whites – combine three
    but keep one separate
500 g (approximately 1 lb 2 oz)
    sifted icing sugar
1 teaspoon glycerine

PREPARATION TIME: *about 3
hours, plus drying*

COOKING TIME: *12 minutes*

For a basic and uncomplicated icing, I've chosen a layer of almond paste topped with a semi-rough royal icing, decorated with almond paste flowers (in this case poinsettias). Ideally the cake should be almond iced at least seven days before the royal icing is put on – to give it a chance to dry out. Otherwise the almond oil may seep through and discolour the royal icing. The thick "snowy" icing in this recipe, however, should keep the oil at bay even if you (like me) find that sometimes you still have the cake decorating to do on Christmas Eve!

1. To make the almond paste, begin by sieving the two sugars into a large bowl and stirring in the eggs and egg yolks. Put the bowl over a pan of barely simmering water and whisk for about 12 minutes until the mixture is thick and fluffy. Then remove the bowl from the heat and sit the base in a couple of inches of cold water.
2. Next whisk in the essence, brandy and lemon juice and carry on whisking until the mixture is cool. Stir in the ground almonds and knead to form a firm paste. Weigh out 175 g (6 oz) of the paste and reserve this (in a bowl covered with cling film) for making the flower decoration.
3. Divide the rest of the paste in half and roll out one piece into a shape approximately 2.5 cm (1 inch) larger than the top of the cake (your working surface should be kept dusted with some sifted icing sugar so that the paste doesn't stick to it). Brush the top of the cake with egg white, then invert the cake to sit centrally on the almond paste and then with a palette knife press the paste up around the edge of the cake. Now turn the cake the right way up and brush the sides with egg white.
4. Roll out the other half of the paste into a rectangle and trim it so that it measures half the circumference of the cake by twice the height of the cake (use a piece of string to measure this). Now cut the paste rectangle in half lengthwise, and lightly press the two strips on to the sides of the cake. Smooth over the joins with a knife, and leave the cake covered with a cloth to dry out.
5. To make the almond paste poinsettias, take out the

paste reserved for decoration. Now using a skewer (so as not to overdo it) colour a small piece about the size of a walnut, yellow. Divide the remaining paste in half, colouring one half of it green, the other red. Using the photograph as a guide, cut out two templates in stiff paper or card, one for the green and one for the red leaf. Roll out both colours of paste to about ⅛ inch (3 mm) thick, then with the aid of the templates cut out 6 red leaves and 6 green. Trace a suggestion of veins on the surface with the back of the knife. Leave the leaves to dry, face upwards over a rolling pin. Model the yellow paste into some small pea-sized balls and leave everything to dry overnight.

6. To make the royal icing,

place the three egg whites in a grease-free bowl. Then stir in the icing sugar, a spoonful at a time, until the icing falls thickly from the spoon. At that point, stop adding any more sugar and whisk with an electric mixer for 10 minutes or until the icing stands up in stiff peaks, then stir in the glycerine. Now spoon half the icing into a screw-top jar and put aside in the fridge. Beat about 2 teaspoons more egg white into the remaining half of the icing.

7. Next use a dab of icing to fix the cake to a 25.5 cm (10 inch) cakeboard, then spread about two-thirds of the remainder on top of the cake. Work the icing back and forth to get rid of any tiny air bubbles, then take a clean plastic ruler and holding it at

each end, glide it once over the surface of the cake to give a smooth finish.

8. Hold the ruler vertically and remove any surplus icing from the top edges of the cake, then spread the remaining icing on to the sides of the cake. Keeping your ruler vertical, turn the cake round in one sweep to smooth the sides – a turntable is ideal for this, but two plates set base to base will also do the job. Now leave the cake for 24 hours for the icing to dry.

9. To finish off: mark the centre of the cake with an 8 cm (3¼ inch) plain circular cutter, then taking your reserved icing from the screw-top jar, spread it thickly outside the marked circle. Use a broad-bladed knife to "spike" the icing into

snow-like peaks. At the edges, bring the peaks over and down to give the effect of hanging snowy icicles (see the photograph). Lastly lay the green almond paste leaves in the centre of the cake, then the red leaves on top of them. Place the small yellow "berries" in the centre, fixing them in place with a little icing. Set the whole effect off with a red ribbon, tied in a bow around the cake.

Above: Christmas Cake made from the Rich Fruit Cake.

SIX

HOLIDAY COOKING

Honey-Grilled Trout

4 rainbow trout, cleaned
75 g (3 oz) butter
1 tablespoon chopped fresh
    parsley
salt
freshly ground black pepper
1½ tablespoons clear honey
2 tablespoons lemon juice

TO GARNISH:
parsley sprigs
lemon wedges

PREPARATION TIME: *10 minutes*
COOKING TIME: *12-16 minutes*

1. Pat the trout dry with absorbent paper. Remove the fins and trim the tails into a neat 'V' shape. Using a sharp knife, make 3 diagonal slashes on both sides of the trout.
3. Cream 25 g (1 oz) of the butter with the parsley and season to taste with salt and pepper. Put a pat of the seasoned butter inside each trout and place in a greased grill pan.
3. Put the remaining butter, honey and lemon juice into a saucepan and heat gently until melted. Pour over the trout, season with salt and pepper and cook under a preheated moderately hot grill for 6-8 minutes on each side, basting from time to time with the cooking juices, until cooked through.
4. Arrange the trout on a warmed serving dish, pour over the juices from the pan and garnish with the parsley sprigs and lemon wedges. Serve hot with brown bread and butter.

Indian Prawn Rice

25 g (1 oz) butter
1 large onion, peeled and
    chopped
3 celery sticks, trimmed and
    thinly sliced
75-100 g (3-4 oz) button
    mushrooms, wiped and
    sliced
100 g (4 oz) long-grain rice
1-2 teaspoons curry powder
450 ml (¾ pint) chicken stock
50 g (2 oz) sliced cooked ham,
    cut into strips
100 g (4 oz) peeled prawns
75 g (3 oz) frozen peas or
    sweetcorn
salt
freshly ground black pepper

PREPARATION TIME: *10 minutes*
COOKING TIME: *about 35 minutes*

1. Melt the butter in a saucepan. Add the onion, celery and mushrooms and fry over a gentle heat for 5 minutes.
2. Add the rice and curry powder and fry for a further 2 minutes, stirring constantly.
3. Stir in the stock and bring to the boil, stirring. Cover and simmer gently for 15 minutes.
4. Stir in the ham, prawns and peas or sweetcorn, cover and cook for a further 10 minutes until the liquid is absorbed. Fluff up with a fork and season to taste with salt and pepper. Turn into a warmed serving dish and serve hot.

VARIATION:
Replace the ham and prawns with crisply fried crumbled bacon and diced cooked chicken. For a tasty vegetarian dish omit the ham and prawns and add 100 g (4 oz) frozen peas and 150 g (5 oz) frozen sweetcorn. Serve topped with grated cheese.

Honey-Grilled Trout; Indian Prawn Rice; Surprise Cheesy Courgettes.

Surprise Cheesy Courgettes

SERVES 3-4

½ tablespoon vegetable oil
12 chipolata sausages
12 medium courgettes, trimmed and halved lengthways
1½ teaspoons mild burger mustard (optional)
50 g (2 oz) butter
1 small onion, peeled and chopped
1 large tomato, chopped
salt
freshly ground black pepper
25 g (1 oz) plain flour
300 ml (½ pint) milk
100 g (4 oz) Cheddar cheese

PREPARATION TIME: *30 minutes*
COOKING TIME: *55-60 minutes*
OVEN: *180°C, 350°F, Gas Mark 4*

An exciting dish with a surprising filling, as the sausages are disguised until the first mouthful.

1. Heat the oil in a frying pan, add the sausages and fry over a gentle heat for 12 minutes, turning often. Remove the sausages from the pan and drain on absorbent paper.
2. Meanwhile, using a teaspoon, remove and reserve the seeds from the halved courgettes, making a channel large enough to take the cooked sausages.
3. Place the courgette halves in a saucepan of boiling, salted water and cook for 2 minutes. Drain, then rinse under cold running water and drain well again. Pat dry with absorbent paper.
4. Brush the sausages with mustard, if using, and sandwich each one between 2 courgette halves.
5. Chop the reserved courgette seeds. Melt half the butter in a saucepan, add the chopped courgette seeds, onion and tomato and fry over a gentle heat for 3 minutes. Place the mixture in a lightly greased shallow ovenproof dish. Arrange the stuffed courgettes on top and season well with salt and pepper.
6. Melt the remaining butter in a saucepan, stir in the flour and cook for 1 minute.

Gradually stir in the milk and bring to the boil, stirring all the time. Lower the heat and cook for 2 minutes, stirring.
7. Grate the cheese and divide into 2 portions. Stir one half into the white suce and season to taste with salt and pepper.
8. Pour the sauce over the stuffed courgettes and sprinkle with the remaining cheese. Ⓐ Cook in a preheated oven for 35-40 minutes until tender and golden-brown. Serve hot with crusty bread.

Ⓐ Can be prepared 3-4 hours in advance, covered with cling film and kept in a refrigerator.

Ham and Spinach Crisps

100 g (4 oz) frozen chopped
   spinach
8 medium-thick slices brown or
   white bread, crusts removed
65 g (2½ oz) butter, softened
15 g (½ oz) plain flour
85 ml (3 fl oz) milk
75 g (3 oz) Cheddar cheese,
   grated
40 g (1½ oz) sliced cooked
   ham, chopped
2 tablespoons single cream
salt
freshly ground black pepper

PREPARATION TIME: *15 minutes*
COOKING TIME: *40-45 minutes*
OVEN: *190°C, 375°F, Gas Mark 5*

These crisp bread 'baskets',
filled with a tasty mixture of
spinach, ham and cheese,
make a nourishing and
substantial snack meal.

1. Cook the spinach
according to packet
instructions and drain very
thoroughly. Set aside.
2. Place the bread slices on a
board and run a rolling pin
firmly across each one to
flatten slightly. Butter each
slice on one side only, using
50 g (2 oz) of the butter.
3. Place 4 of the bread slices,
buttered side down, in 4
Yorkshire pudding tins and
press firmly into the base and
around the sides, leaving the
corners of the bread
protruding. Place the
remaining 4 bread slices,
buttered side down, on top,
at 45° to the previous slices,
to form bread cases with 8
protruding corners. Bake in
a preheated oven for 10-15
minutes until light golden
and crisp. Remove from the
oven and set aside. Ⓐ
4. Melt the remaining butter
in a saucepan, stir in the flour
and cook for 1 minute,
stirring. Gradually stir in the
milk and bring to the boil,
stirring all the time. Lower
the heat and simmer for 2
minutes, stirring. Remove
from the heat and stir in 25 g
(1 oz) of the cheese with the
ham, spinach, cream and salt
and pepper to taste. Ⓐ
5. Spoon the spinach
mixture into the bread cases
and sprinkle with the
remaining cheese. Return to
the oven and cook for a
further 20-25 minutes until
well heated through and the
cheese has melted. Serve
straightaway.

Ⓐ The bread cases can be
prepared several hours in
advance, covered and kept at
room temperature. The
spinach mixture can be
prepared 3-4 hours in
advance, covered with cling
film and kept chilled. Reheat
gently until piping hot
before following the
instructions given in step 5.

Mediterranean Pasta

1 tablespoon vegetable oil
1 medium onion, peeled and
   finely chopped
1 celery stick, trimmed and
   finely chopped
1 garlic clove, peeled and
   crushed
400 g (14 oz) can tomatoes
1 tablespoon tomato purée
½ teaspoon dried marjoram
½ bay leaf
1 teaspoon sugar
salt
freshly ground black pepper
100 g (4 oz) peeled prawns
290 g (10 oz) can baby clams in
   brine, drained
1 tablespoon chopped fresh
   parsley
350 g (12 oz) spaghetti
40 g (1½ oz) butter

PREPARATION TIME: *10 minutes*
COOKING TIME: *30 minutes*

A rich herb and tomato
seafood sauce, spooned over
buttered spaghetti, makes a
delicious meal, served with a
crisp green salad and crusty
bread.

1. Heat the oil in a saucepan.
Add the onion, celery and
garlic and fry over a gentle
heat for 5 minutes until
softened.
2. Stir in the tomatoes with
their juice and break them
up coarsely with a wooden
spoon. Add the tomato
purée, marjoram, bay leaf,
sugar and salt and pepper to
taste. Stir well and bring to
the boil, then lower the heat
and simmer, uncovered, for
15 minutes. Ⓐ
3. Remove and discard the
bay leaf. Stir in the prawns,
clams and parsley and cook
for a further 10 minutes.
4. Meanwhile, cook the
spaghetti in a large saucepan
of boiling, salted water for
10-12 minutes until just
tender. Drain well, then
rinse with boiling water and
drain well again. Melt the
butter in the rinsed out pan,
add the drained spaghetti
and toss lightly until the
spaghetti is thoroughly
coated with butter.
5. Divide the spaghetti
equally between 4 warmed
serving dishes and spoon
over the hot seafood sauce.
Serve at once with a green
salad and crusty bread.

Ⓐ Can be prepared the
previous day, covered with
cling film and kept chilled.

Golden Lamb Lasagne

SERVES 6-8

2 tablespoons vegetable oil
750 g (1½ lb) lean minced
    lamb
1 garlic clove, peeled and
    crushed
2 medium onions, peeled and
    finely chopped
3 celery sticks, trimmed and
    finely chopped
2 medium carrots, scraped and
    finely chopped
1½ tablespoons plain flour
400 g (14 oz) can tomatoes
2 tablespoons tomato purée
¼-½ teaspoon dried mixed
    herbs
salt
freshly ground black pepper
9 lasagne sheets
350 g (12 oz) cottage cheese
50 g (2 oz) Mozarella cheese,
    grated

PREPARATION TIME: *15 minutes*

COOKING TIME: *about 1¼ hours*

OVEN: *180°C, 350°F, Gas Mark 4*

1. Heat the oil in a saucepan. Add the lamb, garlic, onions, celery and carrots and cook over a moderate heat for 5 minutes, stirring frequently.
2. Stir in the flour and cook for 1 minute. Add the tomatoes with their juice and break them up coarsely with a wooden spoon. Stir in the tomato purée and herbs and bring to the boil, stirring. Lower the heat, season to taste with salt and pepper, then cover and simmer gently for 30 minutes. Ⓐ
3. Meanwhile cook the lasagne in a large saucepan of boiling, salted water for 10 minutes. Drain and rinse under cold running water, then drain well again.
4. Cover the base of a shallow greased ovenproof dish with one-third of the lasagne. Cover with one-third of the lamb mixture and half the cottage cheese. Top with half the remaining lasagne and lamb mixture and the remaining cottage cheese. Cover with the remaining lasagne and lamb mixture. Sprinkle over the grated Mozarella cheese. Ⓐ
5. Bake in a preheated oven for 30 minutes until golden brown on top. Serve hot with a tossed mixed salad.

Ⓐ The meat sauce can be prepared several hours in advance, covered and kept chilled.

The lasagne layer can be prepared several hours in advance, covered and kept chilled.

VARIATION:
Replace minced lamb with minced beef if preferred.

Above, clockwise from top left:
Golden Lamb Lasagne; Beefy Layer
Pie; Mediterranean Pasta; Ham and
Spinach Crisps.

Beefy Layer Pie

SERVES 4-5

350 g (12 oz) minced beef
2 medium onions, peeled and
    finely chopped
2 carrots, scraped and finely
    chopped
40 g (1½ oz) butter or
    margarine
25 g (1 oz) plain flour
300 ml (½ pint) milk
½ teaspoon made English
    mustard
100 g (4 oz) Cheddar cheese,
    grated
salt
freshly ground black pepper
225 g (8 oz) cooked
    cauliflower florets
3 medium tomatoes, sliced
450 g (1 lb) cooked potatoes,
    cut into 5 mm (¼ inch) slices

PREPARATION TIME: *20 minutes*

COOKING TIME: *about 1 hour*

OVEN: *190°C, 375°F, Gas Mark 5*

1. Place the beef in a non-stick saucepan and fry (without added fat) for 10 minutes, stirring often. Add the onions and carrots and fry for a further 5 minutes.
2. Add 25 g (1 oz) of the fat to the pan, stir until melted, then stir in the flour and cook for 1 minute. Stir in the milk and bring to the boil, stirring all the time. Lower the heat and cook for 2 minutes, stirring. Remove from the heat.
3. Stir in the mustard, three-quarters of the cheese and salt and pepper to taste. Ⓐ
4. Place half this mixture in a 1.75 litre (3 pint) ovenproof dish. Cover this with half the cauliflower florets, tomato slices and potato slices. Season the layer to taste with salt and pepper.
5. Repeat these 2 layers to finish. Melt the remaining fat and brush over the potatoes. Sprinkle with the remaining cheese. Ⓐ Ⓕ
6. Bake in a preheated oven for 35-40 minutes until golden brown and cooked through. Serve hot.

Ⓐ The meat and cheese sauce can be prepared 3-4 hours in advance, covered and kept chilled.

The pie can be prepared 3-4 hours in advance, covered with cling film and kept chilled.
Ⓕ Freeze for up to 1 month. Thaw overnight in refrigerator then follow instructions given in step 6.
Ⓜ Or microwave on Defrost for 25-30 minutes, then stand for 30 minutes before following the instructions from step 6.

Chinese-Style Cabbage with Pork

2 tablespoons plain flour
salt
freshly ground black pepper
450 g (1 lb) pork fillet, cut into
    thin strips
4 tablespoons vegetable oil
2 medium onions, peeled,
    quartered and separated into
    layers
1 large red pepper, cored,
    seeded and cut into 1 cm
    (½ inch) pieces
350 g (12 oz) Chinese leaves,
    cut into 1 cm (½ inch) slices
2 slices fresh or canned
    pineapple, cut into pieces
1 tablespoon sugar
1 tablespoon soy sauce
1 tablespoon dry sherry
1 tablespoon malt vinegar
1 ½ tablespoons tomato purée
2 teaspoons cornflour
150 ml (¼ pint) chicken stock

PREPARATION TIME: *15 minutes*

COOKING TIME: *10 minutes*

A selection of quick-fried vegetables with evenly-sliced strips of pork fillet and pineapple pieces combine to give this quickly-made dish an excellent flavour and crunchy texture.

1. Spread the flour out on a plate and season with salt and pepper. Add the pork fillet strips and turn to coat thoroughly. Heat half the oil in a frying pan, add the pork and fry over a high heat for 5 minutes, stirring all the time. Remove from the pan with a slotted spoon and keep warm.
2. Heat the remaining oil in the frying pan. Add the onions, red pepper and Chinese leaves and fry over a moderate heat, stirring, for 3-4 minutes. Stir in the pineapple and pork, remove from the heat and keep warm while preparing the sauce.
3. Mix together the sugar, soy sauce, sherry, vinegar and tomato purée in a saucepan. Blend the cornflour with a little of the chicken stock to form a smooth paste. Add the remaining stock and stir into the tomato mixture in the pan. Bring to the boil, stirring all the time, then lower the heat and simmer for 2 minutes, stirring, until the mixture clears and thickens.
4. Pour the sauce over the pork mixture in the frying pan and place over a moderate heat for 2-3 minutes, stirring.
5. Turn the mixture into a warmed serving dish and serve at once with boiled rice or crisp fried egg noodles.

Lamb Chops Provençale

25 g (1 oz) butter
2 tablespoons vegetable oil
3 medium carrots, scraped and
    thinly sliced
1 garlic clove, peeled and
    crushed (optional)
2 medium onions, peeled and
    thinly sliced
450 g (1 lb) potatoes, cut into
    1 cm (½ inch) pieces
1 large green pepper, cored,
    seeded and cut into 1 cm
    (½ inch) pieces
2 celery sticks, trimmed and
    thinly sliced
2 large tomatoes, skinned and
    chopped
1 tablespoon tomato purée
150 ml (¼ pint) chicken stock
¼ teaspoon dried mixed herbs
salt
freshly ground black pepper
4 lamb chops

TO GARNISH:
watercress sprigs

PREPARATION TIME: *10 minutes*

COOKING TIME: *25-30 minutes*

1. Heat the butter and oil in a saucepan. Add the vegetables and fry over a gentle heat for 3 minutes, stirring. Stir in the tomato purée, chicken stock, herbs and salt and pepper to taste.
2. Bring to the boil, then cover and simmer gently for 20-25 minutes until all the vegetables are tender.
3. Meanwhile, place the lamb chops on a grill pan rack, sprinkle with salt and pepper and cook under a preheated moderately hot grill for 15-20 minutes, turning occasionally until cooked through.
4. Place the chops on a warmed serving dish and spoon the hot vegetable mixture around them. Garnish with watercress and serve straightaway.

Lamb Chops Provençale; Chinese-Style Cabbage with Pork.

Stir-Fry Chicken and Vegetables

4 tablespoons vegetable oil
3 medium carrots, scraped, halved and thinly sliced
3 celery sticks, trimmed and sliced
2 medium onions, peeled, quartered and sliced
1 large red or green pepper, cored, seeded and cut into thin strips
100 g (4 oz) button mushrooms, wiped and sliced
450 g (1 lb) chicken breast fillets, cut diagonally into very thin strips
2 teaspoons cornflour
200 ml (7 fl oz) chicken stock
4-5 teaspoons soy sauce
salt
freshly ground black pepper

| PREPARATION TIME: *25 minutes* |
| COOKING TIME: *20 minutes* |

A delicious healthy combination of crisp stir-fried vegetables and chicken which will suit children and adults alike.

1. Heat 3 tablespoons of the oil in a large frying pan. Add the carrots, celery and onions and fry over a gentle heat for 5 minutes, stirring often.
2. Add the red or green pepper and mushrooms to the pan and fry for a further 3 minutes, stirring often. Remove the vegetables from the pan with a slotted spoon and keep warm.
3. Heat the remaining oil in the frying pan, add the chicken and fry over a moderately high heat for 5 minutes, stirring all the time, until the chicken is cooked through.
4. In a bowl blend the cornflour with a little of the stock to form a smooth paste. Stir in the remaining stock with the soy sauce. Stir the mixture into the pan and bring to the boil, stirring all the time. Lower the heat and simmer for 2 minutes, stirring.
5. Return the vegetables to the pan and heat through gently for 2 minutes. Season to taste with salt and pepper and turn the mixture into a warmed serving dish. Serve hot with boiled rice or noodles.

Above: Stir-Fry Chicken and Vegetables; Fan-Tail Tomato and Egg Mayonnaise.

Fan-Tail Tomato and Egg Mayonnaise

4 large firm tomatoes
1 × 7.5 cm (3 inch) piece cucumber, sliced
4 hard-boiled eggs, sliced
150 ml (¼ pint) Mayonnaise (page 32), or good-quality bought mayonnaise
1 teaspoon tomato purée
2-3 tablespoons single cream
salt
freshly ground white pepper

TO GARNISH:
parsley sprigs

| PREPARATION TIME: *15 minutes, plus chilling* |
| COOKING TIME: *10 minutes* |

An unusual and attractive way of serving an egg mayonnaise salad.

1. Slice the tomatoes 5 times vertically almost through to the base, but still keeping the tomatoes whole.
2. Arrange a halved slice of cucumber in each cut in the tomatoes. Keep the remaining cucumber slices whole.
3. Arrange slices of hard-boiled egg and cucumber overlapping to cover a serving plate.
4. Mix together the mayonnaise, tomato purée, cream and salt and pepper to taste. Spoon the mixture evenly over the egg and cucumber.
5. Arrange the tomatoes on top, then garnish with parsley. Serve chilled.

Harlequin Vegetable Pilaff

2 tablespoons vegetable oil
2 medium onions, peeled and chopped
2 medium carrots, scraped and chopped
50 g (2 oz) button mushrooms, wiped and sliced
1 red pepper, cored, seeded and cut into small dice
2 celery sticks, trimmed and sliced
175 g (6 oz) long-grain rice
300 ml (½ pint) boiling chicken stock
300 ml (½ pint) tomato juice
1 bay leaf
salt
freshly ground black pepper
100 g (4 oz) frozen sliced green beans, peas or sweetcorn (or use a mixture of all three)
50 g (2 oz) sultanas
25-50 g (1-2 oz) Cheddar cheese, grated

PREPARATION TIME: *15 minutes*

COOKING TIME: *about 30 minutes*

Serve this colourful savoury rice either as a vegetarian main course, garnished with wedges of hard-boiled egg, or as an accompaniment to chops, sausages or beefburgers.

1. Heat the oil in a saucepan. Add the onions, carrots, mushrooms, red pepper and celery and fry over a gentle heat for 5 minutes.
2. Stir in the rice and fry for 2 minutes, then stir in the stock, tomato juice and bay leaf. Bring to the boil, stirring, and season to taste with salt and pepper. Cover the pan and simmer gently for 10 minutes.
3. Add the frozen vegetables and sultanas to the pan, cover again and cook for a further 12 minutes.
4. Remove and discard the bay leaf and turn the mixture on to a warmed serving dish. Sprinkle with the grated cheese and serve hot.

Three-Bean Tuna Salad

SERVES 6

175 g (6 oz) whole stringless French beans, topped and tailed if fresh
425 g (15 oz) can red kidney beans, drained
200 g (7 oz) can butter beans, drained
200 g (7 oz) can tuna, drained and flaked
2 celery sticks, trimmed and sliced
1 dill pickle, quartered and sliced
1 medium onion, peeled, sliced and separated into rings
150 ml (¼ pint) French Dressing (page 33)
salt
freshly ground black pepper
6-8 crisp lettuce leaves
2 tomatoes, quartered
1 tablespoon chopped fresh parsley

PREPARATION TIME: *7-10 minutes, plus chilling*

COOKING TIME: *8 minutes*

1. Cook the French beans in a little boiling, salted water for 8 minutes. Drain well and rinse under cold running water, then drain well again. Cut the beans into chunky pieces and place in a large bowl.
2. Add the red kidney and butter beans, then stir in the tuna, celery, dill pickle and onion rings. Pour over the French dressing and season to taste with salt and pepper. Toss lightly until all the ingredients are well coated with the dressing.
3. Line a serving bowl with lettuce leaves and spoon the bean and tuna mixture into the centre. Ⓐ Arrange the tomato wedges in a border around the bowl and sprinkle the salad with the parsley. Serve chilled.

Ⓐ Can be prepared several hours in advance, covered with cling film and kept chilled.

Celeriac and Beef Salad Bowl

175 g (6 oz) celeriac, peeled
and cut into matchstick strips
2 green dessert apples, cored
and coarsely chopped
1 ripe avocado, peeled, stoned
and diced
150 ml (¼ pint) prepared
French Dressing (page 33)
175-225 g (6-8 oz) cooked
roast beef, cut into thin strips
100 g (4 oz) button
mushrooms, wiped and
sliced
1 medium onion, peeled,
quartered and sliced
1 carrot, scraped, halved
lengthways and thinly sliced
50 g (2 oz) sultanas or raisins
1 tablespoon mustard seeds
(optional)
salt
freshly ground black pepper
3-4 crisp lettuce leaves

TO GARNISH:
cucumber slices
cherry tomatoes

PREPARATION TIME: *15 minutes*

1. Place the celeriac, apples
and avocado pear in a bowl.
Pour over the French
dressing and toss lightly.
2. Add the remaining
ingredients, except the
lettuce leaves, and toss
lightly again until all the
ingredients are well coated
with the dressing.
3. Spoon the salad into a
bowl. Arrange the lettuce
leaves at the side and garnish
with cucumber slices and
tomatoes. Serve chilled, with
hot French bread.

VARIATION:
If celeriac is unavailable use
350 g (12 oz) cooked diced
potatoes, mixed with 2 sliced
celery sticks.

Left: Harlequin Vegetable Pilaff; Three-
Bean Tuna Salad. **Right:** Pasta Salad
Mix; Celeriac and Beef Salad Bowl.

Pasta Salad Mix

SERVES 4-6

175 g (6 oz) small pasta bows,
twists or shells
1 tablespoon vegetable oil
7.5 cm (3 inch) piece
cucumber, quartered
lengthways and sliced
8 spring onions, trimmed and
chopped
100 g (4 oz) radishes, trimmed
and quartered
1 large carrot, scraped and
grated
2 celery sticks, trimmed and
sliced
150 ml (¼ pint) Mayonnaise
(page 32) or good-quality
bought mayonnaise
2 tablespoons single cream
2 tablespoons tomato purée

1 garlic clove, peeled and
crushed (optional)
salt
freshly ground black pepper
50 g (2 oz) cooked ham,
chopped
100 g (4 oz) Cheddar or Edam
cheese, cubed
50 g (2 oz) salted peanuts

TO GARNISH:
mint sprigs

PREPARATION TIME: *15 minutes,
plus chilling*

COOKING TIME: *12-15 minutes*

1. Cook the pasta shapes in a
saucepan of boiling, salted
water for 12-15 minutes or
until just tender. Drain well,
rinse with boiling water,
then drain well again. Toss
the pasta in the oil in a bowl
and leave to cool for 20
minutes.
2. Add the vegetables to the
pasta and stir lightly to mix.
3. Mix together the
mayonnaise, cream, tomato
purée, garlic, if using, and
salt and pepper to taste. Stir
in the ham and cheese and
add the mixture to the pasta
and vegetables. Toss lightly
until all the ingredients are
coated with the mayonnaise
mixture.
4. Turn the pasta salad into a
serving bowl, sprinkle with
the peanuts and garnish with
mint. Serve chilled.

Italian Beef Bake

SERVES 4-5

350 g (12 oz) minced beef
4 rashers streaky bacon, rinded, boned and chopped
1 medium onion, peeled and finely chopped
1 celery stick, trimmed and finely chopped
50 g (2 oz) button mushrooms, wiped and finely chopped
1 garlic clove, peeled and crushed
½ tablespoon plain flour
225 g (8 oz) can tomatoes
1 tablespoon tomato purée
¼ teaspoon dried marjoram
150 ml (¼ pint) beef stock
salt
freshly ground black pepper
good pinch of grated nutmeg (optional)
225 g (8 oz) spaghetti
75 g (3 oz) Mozzarella cheese, grated
15 g (½ oz) grated Parmesan cheese
3 medium tomatoes, sliced

PREPARATION TIME: *15 minutes*	
COOKING TIME: *about 1 hour*	
OVEN: *190°C, 375°F, Gas Mark 5*	

A very useful way of using up leftover cooked spaghetti.

1. Put the beef and bacon in a non-stick saucepan and fry without added fat for 5 minutes, stirring often. Add the onion, celery, mushrooms and garlic and fry over a moderate heat for 3 minutes, stirring often.
2. Add the flour and cook for 1 minute, then add the tomatoes with their juice, breaking them up coarsely with a wooden spoon. Stir in the tomato purée, marjoram, stock, salt and pepper to taste and the nutmeg, if using. Bring to the boil, then lower the heat and simmer, uncovered, for 15 minutes. Ⓐ
3. Meanwhile, cook the spaghetti in a large saucepan of boiling, salted water for 10-12 minutes or until just tender. Drain well, then rinse with boiling water and drain well again.
4. Place the cooked spaghetti in a greased, shallow ovenproof dish, spoon over the meat sauce and sprinkle with the Mozzarella and Parmesan cheeses. Ⓕ Arrange the sliced tomatoes on top. Ⓐ
5. Bake in a preheated oven for 25-30 minutes until golden brown. Serve hot with a green salad.

Ⓐ The meat sauce can be prepared several hours in advance, covered and kept chilled.
   The dish can be prepared in the morning, covered with cling film and kept chilled before proceeding from step 5.
Ⓕ Freeze for up to 1 month. Thaw for 2 hours at room temperature before covering with the sliced tomatoes and proceeding from step 5.
Ⓜ Or microwave on Defrost for 20-25 minutes, then stand for 20 minutes before proceeding from step 5.

Mexican Espresso Beef

½ tablespoon vegetable oil
350 g (12 oz) minced beef
1 large onion, peeled and chopped
2 celery sticks, trimmed and chopped
1 garlic clove, peeled and crushed
¼-½ teaspoon chilli powder
2 teaspoons plain flour
300 ml (½ pint) tomato juice
150 ml (¼ pint) beef stock
½ tablespoon tomato purée
salt
freshly ground black pepper
425 g (15 oz) can red kidney beans, drained
1 medium green pepper, cored, seeded and diced
225 g (8 oz) long-grain rice

TO GARNISH:
4 cream crackers

PREPARATION TIME: *10 minutes*	
COOKING TIME: *38 minutes*	

1. Heat the oil in a saucepan, add the beef, onion, celery and garlic and cook over a moderate heat for 5 minutes, stirring often.
2. Stir in the chilli powder and flour and cook for 1 minute. Stir in the tomato juice, stock and tomato purée and bring to the boil, stirring all the time. Season to taste with salt and pepper, then lower the heat and simmer, uncovered, for 20 minutes.
3. Stir in the red kidney beans and green pepper and cook for a further 15 minutes. Ⓐ Ⓕ
4. Meanwhile, cook the rice in a saucepan of boiling, salted water for 12-15 minutes or until tender. Drain the rice well, rinse with boiling water, then drain well again.

Left to right: Italian Beef Bake; Mexican Espresso Beef; Chicken Cheese Fries.

5. Divide the rice equally between 4 warmed individual serving bowls, spoon over the chilli mixture and top with the cream crackers coarsely crushed. Serve hot.

Ⓐ Can be prepared the previous day, covered with cling film and kept chilled. Reheat gently while cooking rice proceeding from step 4.
Ⓕ Freeze for up to 1 month. Thaw overnight in the refrigerator, then follow from step 4.
Ⓜ Or microwave on Defrost for 15-20 minutes, breaking up gently as soon as possible, then stand for 10 minutes before proceeding from step 4.

Chicken Cheese Fries

MAKES 12

25 g (1 oz) butter or hard margarine
40 g (1½ oz) plain flour
150 ml (¼ pint) milk
225 g (8 oz) cooked chicken, finely chopped
1 medium onion, peeled and finely chopped
75 g (3 oz) Cheddar cheese, grated
1 tablespoon chopped fresh parsley
salt
freshly ground black pepper
1 egg, beaten
50 g (2 oz) soft fresh white breadcrumbs
vegetable oil, for deep frying

PREPARATION TIME: *10 minutes*
COOKING TIME: *6-7 minutes*

Serve these tasty fries either hot or cold.

1. Melt the butter or margarine in a saucepan, add 25 g (1 oz) of the flour and cook for 1 minute, stirring. Remove from the heat and gradually stir in the milk. Return to the heat and bring to the boil, stirring. Lower the heat and cook for 2 minutes, stirring.
2. Remove from the heat and stir in the chicken, onion, cheese, parsley and salt and pepper to taste. Leave aside to cool for 30 minutes. Ⓐ
3. Divide the mixture into 12 equal pieces and shape each one into a ball, using lightly floured hands. Roll each ball in the remaining flour, then dip in beaten egg and coat in the breadcrumbs, pressing on firmly with the palms of the hands.
4. Heat the oil in a deep fat fryer to 180°-190°C/350°-375°F or until a stale bread cube browns in 30 seconds. Add half the balls and fry for 6-7 minutes, turning, until golden brown and cooked through. Drain well on absorbent paper and keep warm while frying the remainder in the same way. Serve hot with chips or creamed potatoes and peas, or cold with salad.

Ⓐ Can be prepared the previous day, covered with cling film and kept chilled.

Raspberry Trifle Cream

SERVES 4-5

500 g (1¼ lb) raspberries, thawed if frozen
1½ tablespoons lemon juice
175 g (6 oz) caster sugar
8 trifle sponges, each split into 3 thin slices
150 ml (¼ pint) whipping cream

TO DECORATE:
toasted blanched almonds

PREPARATION TIME: *15 minutes, plus chilling overnight*

COOKING TIME: *5 minutes*

A delicious, simple-to-make variation on Summer Pudding, using trifle sponges instead of bread.

1. Place the raspberries, lemon juice and sugar in a saucepan and simmer gently for 5 minutes until the sugar is dissolved. Strain, reserving the juice, and leave to cool for 10 minutes.
2. Quickly dip the trifle sponge slices into the reserved juice and use two-thirds of them to line the base and sides of a 900 ml (1½ pint) pudding basin, overlapping them to come within 1 cm (½ inch) of the top of the basin.
3. Turn the fruit into the prepared basin and cover with the remaining trifle sponge slices. Place a saucer on top of the pudding, weight down and chill overnight in the refrigerator.
4. Run a knife all the way round the pudding and turn on to a serving plate. Stiffly whip the cream and use to fill a piping bag fitted with a large star nozzle. Pipe the cream attractively on to the pudding and decorate with toasted blanched almonds. Serve chilled.

VARIATION:
Replace 225 g (8 oz) of the raspberries with the same quantity of strawberries, blackberries or a mixture of red and blackcurrants.

Jubilee Ice Cream Sundaes

225 g (8 oz) raspberries
50 g (2 oz) icing sugar (optional)
150 ml (¼ pint) whipping cream (optional)
2 drops red food colouring (optional)
8 scoops or slices of vanilla ice cream
2 medium bananas, peeled and sliced
175 g (6 oz) strawberries, hulled and halved
1 tablespoon desiccated coconut, toasted
4 glacé or maraschino cherries (optional)

PREPARATION TIME: *7 minutes*

1. Place the raspberries and icing sugar in a blender goblet and process for 30 seconds until smooth. Pass the mixture through a sieve. Ⓐ Ⓕ
2. Stiffly whip the cream with the red food colouring, if using, and place in a piping bag fitted with a large star nozzle.
3. Place 2 scoops or slices of ice cream in each of 4 sundae dishes. Arrange the bananas and strawberries around the edge. Spoon over the raspberry sauce and top each sundae with a swirl of whipped cream, if using.
4. Decorate with toasted shredded coconut, if using. Serve at once with wafers.

Ⓐ Can be prepared the previous day, covered with cling film and kept chilled.
Ⓕ Freeze for up to 3 months. Thaw for 2 hours at room temperature.
Ⓜ Or microwave on Defrost for 8-10 minutes, stirring gently as soon as possible. Stand for 10 minutes before using.

VARIATION:
Replace the bananas and strawberries with other fresh fruits such as sliced pineapple, sliced peaches, mango, kiwi fruit or diced melon.

Kissel Cream Layer

150 ml (¼ pint) fresh orange juice, strained
100 g (4 oz) caster sugar
225 g (8 oz) blackcurrants, topped and tailed if fresh, thawed if frozen
225 g (8 oz) redcurrants, topped and tailed
1½ tablespoons cornflour
2 tablespoons cold water
16 ratafias
150 ml (¼ pint) whipping cream

TO DECORATE:
4 ratafias (optional)

PREPARATION TIME: *10 minutes, plus chilling*

COOKING TIME: *5 minutes*

These refreshing desserts are simple to make and delicious to eat. If redcurrants are unavailable, use double the quantity of blackcurrants.

1. Place the orange juice, sugar, blackcurrants and redcurrants in a saucepan and cook over a gentle heat, stirring occasionally, until the sugar is dissolved. Bring to the boil, then lower the heat and simmer for 5 minutes. Remove from the heat.
2. Strain the fruit, reserving the juice. Place the juice in a saucepan. Blend together the cornflour and water to form a smooth paste. Add the blended cornflour to the juice and bring slowly to the boil, stirring all the time. Lower the heat and simmer for 2 minutes, stirring. Remove from the heat and stir in the fruits. Allow to cool slightly.
3. Place 4 ratafias in each of 4 individual glass serving dishes, spoon over the fruit mixture and smooth the surfaces. Leave to cool for 30 minutes. Ⓐ
4. Whip the cream until soft peaks form and spoon a thick layer on to each fruit-filled glass. Chill for 2 hours before serving. Decorate each one with a ratafia, if using.

Ⓐ Can be prepared 3-4 hours in advance, covered with cling film and kept chilled.

Top to bottom: Jubilee Ice Cream Sundaes; Kissel Cream Layer; Raspberry Trifle Cream.

Summer Fruit Cup with Yogurt Cream

SERVES 4-5

2 tablespoons redcurrant jelly
150 ml (¼ pint) cold water
1 tablespoon lemon juice
225 g (8 oz) strawberries, hulled and halved
225 g (8 oz) cherries, halved and stoned
100 g (4 oz) black or green grapes, seeded and halved
2 peaches, stoned, peeled and sliced
85 ml (3 fl oz) whipping cream
½-1 tablespoon icing sugar, sifted
150 ml (¼ pint) plain unsweetened yogurt

PREPARATION TIME: *15 minutes, plus chilling*

COOKING TIME: *3 minutes*

1. Place the redcurrant jelly, water and lemon juice in a saucepan and bring slowly to the boil, stirring until the jelly is dissolved. Remove from the heat and leave to cool for 10 minutes. Ⓐ
2. Place the fruits in a serving bowl and pour over the cooled redcurrant syrup; stir well. Cover and chill for 1-2 hours before serving. Ⓐ
3. Stiffly whip the cream with the icing sugar, then fold in the yogurt. Chill before serving with the fruit salad.

Ⓐ The syrup can be prepared the previous day, covered with cling film and kept chilled.

The fruit salad can be prepared several hours in advance, covered and kept chilled.

VARIATION:
Use any mixture of fresh or canned fruits, as liked.

Rich Chocolate Fondue

SERVES 6-8

400 g (14 oz) can evaporated milk
15 g (½ oz) caster sugar
175 g (6 oz) plain chocolate, finely chopped
25 g (1 oz) toasted chopped blanched almonds (optional)

PREPARATION TIME: *5 minutes*

COOKING TIME: *15 minutes*

This would make a super birthday treat at a children's party – provided, of course, an adult is there to watch the fondue. All you do is spear a marshmallow or a piece of fruit, such as a whole strawberry, a chunk of banana or a cube of melon with a fondue fork and dunk into the luscious chocolate sauce until well coated. Nice, too, served with sponge finger (boudoir) biscuits for 'dunking'.

1. Place the evaporated milk, sugar and chocolate in a metal fondue pot or a saucepan and heat very gently over a spirit burner or very low heat, stirring until the chocolate melts.
2. Bring to the boil, then lower the heat and simmer for about 8 minutes, stirring constantly until the mixture thickens to a coating consistency.
3. Stir in the chopped nuts, if using, and serve at once.

Rich Chocolate Fondue; Summer Fruit Cup with Yogurt Cream.

Boodles Orange Fool

SERVES 6

150 ml (¼ pint) fresh orange juice
2 tablespoons lemon juice
¼ teaspoon finely grated orange rind
¼ teaspoon finely grated lemon rind
2 tablespoons caster sugar
300 ml (½ pint) whipping cream
6 trifle sponges, chopped

PREPARATION TIME: *10 minutes, plus chilling*

This lovely tangy dessert needs to stand for at least 3 hours before serving to allow time for the fruit juices to soak through to the sponge layer beneath.

1. Place the orange and lemon juices and rinds in a bowl and stir in the sugar.
2. Stiffly whip the cream and gradually fold in the fruit juice mixture, until well combined.
3. Place the trifle sponges in a serving bowl. Spoon over the fruit cream mixture and chill in the refrigerator for at least 3 hours before serving.

Boodles Orange Fool; Crunch Nut Crumble.

Crunch Nut Crumble

SERVES 4-5

225 g (8 oz) blackberries
2 medium cooking apples, peeled, cored and sliced
2 teaspoons cornflour
100-150 g (4-5 oz) sugar
100 g (4 oz) plain flour
50 g (2 oz) hard margarine, diced
50 g (2 oz) demerara sugar
25 g (1 oz) bran flakes, coarsely crushed
50 g (2 oz) chopped mixed nuts

PREPARATION TIME: *20 minutes*
COOKING TIME: *40-45 minutes*
OVEN: *190°C, 375°F, Gas Mark 5*

1. Place the blackberries and apple slices in a bowl. Mix together the cornflour and sugar and sprinkle over the fruit. Toss well until thoroughly coated. Turn the mixture into a 1.2 litre (2 pint) pie dish.
2. Sift the flour into a mixing bowl, add the margarine and rub in with the fingertips until the mixture resembles coarse breadcrumbs. Stir in the demerara sugar, bran flakes and chopped nuts. Spoon the mixture over the fruit and flatten slightly with the back of a spoon. Ⓐ Ⓕ
3. Cook in a preheated oven for 40-45 minutes until the fruit is tender and the topping light golden. Serve hot or cold.

Ⓐ Can be prepared the previous day, covered with cling film and kept chilled.
Ⓕ Freeze for up to 1 month. Cook from frozen, covering with foil to prevent over-browning, for 50-55 minutes until cooked thoroughly and lightly golden.
Ⓜ Or microwave on Defrost for 13-15 minutes, then stand for 10 minutes before following step 3.

Rose Elliot's
Midsummer Supper

═══ MENU ═══

CHILLED CUCUMBER SOUP

HOT HERB BREAD

SPINACH ROULADE WITH MUSHROOM FILLING

PUREE OF SUMMER CARROTS WITH FRESH HERBS

RODGROD

ALMOND BUTTER BISCUITS

This is a cool, refreshing meal to celebrate midsummer. It is typical of the type of food I would serve for a dinner party. I like to have something a bit dramatic and unusual as the centrepiece of the meal and the spinach roulade is ideal.

Both the first course and the pudding can be made in advance, which is helpful, and though the home-made herb bread is best served still warm from the oven – its warmth and herby flavour providing the perfect contrast to the cool cucumber soup – it is a very quick, no-knead recipe.

Hot Herb Bread

MAKES one 450 g (1 lb) loaf

butter, for greasing
250 g (9 oz) plain wholemeal flour
1 teaspoon salt
1 teaspoon sugar
1 small onion, peeled and finely chopped
1 teaspoon dried dill weed
½ teaspoon dried rosemary, crushed
1 packet easy-blend dried yeast (equivalent to 25 g (1 oz) fresh yeast)
250 ml (8 fl oz) tepid milk

PREPARATION TIME: *15 minutes, plus rising*
COOKING TIME: *35 minutes*
OVEN: *200°C, 400°F, Gas Mark 6*

This fragrant savoury bread is very easy to make and requires no kneading. It is essential to use wholemeal flour, and the bread is best eaten while still warm.

1. Grease a 450 g (1 lb) loaf tin generously with butter.
2. Put the flour into a large bowl, together with the salt, sugar, onion and herbs. Sprinkle in the yeast, then make a well in the centre and pour in the milk. Mix with a wooden spoon until a soft dough is formed. (The dough will be wetter than normal.)
3. Spoon the dough into the prepared tin: the dough should half fill the tin. Cover the top of the tin with clingfilm, then leave until the dough has risen to within 1 cm (½ inch) of the top of the tin: 20 minutes in a warm place, 30-40 minutes at room temperature.
4. Bake the loaf in a preheated oven for 35 minutes. Turn out on to a wire tray to cool. Serve warm. Ⓐ Ⓕ

Ⓐ Bake and cool loaf a few hours in advance. Before serving, wrap in foil and place in a moderate oven, 180°C, 350°F, Gas Mark 4, for 15-20 minutes, to warm through.

Ⓕ Freeze for up to 4 weeks. To serve, remove wrappings, stand loaf on wire tray and allow to thaw for 3-4 hours. Reheat before serving as described for Ⓐ
Ⓜ Or microwave on Defrost for 5-8 minutes. Stand for 15 minutes before reheating as for advance preparation note above.

Chilled Cucumber Soup

SERVES 4-6

1 large cucumber, peeled and diced
1 onion, peeled and chopped
4 sprigs fresh mint
900 ml (1½ pints) light vegetable stock, or 900 ml (1½ pints) water and a vegetable stock cube
2 teaspoons arrowroot or cornflour
6-8 tablespoons single cream
salt
freshly ground black pepper
few drops green food colouring (optional)

TO GARNISH:
mint sprigs
2-3 radishes, trimmed and sliced into thin rounds

PREPARATION TIME: *20 minutes, plus chilling*
COOKING TIME: *20 minutes*

This refreshing, pale green soup is delicious served with the Hot Herb Bread.

1. Put the cucumber, onion and mint into a large saucepan with the stock or water and stock cube and bring to the boil. Cover and simmer for 15 minutes.
2. Remove the mint sprigs, liquidize the soup and return to the pan. Reheat gently.
3. Put the arrowroot or cornflour into a small bowl with 4 tablespoons of the cream and mix to a smooth paste. Stir in a little of the hot soup, then pour back into the pan. Bring to the boil, stirring all the time, and cook for 1-2 minutes, until thickened slightly.
4. Season with salt and pepper and add a few drops of green food colouring, if using. Pour the soup into a bowl, cool, cover with clingfilm and chill for several hours. Ⓐ
5. Stir the soup, then taste and adjust the seasoning. Spoon into chilled individual bowls. Garnish with a swirl of the remaining cream, a sprig of mint and 2-3 slices of radish to each bowl.

Ⓐ Can be made the day before and kept in the refrigerator until required.

Hot Herb Bread; Chilled Cucumber Soup.

Spinach Roulade with Mushroom Filling

SERVES 4-6

25 g (1 oz) butter, melted
450 g (1 lb) frozen leaf spinach, thawed
4 eggs, separated
salt
freshly ground black pepper
freshly grated nutmeg
3 tablespoons grated Parmesan cheese

FOR THE FILLING:
225 g (8 oz) button mushrooms, washed and chopped
15 g (½ oz) butter
1 teaspoon cornflour
150 ml (¼ pint) single cream
1 tablespoon lemon juice
salt
freshly ground black pepper
freshly grated nutmeg

PREPARATION TIME: *25 minutes*
COOKING TIME: *20-25 minutes*
OVEN: *220°C, 425°F, Gas Mark 7*

This roulade is much easier than it sounds and makes a delicious summer meal, served with the Purée of Summer Carrots and some buttered baby new potatoes.

1. Line a 24×33 cm (9½×13 inch) Swiss roll tin with greaseproof paper to extend 5 cm (2 inches) at the edges. Brush with half of the melted butter.
2. Using your hands, squeeze as much liquid from the spinach as possible, then put it into a bowl with the remaining butter and the egg yolks and mix well.
3. Whisk the egg whites until stiff but not dry. Stir a tablespoonful of egg white into the spinach mixture, then fold in the rest. Season with salt, pepper and nutmeg. Pour the mixture into the prepared tin, spreading gently to the corners and levelling the top with a knife. Sprinkle with 1 tablespoon of the Parmesan cheese. Bake in a preheated oven for 10-15 minutes, until the top is golden brown and feels firm in the centre.
4. Meanwhile prepare the filling. Fry the mushrooms over a gentle heat in the butter for 3-4 minutes, then add the cornflour. Stir for a few seconds, then pour in the cream. Stir for 2 minutes, until thickened. Add the lemon juice and salt, pepper and nutmeg to taste. Keep warm over a gentle heat until required.
5. When cooked, turn the roulade out on to a piece of greaseproof paper which has been sprinkled with 1 tablespoon of the Parmesan cheese. Carefully remove greaseproof paper from the top of the roulade.
6. Spread the filling over the roulade, then quickly roll up, starting at one of the short edges, and using the greaseproof paper to help. Place on a warm serving dish, sprinkle with the remaining cheese Ⓐ and serve at once.

Ⓐ Finished roulade can be lightly covered with foil and kept warm in a moderate oven, 160°C, 325°F, Gas Mark 3, for 15-20 minutes before serving if necessary.

Below: Spinach Roulade with Mushroom Filling; Purée of Summer Carrots with Fresh Herbs. **Right:** Almond Butter Biscuits; Rodgrod.

Purée of Summer Carrots with Fresh Herbs

SERVES 4-6

750 g (1½ lb) carrots, scraped and sliced
1 medium potato, about 150 g (5 oz), peeled and diced
15 g (½ oz) butter
2-3 teaspoons sugar
1-2 teaspoons lemon juice
salt
freshly ground black pepper
1 tablespoon chopped fresh herbs (e.g. chervil, tarragon, parsley, chives – as available)

PREPARATION TIME: *20 minutes*
COOKING TIME: *20-25 minutes*

A useful vegetable dish which adds both colour and moisture to a meal, cutting out the need for extra sauces.

1. Put the carrots and potato into a large saucepan with cold water to cover and bring to the boil. Simmer, covered, for 15-20 minutes, until the vegetables are tender. Drain, reserving the liquid.
2. Put the vegetables into a liquidizer goblet or food processor with the butter and 150 ml (¼ pint) of the reserved cooking liquid.

Blend to a smooth purée.
3. Return the mixture to the pan. Add the sugar, lemon juice and salt and pepper to taste. Reheat gently, then pour into a heated serving dish. Ⓐ Sprinkle with the chopped herbs and serve at once.

Ⓐ Can be lightly covered with foil and kept warm towards the bottom of a moderate oven, 160°C, 325°F, Gas Mark 3, for 15-20 minutes. Sprinkle with the herbs before serving.

Almond Butter Biscuits

MAKES 24

175 g (6 oz) butter
75 g (3 oz) caster sugar
175 g (6 oz) flour
25 g (1 oz) ground almonds
25 g (1 oz) flaked almonds

PREPARATION TIME: *20 minutes*
COOKING TIME: *20 minutes per batch*
OVEN: *160°C, 325°F, Gas Mark 3*

These crunchy, buttery biscuits are delicious with the Rodgrod or with any creamy pudding.

1. Grease 2-3 large baking sheets.
2. Beat the butter and sugar until light and fluffy, then add the flour and ground almonds, mixing gently to a firm dough.
3. Roll walnut-sized pieces of the mixture into balls, flatten between your palms, then place well apart on the prepared baking sheets. Press a few flaked almonds into the top of each biscuit.
4. Bake in a preheated oven for about 20 minutes, or until biscuits are golden brown.

Allow to cool on the baking sheet for 1-2 minutes, then using a spatula, transfer to a wire tray to cool. Ⓐ Ⓕ

Ⓐ Store in an airtight tin for up to 10 days.
Ⓕ Freeze for up to 4 weeks. Pack biscuits carefully to avoid accidental breakage. To serve, spread biscuits out on a wire tray for about 30 minutes, until thawed.
Ⓜ Or microwave 8 at a time on Defrost for 45-60 seconds. Stand for 5 minutes before serving.

Rodgrod

SERVES 4-6

250 g (10 oz) fresh or frozen strawberries, hulled
225 g (8 oz) fresh or frozen redcurrants, stalks removed
150 g (5 oz) caster sugar
600 ml (1 pint) water
50 g (2 oz) cornflour
3 pieces pared lemon rind

TO DECORATE:
150 ml (¼ pint) whipping cream, whipped
a little chocolate flake, lightly crushed

PREPARATION TIME: *20 minutes, plus chilling*
COOKING TIME: *5 minutes*

A pretty summer pudding which makes the most of a small quantity of fruit. Serve with the Almond Butter Biscuits.

1. Reserve 4-6 strawberries. Put the remaining fruit and the sugar into a liquidizer goblet or food processor with the water and blend to a purée, then sieve to remove the pips and skins.
2. Put the cornflour into a small bowl and blend to a paste with a little of the fruit purée. Leave to one side.
3. Put the remaining purée into a saucepan with the pared lemon rind and bring to the boil. Pour a little of this boiling purée over the cornflour mixture. Blend thoroughly, then pour into the pan. Stir for 2-3 minutes, until the mixture has thickened. Take the pan off the heat and then remove the lemon rind.
4. Pour into 4 or 6 individual bowls, cool, then chill. To serve, spoon or pipe whipped cream on to the centre of each, add one of the reserved strawberries and sprinkle with a little chocolate flake.

Index

ACKNOWLEDGEMENTS

PHOTOGRAPHY: Laurie Evans
PHOTOGRAPHIC STYLING: Sue Russell
PREPARATION OF FOOD FOR
    PHOTOGRAPHY:
    Louise Steele, Clare Gordon-Smith,
    Elizabeth Seldon and Elizabeth Holmes.

The publishers would also like to thank
the following companies for the loan of
props for photography:
Elizabeth David, 46 Bourne Street,
    London S.W.1
Divertimenti, 68 Marylebone Lane,
    London W.1
David Mellor, 4 Sloane Square, London
    S.W.1

Recipes by Delia Smith on pages 118-121
    taken from *DELIA SMITH'S COMPLETE
    COOKERY COURSE* and reprinted with
    the permission of BBC Publications.